Bumper Book of

GREETINGS CARDS & GIFT-WRAP

Bumper Book of

GREETINGS CARDS & GIFT-WRAP

More than 80 step-by-step projects

Vivienne Bolton

contents

introduction

I love working with paper, and designing new greetings cards and gift-wrap is a task I have always found most enjoyable. Christmas is my busiest card production period, but I make cards throughout the year, for birthdays, anniversaries and new arrivals. Every now and again I spend time just being creative, experimenting with interesting paper, a special photograph or a new stamp to produce something really unusual.

There is such a wealth of materials constantly appearing on the market that there is always something to provide inspiration for the cardmaker. There is no shortage of new techniques to try, either. Some of these, such as stencilling, stamping and punching, are simple and suited to mass-production. Others, including quilling and cross stitch, are more time-consuming and intricate, and are best for one-off cards made to celebrate special occasions. I have tried to include as many of these exciting crafts and materials as possible in this book.

I am fortunate to live in a city that is well provided with both small, independent arts and crafts shops and larger outlets. Still, I always keep an eye out for inspiration and new materials and information, even when I am shopping in the unlikeliest places. Experience has taught me to always keep an open mind. I store absolutely everything that I think could be of use one day. With cardmaking as a hobby, you too will have the perfect excuse to collect and use beautiful handmade and printed papers, and colourful sequins and ribbons. You may even end up like me, with only the storage space that you have available controlling your stock of craft materials!

I do hope you enjoy this book and learn a few new skills from it. But above all, I hope you will try out the ideas and then use them as a springboard for your own creativity. Be inspired and adventurous, design your own masterpieces, become a collector of 'useful things', and make cardmaking a hobby you can share with friends and family.

Happy crafting.

Vivienne Bolton

getting started

When starting any new hobby, equipping yourself with the basic tools and materials is part of the fun. This is particularly the case with card-making as there are so many wonderful things now available for the card-maker to buy. Start small with good-quality cutting equipment and a selection of paper, card, adhesive tape and glue. As you work your way through the projects in this book you will find that your collection of tools and materials will grow and that your scrap box of bits and pieces will be bursting with all of those interesting things that you've found.

Search out good suppliers, both local stores and mail-order companies (a reliable mail-order supplier is invaluable). As well as checking out craft suppliers, look in cake decorating shops and art material outlets. Small stores are often better as they have time for customers and often specialize in certain areas.

If you are fortunate enough to have the space, create a permanent work surface for yourself and devote a cupboard or shelf to the storage of your materials. If space is an issue in your house, make yourself a portable "craft workshop" – a couple of box files to hold materials and equipment, along with a protective surface cover and a large cutting mat. Decorate and label your storage boxes and keep things filed for easy access. I can't emphasize enough how important it is to keep your tools and materials in good order and condition. No matter how much time you spend making a card, it won't look good if the paper is creased or marked or your craft knife is blunt.

The Getting Started section looks at all of the materials and equipment that you will need to complete the projects in this book. Also demonstrated are the basic techniques of scoring, folding and tracing templates. There are sections on card design, decorating envelopes and making gift-wrap.

paper and card

A wide range of paper and card is available in good stationery and craft stores, and through mail-order suppliers (see pages 236–7). Paper and card come in standard sizes graded from A5 to A1 (A4 is the standard size for most letterhead paper). Although I occasionally purchase paper in larger sheets, I find that A5 (148 x 210mm / 5 13/16 x 8¼in) and A4 (210 x 297mm / 8¼ x 11 11/16in) sheets are easiest to handle and are less likely to be damaged in transit or storage. Paper and card cut to A4 size is the most widely available commercially.

From the finest tissue to the thickest card, paper and card are available in almost any shade, weight, quality and texture. I always have a selection of textured and plain white and cream card in stock as many designs seem to begin with a white or cream card base. I also often prepare coloured A5 card bases and store them in a special basket filed by colour.

Consider the texture and thickness of cardboard when choosing sheets for particular projects. While you will need good-quality card for a base, paper or thin card is suitable for framing a central feature or for creating layers. I purchase sheets of gift-wrap whenever I see something that inspires me and I save used Christmas and birthday wrapping; you never know when something will be useful. Gift-wrap can be used as a card base but you will need to back it first to give it some stability.

Paper and card are the key raw materials of card-making so you will need a good storage system. Store paper flat and divide it by size, colour and quality so that it is easy to find when you're working. If paper becomes creased you can try smoothing it with a warm iron to restore it to near-perfect condition. Never throw scraps of paper and card away – keep a small box of off-cuts as they will be useful for small projects, collages and layering.

Corrugated card and patterned paper

Sugar paper

This thick, slightly textured paper comes in muted shades and is one of the cheapest papers available. Sugar paper is best used as a feature rather than a card base.

Corrugated card and paper

This comes in a variety of corrugations and colours. Use it as a card base or in layering. It is also great for making your own cut-outs and motifs, and is effective wrapping for cylindrical-shaped objects.

Handmade paper

It is available in soft, pastel colours, through to rich, jewel-like shades. The prettiest papers often have flower petals and leaves embedded in them, giving the papers a wonderful texture. Handmade paper comes in a variety of weights and the thicker papers can be used to create the card blank. Used in layering or to create backgrounds handmade paper always creates an interesting feature.

Mulberry paper

This is a light, opaque paper that is handmade from mulberry leaves and contains strands of silk. It is available in many colours, is lightweight and has a slight textured pattern that can be very effective when used creatively. Mulberry paper can be attached with aerosol glue.

Metallic paper

These papers are good highlighters and are effective when used to create borders, frames and cut-outs. They come in a variety of finishes – some muted, others glossy. Metallic paper is easily damaged and so should be stored properly. It is advisable to put layers of tissue paper between each sheet.

Translucent paper

I love the softness and depth you can create with these papers. When layered on other colours or white they bring a special quality to cards. Translucent paper can be used as a card base but it should be backed with card to give it some substance.

Vellum

This is a semi-opaque paper available plain or patterned. It is very useful for layering.

Plasma

Plasma is a versatile heavyweight, translucent plastic. It is very flexible so is useful for pop-ups. Attach with double-sided tape or glue dots.

Patterned paper

Commercially available patterned paper and gift-wrap can be the basis of wonderful cards. They are useful for backgrounds or to cut motifs from. Make bags and cover gift-boxes with gift-wrap to create coordinated gift sets. Store gift-wrap rolled or flat.

Table napkins and paper hankies

These are a delightful decorative material source. I have found paper hankies printed with frogs, umbrellas and roses; table napkins are also available in a wide variety of designs. Use aerosol glue to attach these materials to cards and don't forget to separate the patterned layer first.

Angel hair paper

This stiff, gauzy paper/fabric is very useful for layers.

Angel hair

The notes on pages 9–15 are general information on the variety of products and materials that are available to the card-maker. You should always follow the manufacturer's instructions for the specific products that you buy.

pens, pencils and paints

Pens

I always have a good handwriting pen and a black and blue fine liner to hand. Fine liners come in a wide range of colours.

Pencils

Pencils are graded by the hardness of the lead. HB is the all-purpose pencil – the lead is neither hard nor soft. If you want a fine line choose an H or HH; if you need a soft, dark line then go for a 3B or 4B. I always keep a selection of pencils. My favourite pencil is a propelling one that contains a soft lead. It is easy to erase when marking up and is lovely to write with and to draw out rough designs.

Marker pens

These are useful for creating designs on plasma or vellum. A double-ended fine/broad point pen in black is my favourite. I use a marker pen when transferring patterns as the marks are clear, clean and easy to see.

Silver and gold pens

I find fine nib silver and gold pens very useful when writing on cards, particularly on black paper or card. Liquid silver and gold pens are also useful but test them out on your paper first as the ink sometimes bleeds. It is important to replace the lid immediately after use.

Gel pens

These highly versatile pens are lovely to decorate cards with. The quality of the ink is very good and the colours are amazing. You can write with one gel pen over another and they are effective on light and dark papers.

Felt-tip pens

Felt-tip pens are always useful as they come in such a variety of thicknesses and colours, and are an economical option. They are good for marking up edgings; try creating rainbow borders with different shades. Use them for highlighting, writing messages inside cards and to ink up intricate rubber stamp designs in place of an inkpad.

3D Paint

3D paint can be used as a paint or a glue and comes in a rainbow of colours. Use it to decorate, embellish or stick. It is also great for highlighting, patterns and corner features. A gem effect can be created using coloured, translucent 3D paints.

Pencil

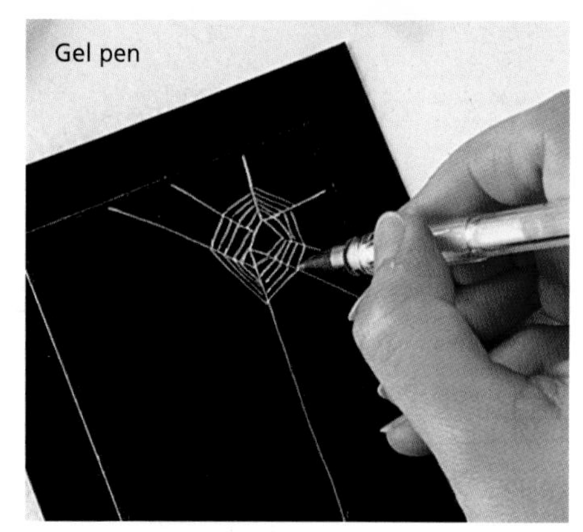

Gel pen

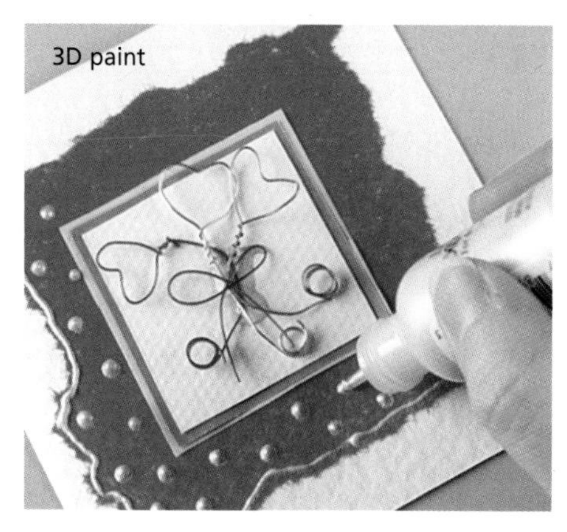

3D paint

cutting and scoring equipment

Scissors

Make sure you have small and large paper scissors, fine-tipped scissors for cut-outs and other intricate work and scissors with a patterned edge. Keep a pair of scissors specifically for cutting fabric. My Fiskars non-stick scissors are one of my most useful tools. I use them for cutting glued surfaces and sticky tape.

Craft knife

A sharp craft knife is essential for cutting neat edges. Great care should be taken when using them – always use a metal ruler, work on a cutting mat and don't cut towards your body. Replace the safety lid after use and keep the knife in a safe place well out of the reach of children.

Cutting mat

Invest in a cutting mat marked with clear measure lines.

Stylus

Use a stylus to ensure a neat fold line is scored on paper and card.

Rulers and measuring

Buy a metal ruler for cutting against and a clear plastic ruler for taking measurements. A set square is essential for drawing accurate right angles.

Shape cutters and templates

I find shape cutting tools and templates extremely useful and often wonder what I did without them. They make cutting out shaped windows and frames so much easier. Once you have mastered the technique of using the tools, squares, circles, ovals and rectangles are quick and easy to cut. Always cut on a board or a mat. Practise on scrap paper and card in order to produce good finished pieces. I have used these tools throughout the book, but don't worry if you don't have them; you can just cut the ovals, squares etc. using scissors or a craft knife. I have included templates where appropriate.

adhesives

Keep a selection of adhesives at hand. Always replace lids and store them correctly.

PVA glue
This glue becomes transparent when dry and is useful for sticking paper to card or card to card. I transfer a quantity of PVA glue to a small squeezy applicator for ease of use. I find this useful when small quantities of glue are necessary and the narrow applicator tube is easy to keep clear and covered.

Glue stick
A glue stick is a useful alternative to PVA glue or adhesive tape. Keep the glue stick clean and always replace the lid to prevent the glue drying out.

Aerosol glue
This is useful when sticking tissue paper, mulberry paper, fabric or opaque paper. When working with this type of adhesive I use what I call a "glue box". This is a cardboard carton approximately 40cm (16in) square. Place the item to be sprayed in the base of the box. Spray it with adhesive then close the lid of the box to minimize the inhalation of fumes and glue particles. Remove the sprayed item after a few minutes. Always follow the glue manufacturer's instructions.

Glue marker pen
This is perfect for attaching decorative motifs and other small items. When a little sparkle is required draw lines/patterns or write text with the glue marker pen and then sprinkle glitter over the glue. For a raised finish sprinkle with embossing powder and fix with a precision heat tool (see page 14).

Glitter glue
Useful as an embellishment, glitter glue can be used to attach acetate decoratively.

Adhesive tape
This comes in a selection of widths. A good, clear, low-tack tape is very useful.

Double-sided tape
Double-sided tape is wonderful. I love it. You will see how much I love it by how many times I've used it in the projects in this book! Quick and easy to use, double-sided tape comes in a variety of widths and is also available in dispensers, which save you cutting little pieces. Use double-sided tape instead of glue for a clean finish.

3D tape
This is a double-sided tape with an added spongy layer enabling you to create raised pictures or embellishments.

Glue dots
These are excellent when a 3D effect is needed and are good for attaching buttons etc. Be careful, as they are very sticky!

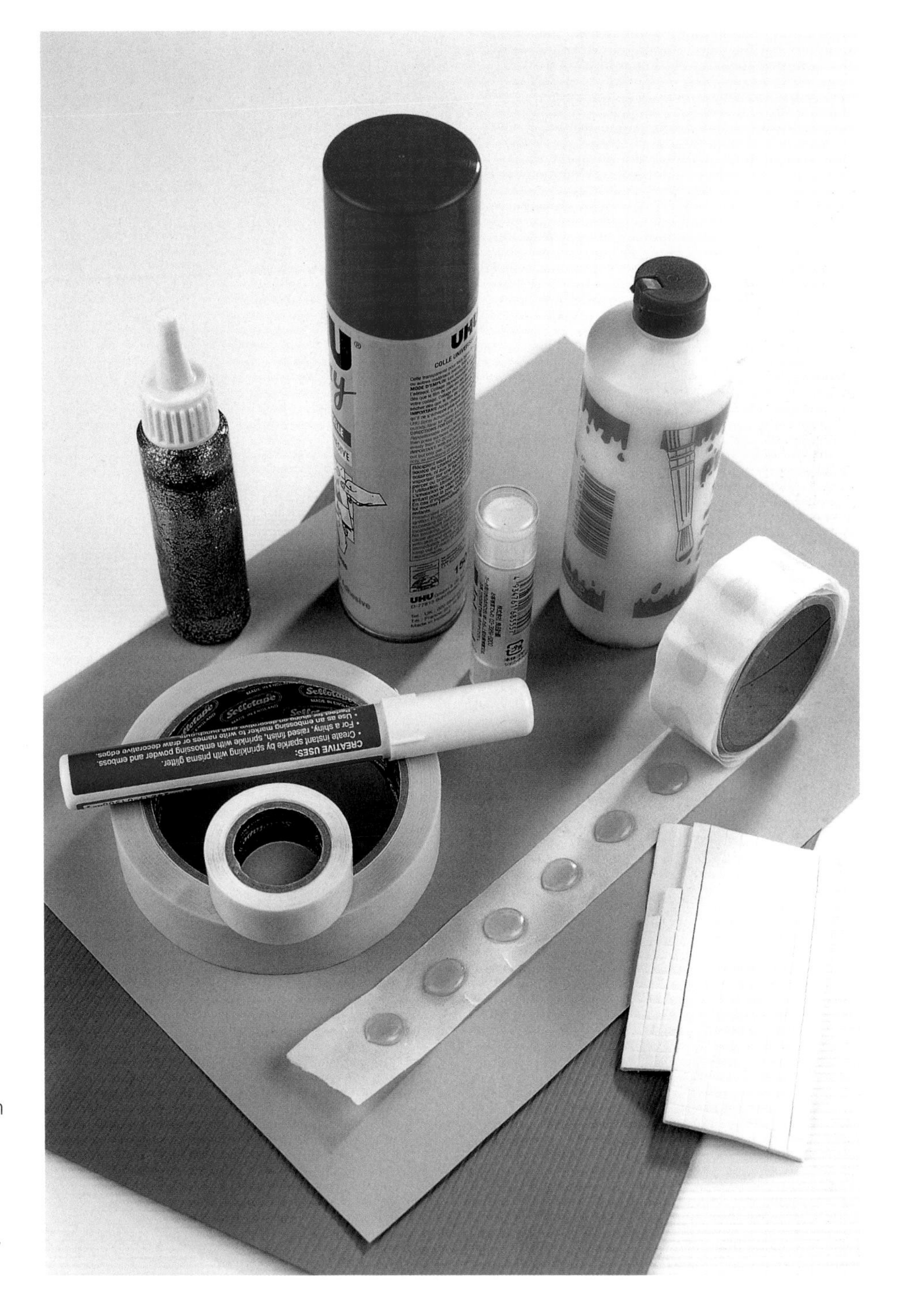

stamps and punches

Stamps

Stamps are available in a huge variety of styles and designs; some even have messages on them. Some stamps are extremely versatile, while you may find you only use others once or twice. Use stamps to create your own motifs and borders. Always keep them clean; wash them in warm soapy water or use stamp cleaner.

Coloured ink pads

Use coloured ink pads or felt-tip pens to colour rubber stamps.

Embossing pads

These can be clear or coloured. You simply stamp your design on to the card and sprinkle it with embossing powder.

Embossing pen

Use an embossing pen along with embossing powder for freehand embossing. Do not use regular felt-tip pens as their ink dries too quickly.

Embossing powders

Embossing powders used with stamps are such fun. Always sprinkle embossing powder over a sheet of scrap paper, shake and return any surplus powder to the container for reuse.

Precision heat tool

A heat tool is necessary to fix embossing powder. These tools get extremely hot so do take care. Keep your hands and the paper or card that is being heated a safe distance from the heat source (try holding the paper with tweezers or tongs). Take care not to singe the paper. Always follow the manufacturer's instructions.

Homemade stamps

Cut out simple designs from a foam sheet and use double-sided tape to attach them to a piece of card or sponge board. Use them as you would a commercial stamp. The holly printed gift-wrap on pages 210–11 was made using a homemade stamp.

Punches

Punches are such fun. You can punch out patterns and motifs. Use the punched out shapes to create your own motifs and to decorate cards, boxes, bags and wrapping paper. A simple hole punch can be a useful tool too.

decorative materials

Rivets and eyelets

These are great to use in card designs. You usually buy the rivets and eyelets in a kit along with a hole maker and a tool to hammer the reverse of the eyelets flat. Kits are obtainable from craft and dress-making shops. You will need a hammer and a sturdy board to work on. I use a wooden breadboard and a lightweight hammer.

Wire

This comes in a variety of colours and thicknesses. Some outlets stock little peg boards that can be used for shaping wire. To cut wire you will need a small pair of pliers or a pair of scissors kept specifically for this purpose.

Buttons and beads

An interesting bead or button can be the focus of a special card. I purchase them in junk shops, cut them off old clothes and seek them out in haberdashery stores.

Braid, ribbon and mesh

Ribbons, strings, threads and yarns are useful for making handles on gift-bags and as extra decoration on a card.

Gems

Faux gems add a little luxury to your cards and can be used as accents. Try haberdashery departments for a selection of unusual stick-on gems.

Glitter

Glitter or sparkle is useful when embellishing cards or making motifs. I prefer the finer glitters and occasionally use glittery embossing powder as glitter.

Oven-bake clay

This material gives you a chance to craft something unique. It is useful for making small hearts, flowers, stars etc. Follow the manufacturer's instructions.

Transfers

There is a huge variety of designs available in many different styles – beautiful illustrations, comic characters, patterns etc. Transfers are an extemely quick way to make an original card. Peel-offs are widely available and can be used on acetate or vellum and decorated with felt-tip pens to create stained glass effects.

Motifs, cut-outs and stickers

There is such a wide variety of motifs and cut-outs available, you are bound to find something to suit your needs. Some are adhesive, while you will need to glue others on. Look in haberdashery departments, cake decorating stores and stationery and craft shops.

card design

Crafters are always on the lookout for new ideas. I keep a journal where I note down and sketch out ideas for all sorts of things from greetings card designs to ideas for fundraiser sales, wedding cake designs, sketches of baby knits or ideas for new recipes. Very often, something that I had intended for one project, works for another. I tape in bits and pieces torn from magazines and inspirational photos taken on holiday. When I have a new project to create a design for, the first place I go to for inspiration is my journal. It is amazing how the roughest of sketches will remind me of a jumper I saw someone wearing when I was travelling on the Paris Metro or a beach bag I noticed on a trip to the seaside. Simply make a record of anything that catches your "design" eye, as you never know when you might be able to use it.

I also have a large noticeboard where I pin up an on-going collection of inspirational pictures and tear-outs. I position it so that I can see it from where I'm working, so my brain is always thinking of new ideas. When the noticeboard becomes overcrowded I tape the most useful images into some sort of order in my journal.

I file bits and pieces of paper and card left over from design projects in themes and colourways. For example, scraps of Christmas gift-wrap, brightly coloured sweet wrappers, the foil from Christmas crackers, Christmas stickers, used Christmas postage stamps torn from envelopes and Christmas cards to be cut up and recycled get put in a box file and labelled "Christmas". When the festive season is approaching I sit down and go through the box searching for inspiration. I also keep themed boxes for spring, flowers, new baby and things suitable for children's cards. Having everything in one place is very useful, particularly when making homemade motifs.

Homemade motifs

I find commercially available motifs very useful and would not be without them. However, occasionally when I have the time, I make my own motifs. I find this very creative as it gives me a chance to play with my materials when I am not under pressure to produce a card for a particular person or client. I save scraps left over from other projects and store them in a large box; my "motif" box. I keep punched out shapes, interesting scraps of paper and card, stickers, ribbons, buttons – basically I don't throw anything away.

A few ideas as to the kinds of motifs that you can make are shown in the photograph below. Take the black cat motif for example. One is made from a stamped image decorated with green gel pen eyes. The image is layered up on paper and card which outline and frame the picture. The other is a silver embossed cat, layered on to different coloured cards. You can use the same stamp, punch, sticker or paper to create many different motifs. Change the colour of the ink, card, paper or pen or cut the backing layers into different shapes and sizes.

scoring and folding

Scoring makes folding card and paper easy and gives your finished cards a professional appearance.

Use a stylus to score paper and card. You should score on the outside of the card.

Hill and valley folds are basic origami folds and are useful to the cardmaker. I have used them in the Winter Wonderland card on pages 212–13.

A hill fold is scored on the front of the card and folded so that the fold peaks towards you.

A valley fold is scored on the underside of the card so that the fold points away from you.

Hill fold

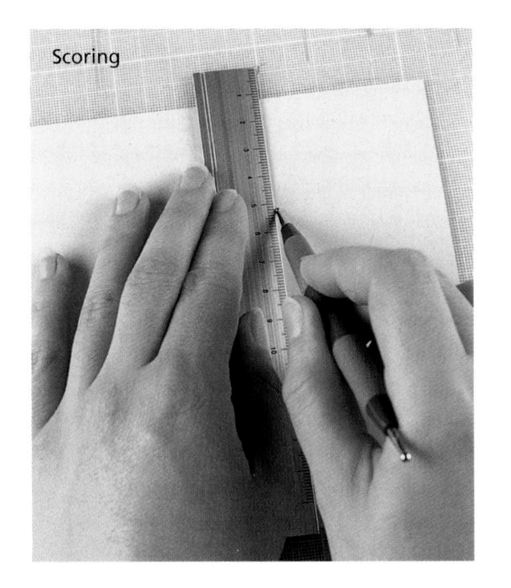
Scoring

Valley fold

tracing templates

There are several ways of doing this, and you may already have your own way that you're happy with, so carry on! I like to trace templates and patterns on to acetate using a marker pen, especially when I'm making templates for envelope inserts, gift pouches, bags – indeed any pattern that I intend using more than once. Obviously you can using tracing paper, but acetate is more robust and your templates will stay in good condition for longer.

decorating envelopes

I'm not going to show you how to make envelopes as they are available to buy in just about every size and colour imaginable. I think it is more efficient to spend your time decorating envelopes to match your cards. Use stickers or motifs to decorate envelope covers. It is also fun to create inserts. You can use decorative paper, or line the envelope with tissue or mulberry paper and then use punches, stamps, gel pens, whatever you can think of, to embellish the lining. Have fun and let your imagination run away with you.

1 Select an envelope that you want to decorate and use it to create a template for the lining. Do this with acetate and a marker pen.

2 Use the template to cut out an insert from your chosen paper.

3 Use aerosol glue (or double-sided tape) to attach the insert inside the envelope.

1

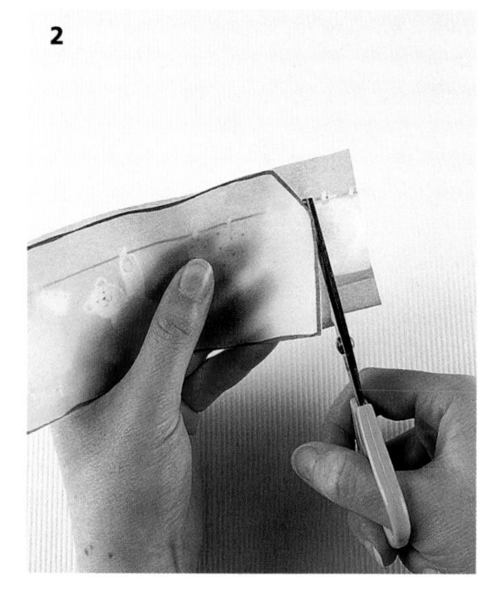

2

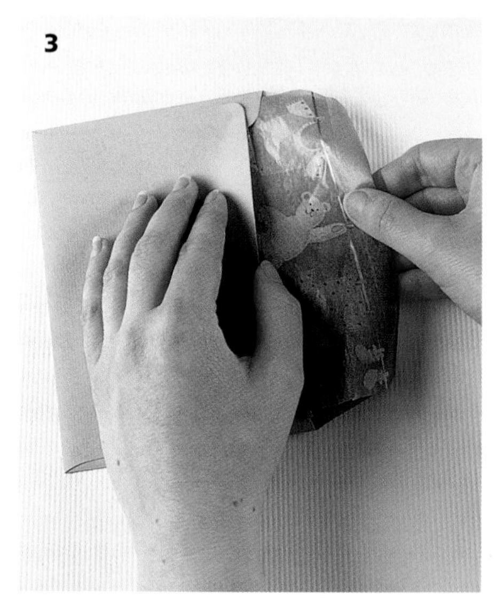

3

gift-wrap

Making gift-wrap to coordinate with your cards is another way to use your design skills. It's your chance to create gorgeous wrapping papers, boxes, bags and pouches that are much more desirable than anything you'll find in the shops. Obviously you need to think about how you can take the design elements on the card and carry them through. I often use the feature stencil, stamp or theme of the card. For example with Flower Power (pages 148–9) simply sticking the punched flowers on paper looked good; while for Holly Berries (pages 210–11) I made my own stamp. The foil decorated card Star Bright (pages 214–15) looks great paired with embossed gold snowflake stamped tissue paper.

Take care to ensure that the shades of paper or card you use are the same as those on your card, or complement the card. Also, remember to use the same embossing powders, paints and pens. It is this attention to detail that will give your work a professional look.

Creating decorative gift-wrap

The ways in which you can decorate gift-wrap are virtually limitless. Paper can be stamped, embossed, stencilled, decorated with punched shapes, covered in stickers – the list goes on and on. Look carefully at the card that you have made and decide how you can use part of the design on your gift-wrap and choose what paper to use as a base.

Tissue paper is my favourite wrapping medium as it is a great background for all sorts of embellishment. It is widely available in a huge range of colours and shades so you'll always find something suitable. I usually use two layers of tissue paper to wrap a gift – one is decorated and the other is plain backing. Use single sheets of decorated tissue to pack out boxes containing delicate or smaller gifts such as lingerie, baby clothes or jewellery.

Brown paper printed or stencilled with gold or silver seasonal motifs makes great Christmas wrapping. White butcher's paper or lining paper looks great printed in primary colours – children's handprints or paint splatters look particularly effective.

Pouches, bags and boxes

Decorating commercially available gift-bags, boxes and pouches is quick and fun. They are available in all shapes, sizes and colours and you can add your own personal touches to them in a matter of minutes. Although it is nice to make your own bags and boxes, buying blanks is certainly the easiest option if you need to decorate 30 party bags or 100 wedding favours. However, even very plain gift-bags can be expensive so look out for other bags that you could use. Plain brown and white paper bags are cheap to buy and make great party bags; recycle gift-bags and boxes that are given to you. Everything that you buy these days seems to come with loads of packaging, so think about how you can reuse it.

If you need a bag of a particular size you may need to make one yourself (see page 21 for instructions). If you need a large bag make it from heavier paper. If this isn't possible, line the paper before you begin construction.

gift pouch

This simple gift pouch is easy to make and fun to decorate. Make pouches in different colours and decorate them to coordinate with your card or gift-wrap.

you will need

A5 sheet acetate
Marker pen
Craft knife
Cutting mat
A5 sheet medium-weight card
Low-tack masking tape
Scissors
Pencil
Stylus
Metal ruler
Eraser
Double-sided tape

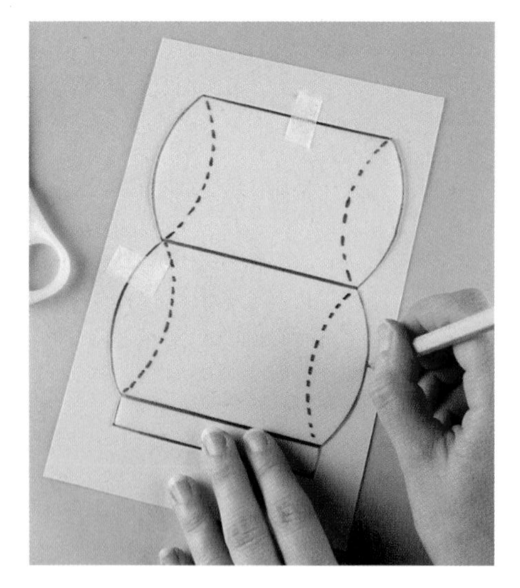

1 Trace the template on page 228 on to acetate using the marker pen. Cut out the template. Lay the template on to the sheet of card and tack in position using low-tack masking tape. Draw around the template in pencil.

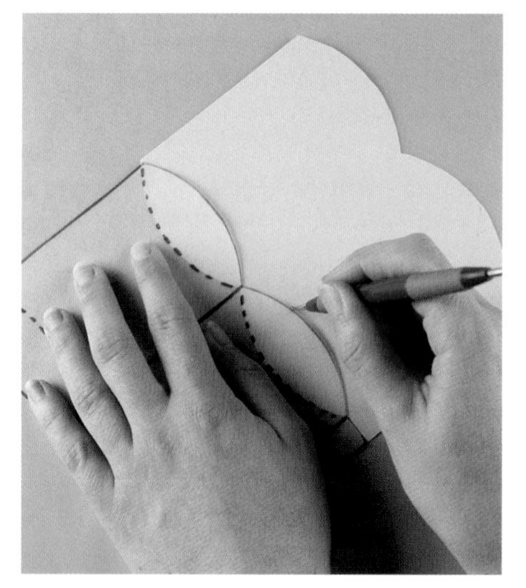

2 Use the stylus (and ruler when appropriate) to score the fold lines. Erase any visible pencil lines carefully before folding the scored lines.

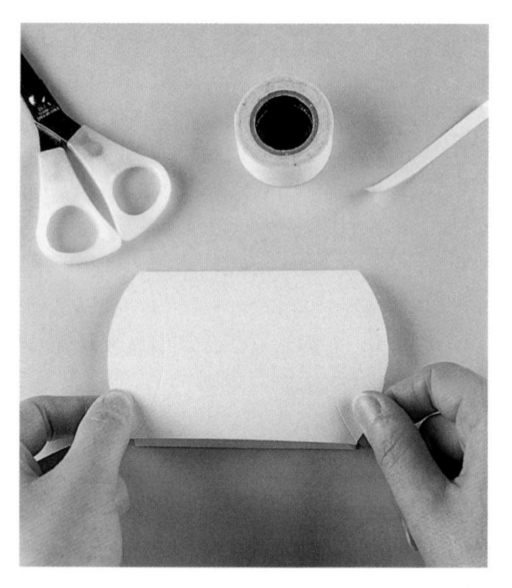

3 Place a line of double-sided tape on the flap, fold over and stick. Your pouch is now ready to decorate.

gift-bag

Making a gift-bag is simple. Use plain or patterned paper and make handles from string, rolled paper or ribbon. The main thing to remember when making a gift-bag is that the side folds should be the same depth as the bottom fold. Once you have mastered the technique making bags will be quick and easy. Choose the size of your piece of paper to suit the gift that you want to put in the bag. You can punch holes in the top of the bag and thread ribbon through it or attach bought or homemade handles using PVA glue.

you will need

Sheet of paper
Double-sided tape
Scissors

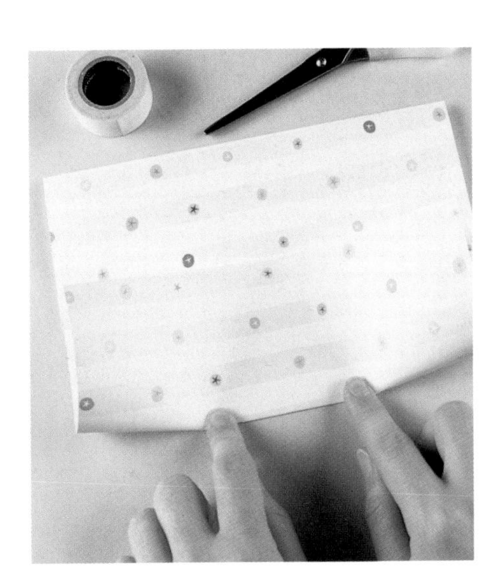

1 Take the side of the paper furthest away from you and fold it down towards the centre. Then fold the side of the paper nearest to you up towards the centre. Make sure that the ends overlap slightly. Use double-sided tape to stick down.

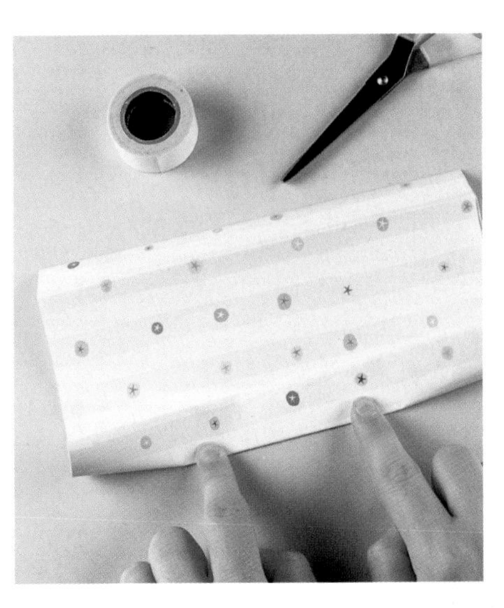

2 Fold the far side in 2cm (¾in). Press down on the fold firmly. Fold the near side in 2cm (¾in) and once again press down on the fold firmly.

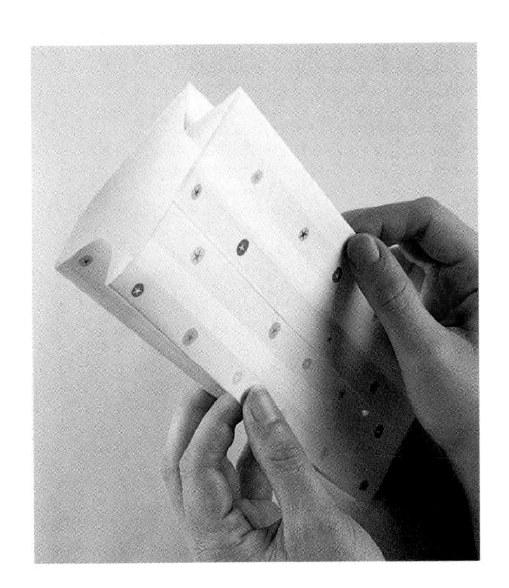

3 Open out and push the folds that you have just made, inwards.

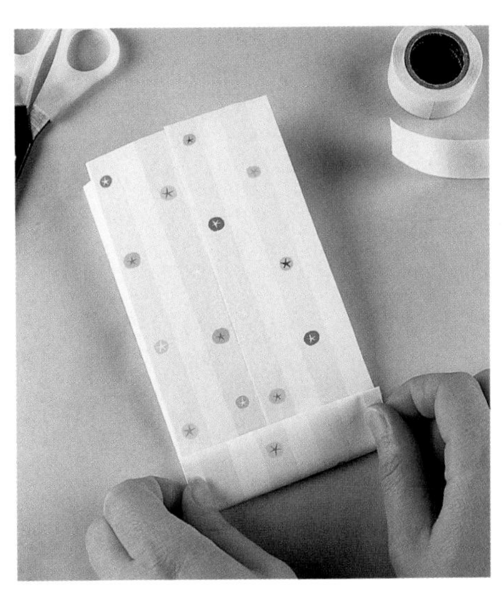

4 Place the folded bag on the surface in front of you. Fold the base of the bag up by 2cm (¾in). Press along the fold firmly. Make a second 2cm (¾in) fold upwards and stick in place with double-sided tape.

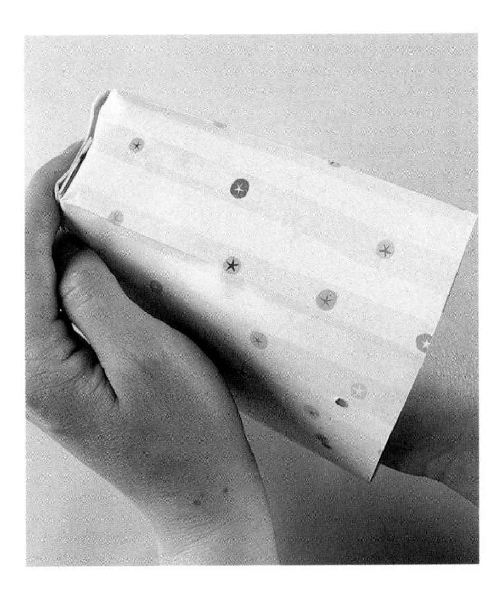

5 Open up the bag by slipping your hand inside it and gently pressing out the corners.

paperwork

projects

celebration collage

This card is effortlessly simple to make and requires only the most basic materials. Artfully placed scraps of torn sugar paper and snippets of gold foil make up this colourful celebration collage.

you will need

- A5 sheet of blue handmade paper
- Pale green, red, yellow, dark green and purple sugar paper
- Metal ruler
- Glue stick
- Scissors
- Scraps of gold and green foil or recycled chocolate wrappers
- Black outliner

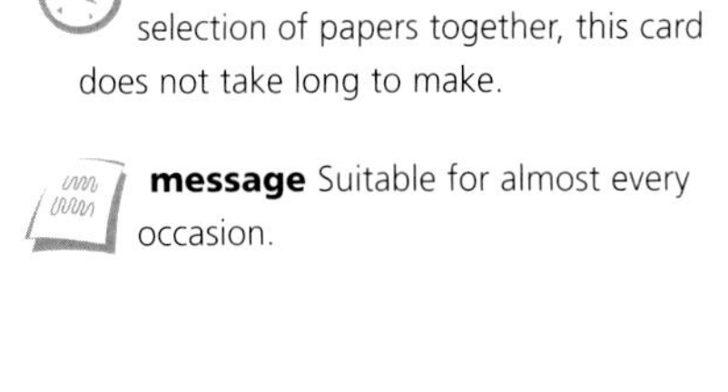

timing Once you have gathered a selection of papers together, this card does not take long to make.

message Suitable for almost every occasion.

1 Fold the sheet of blue handmade paper in half to create the basic card shape. Tear 8 x 3cm (3¼ x 1¼in) pieces from the pale green and the red sugar papers. Next, tear a piece of yellow sugar paper 8 x 3cm (3¼ x 1¼in). Fold it in three and tear off the corners from one end.

2 Open out the folded yellow paper. Using the photo as a guide, glue all three pieces of torn sugar paper in place on the card.

3 Tear three narrow strips of dark green sugar paper and glue in place on top of the pale green rectangle. Next tear a simple 8 x 3cm (3¼ x 1¼in) rectangle from the purple sugar paper and then carefully tear out the wriggly shape. Glue in place on top of the yellow paper. Use scissors to cut out a simple 8 x 2cm (3¼ x ¾in) pattern from gold foil and glue at the base of the collage.

4 Cut three small triangular shapes from gold foil and glue at the top of the yellow panel. Cut out a narrow strip of gold foil and glue at the bottom of the green panel. Tear three 1cm (½in) squares of red paper and glue diagonally on the green panel. Place a small square of green foil on the centre of each square. Stick tiny snippets of gold foil around the edge of the card. Make five crosses from the gold foil and glue them on to the red paper. Highlight the collage with black outliner.

Use miniature collages as gift tags.

newborn baby

Four baby's nappies pegged up on a silver washing line flutter across the sky, surrounded by tiny teddy bears, all set in richly textured card. This magical newborn baby card will delight a mother or grandmother at this special time.

Make these dainty gift tags from scraps of handmade paper and silver bits and pieces.

you will need

- Textured white card
- Pencil and metal ruler
- Craft knife
- Cutting board
- Lilac handmade paper
- Glue stick
- Scissors
- Scrap of silver thread
- PVA glue
- White tissue paper
- Slivers of wood (a matchstick would do)
- Silver teddy bear confetti shapes
- Tweezers

timing This imaginative card will take no time at all to make.

message Send this card to a new mother with a message of love.

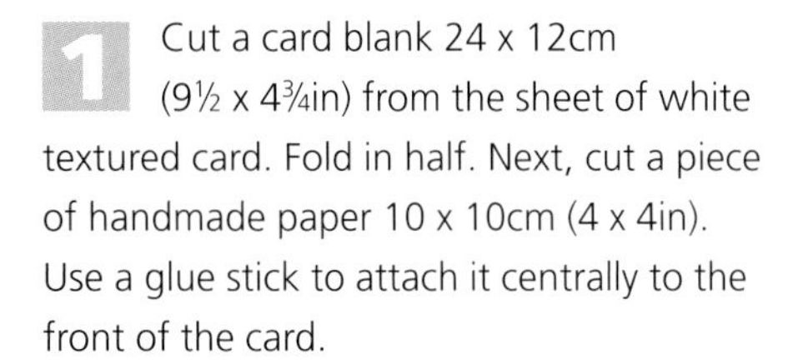

1 Cut a card blank 24 x 12cm (9½ x 4¾in) from the sheet of white textured card. Fold in half. Next, cut a piece of handmade paper 10 x 10cm (4 x 4in). Use a glue stick to attach it centrally to the front of the card.

2 Cut a length of silver thread. Put a spot of PVA glue on to a piece of scrap card and lightly pull the thread through the glue. Carefully lay the thread across the card, so it loops across the sky. Trim the ends level with the lilac square.

3 Glue together a double layer of white tissue paper. Cut some small nappy shapes from the double layer and 'hang' them on the line using a glue stick.

4 Use the craft knife to slice some tiny slivers of matchstick wood and glue them to the nappies to represent the clothes pegs.

5 Use PVA glue to attach six silver teddy bears to the front of the card. It is easiest to do this by holding the bears with the tweezers, touching them into the glue and then placing them on the card.

good luck wish

This card has a sense of the Orient, with the black card providing a mysterious background for the opulent reds and golds. This good luck symbol was cut using a commercial punch. Have a look around your local craft and art shops for something similar, or try one of the mail-order suppliers. I have also made and decorated a coordinating envelope and gift tags.

you will need

- A5 sheet of black card
- Pencil and metal ruler
- Handmade speckled red paper
- Scissors
- Glue stick
- A5 sheet of lightweight white paper
- Paper punch with good luck symbol
- A5 sheet of black paper
- A5 sheet of gold mottled card
- A5 sheet of red paper

timing Once you have located a suitable punch, this card is simple and quick to make.

message Send a good luck greeting to a friend about to sit an exam. This card also makes a very stylish birthday greeting.

1 Fold the black card in half to create the card blank. Cut out a 5 x 5cm (2 x 2in) square from the red handmade paper and use the glue stick to attach it to the lightweight white paper. Cut carefully around the edges.

2 Insert the glued-together red and white paper into the punch and cut out the shape.

3 Cut out a square around the shape and glue a small piece of black paper to the reverse side of the symbol. Next, glue this on to a piece of gold card measuring 6 x 6cm (2½ x 2½in).

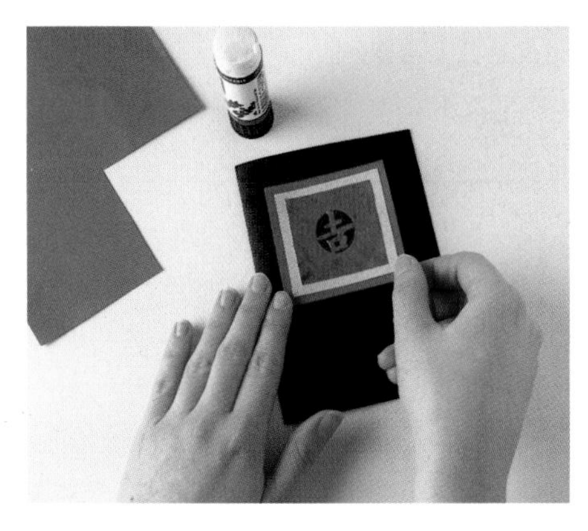

4 Cut a 7 x 7cm (2¾ x 2¾in) square from the red paper and glue this behind the gold card. Using the glue stick, attach the prepared motif in a high central position on the greetings card.

5 Make a matching envelope. Punch a good luck symbol on the back flap and back the cut-out with black paper. Punch another symbol in one of the bottom corners of the envelope.

6 Slide the card into the envelope so that the black of the card shows through the punched holes.

pretty in pink

Send this card as a birthday greeting, a romantic note or simply to say hello to a friend. Pretty pink translucent paper layered over rose pink card and decorated with silver gel pen makes this incredibly simple and quick to achieve. You might want to draw different shaped balloons, for example circles or stars, if these are more appropriate to the greeting.

you will need

- A5 sheet of pink card
- Pencil and metal ruler
- Set square
- Craft knife
- Cutting board
- Scissors
- Pink translucent paper
- Glue stick
- Silver gel pen

timing This is so quick and easy to make that you might like to try a few ideas of your own using translucent paper and metallic pens.

message This stylish card can be used to send almost any greeting.

Use ribbon to tie these elegant gift tags to pink tissue paper-wrapped presents.

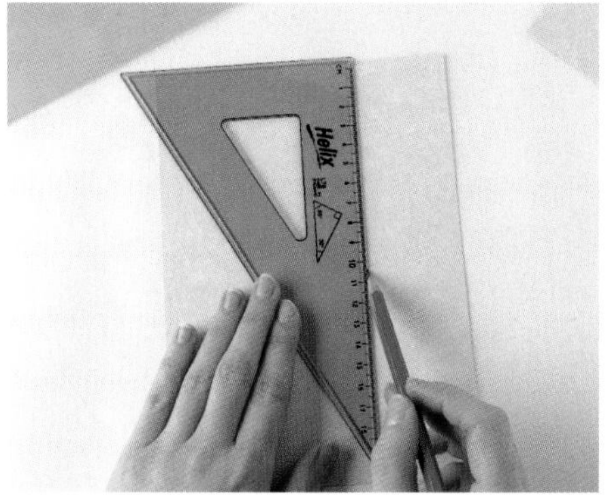

1 Measure a rectangle 21 x 10cm (8½ x 4in) on the pink card. Cut out and fold in half. This is your basic card. Cut a piece of pink translucent paper to the same size. Fold in half, then open up.

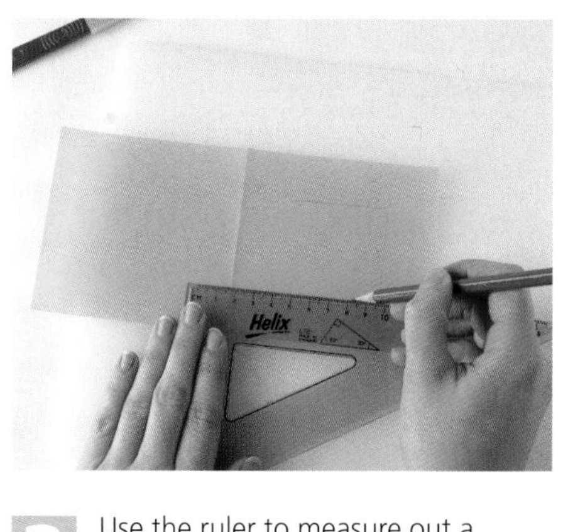

2 Use the ruler to measure out a window 5.5 x 5.5cm (2¼ x 2¼in) in the centre of the front of the translucent paper.

3 Use a craft knife to carefully cut out the window in the translucent paper. Keep the square you have cut out.

4 Run the glue stick down the spine of the pink card and fix it inside the folded translucent paper.

5 Use a silver gel pen to draw swirl shapes and a freehand silver border around the cut-out square.

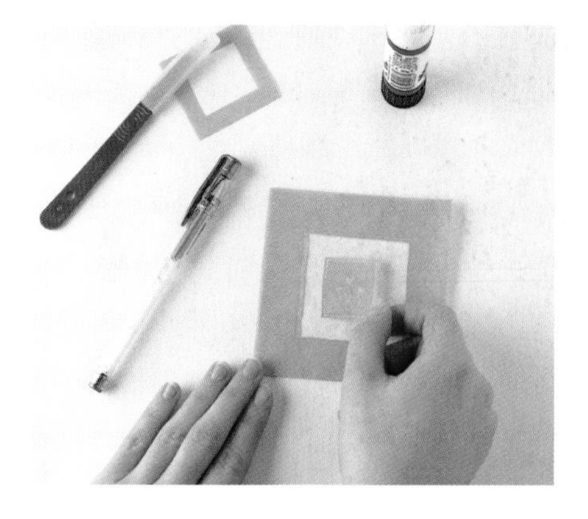

6 Using the 'window' of translucent paper you removed earlier, cut out a square shape roughly 3 x 3cm (1¼ x 1¼in). Attach centrally using the glue stick. Use the silver gel pen to draw on three heart-shaped balloons and a border.

host of angels

These stylish cut-and-fold paper angels will look great on the mantelpiece at Christmas. Paper-cutting is always a favourite with children, so get them involved and see what they come up with. Once you have made the template this card is quick and easy to make, so start a production line and make them for all your friends.

you will need

- Pencil
- Tracing paper
- Scissors
- A4 sheet of white cartridge paper
- Gold marker pen
- A4 sheet of gold paper
- Glue stick

timing Quick and easy to make.

message Paper cut-outs are great fun to make – you may want to make all your Christmas cards this way next season.

1 Use a pencil and tracing paper to trace the angel template on page 220. Cut around the tracing to make the template. Fold a sheet of white A4 cartridge paper in half, then open flat. Now fold from each side in towards the centre and run your finger along the folds to flatten them. Re-fold the centre to create a zigzag fold with four sections.

2 Place the angel template on the front of the folded sheet. Use the pencil to draw around the shape.

3 Cut out the angel, making sure you do not trim the folds where the hands and the bottom of the skirts meet – these points hold the card together. Open out.

4 To decorate the angels, use the gold pen to draw an outline and to add the details (see the photo on page 32 for guidance).

5 Fold the gold paper into a four-section zigzag (as in step 1). The width of the folds should be the same as the width of the angels, but the depth of the card needs to be approximately 2cm (¾in) greater. Trim if necessary.

6 Use the glue stick to attach the angel cut-outs to the gold paper, carefully matching the fold lines. Re-fold the card to fit into an envelope.

decorate the tree

Corrugated card comes in a variety of colours and the size of the corrugations can vary. Two styles of corrugated card are used to make this bright seasonal card. To emphasize the textures, I have used a very simple Christmas tree design decorated with foil stars. I cut the red card so that the lines run horizontally, but you could change the direction of the lines if you wish.

you will need

- Red corrugated card
- Pencil and ruler
- Craft knife
- Cutting board
- Tracing paper
- Green handmade paper
- Brown corrugated card
- Glue stick
- Tweezers
- Gold and red foil stars
- Glue pen

timing Quick to make, but glueing on the stars will slow you down a little.

message A very stylish Christmas card.

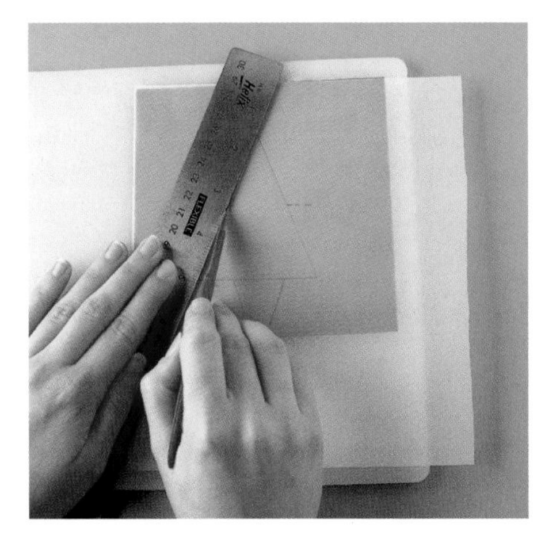

1 Measure a 14 x 14cm (5½ x 5½in) square of red corrugated card. Cut out the square using a craft knife. Trace the template on page 220. Lay the template directly on the card with the top of the tree 3cm (1¼in) from the top of the card and, using a craft knife, cut the triangle as far as the fold line. Fold the card into shape.

2 Cut out the original tracing. Use the templates to cut out the tree from green paper and the pot from brown corrugated card. It is best to draw on the reverse side of the paper and card.

3 Using the glue stick, neatly glue the tree and pot in position on the front of the card.

4 Using tweezers, pick up the foil stars, run them over the tip of the glue pen and stick them in position on the Christmas tree.

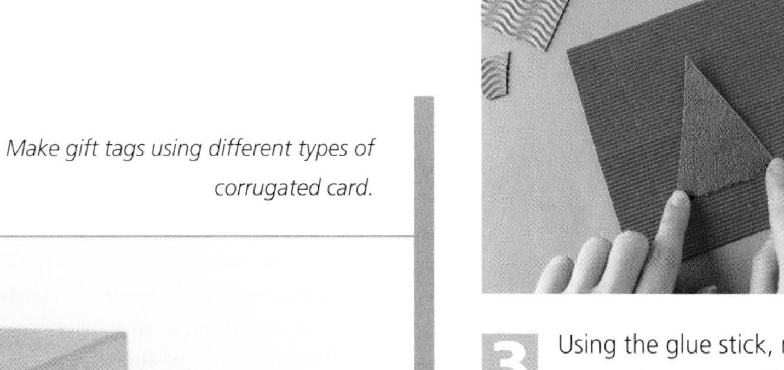

Make gift tags using different types of corrugated card.

gardener's memory album

Decoupage and flower-pressing are great hobbies, and come together to make an excellent card for a gardening friend. This is the ideal card to send to someone with green fingers, and you might like to enclose a real packet of seeds!

you will need

- A5 sheet of aubergine-coloured card
- Pencil and metal ruler
- Craft knife
- Cutting board
- A4 sheet of thin brown card
- Set square
- Glue stick
- Suitably decorated gift-wrap
- Selection of dried flowers
- Tracing paper
- Thin brown paper
- Seeds

timing Collecting the various elements of this card together is what takes the time.

message Send greetings to your gardening friends. You can make this card as seasonal as you like by varying the gift-wrap.

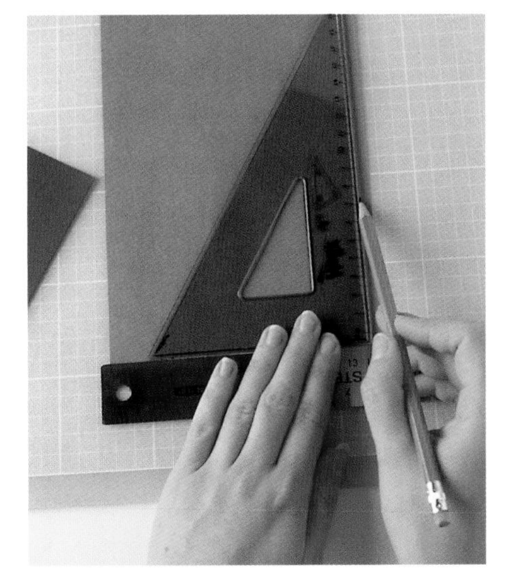

1 Score and fold the aubergine-coloured card in half to create the card base. From the thin brown card, measure and cut a piece 20 x 14cm (8 x 5½in), score and fold in half. Using a glue stick, glue on top of the aubergine-coloured card, matching up the fold lines.

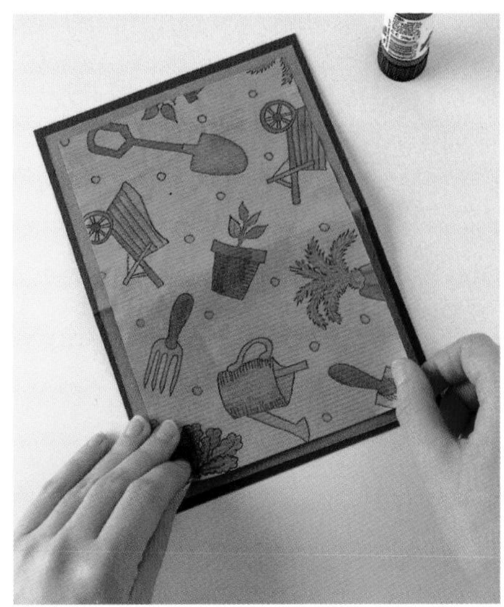

2 Measure and cut a piece of gift-wrap 19 x 13cm (7½ x 5in). Consider which elements of the gift-wrap design you would like to see on the card before you do this. Be sure to save a motif to decorate the centre of the card. Glue this centrally on top of the thin brown card.

3 Next, measure a piece of thin brown card 8.5 x 10.5cm (3¼ x 4¼in) and use the craft knife and cutting board to cut it out. Spread the back with glue and attach centrally on the front of the card. Cut a suitable motif from the gift-wrap and use the glue stick to attach it on the lower left hand side of the card. Add a spray of dried flowers to the right-hand edge of the card.

4 Now make the seed packet. Trace the template on page 220. Cut the seed packet shape from brown paper, fold into shape and use the glue stick to hold in place. Glue the seed packet on to the top left-hand side of the card. Use a small quantity of glue to attach a few seeds, as if they have spilled out of the open packet.

looking through the garden gate

This pretty card is made using shaped pieces of coloured paper to create a simple yet very effective image. Once you have made this card, why not try to create your own design?

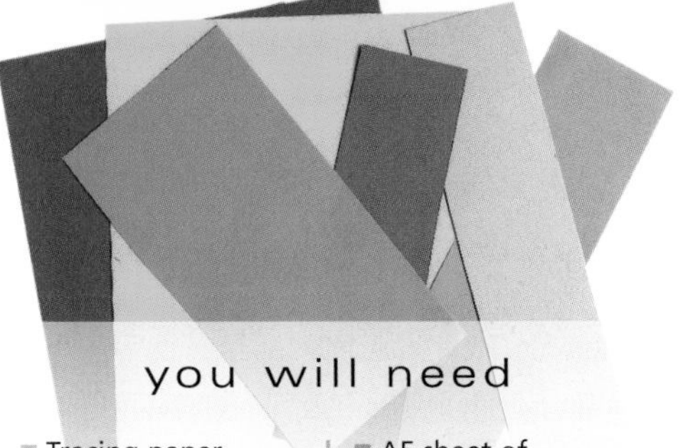

you will need

- Tracing paper
- Pencil
- Spray adhesive
- Scrap of card for template
- Scissors
- A5 sheet of textured white card
- Paper in yellow, purple, dove grey, lilac, green and violet
- Glue stick

timing Paper-cutting takes time and patience, so make this card when you have plenty of time and won't feel rushed.

message Send birthday greetings on this handsome card.

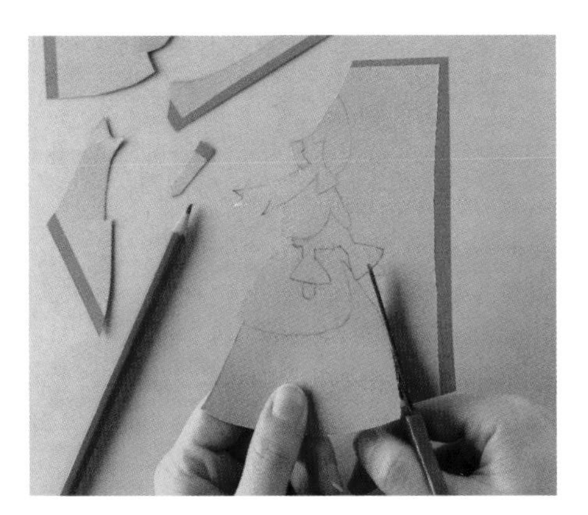

1 Trace the template of the lady on page 221 on to tracing paper. Using spray adhesive, attach the tracing paper to a piece of scrap card and cut around the shape of the lady.

2 Fold the white card in half to form the card blank. Trace around the whole template on yellow paper and cut out. Cut within the pencil lines so you don't get any marks and the template doesn't get bigger. Use the glue stick to attach the lady to the card blank.

3 Cut out the individual items of clothing from the template – you need to cut extremely accurately. Referring to the photograph, put the templates on to the appropriate pieces of coloured paper. Keep the tracing paper on the templates to remind you which is the right side. Draw around the templates and cut out.

4 Trace the tree template on page 221 twice. Cut out from green paper and using the marks on the template as a guide, stick on to the main picture, sliding slightly underneath the lady.

5 Start positioning and sticking the clothes on to the main picture. Start from the bottom and work upwards – overskirt, sleeves, hands, cape, and so on.

6 Cut four 5mm (¼in) wide lengths of violet paper. Glue them around the edges of the card to form a border and then cut off the excess.

spring surprise

Lemon yellow, spring green and crisp white – this parchment card is just the thing to brighten up an early spring birthday. This Victorian craft has enjoyed a revival and materials and equipment are available in most craft shops. I have united the old with the new in the form of modern gel pens and traditional parchment to create this delightful card.

you will need

- A5 sheet of light green paper
- Tracing paper
- Pencil
- A5 sheet of plain parchment
- Non-permanent adhesive tape
- Small, sharp scissors
- A5 sheet of white paper
- Small ball embossing tool
- Metal ruler
- Embossing pad
- Daisy tool
- Gel pens in white, lemon and green
- Yellow felt-tip pen
- Clear glue
- Scrap piece of coloured paper

timing Parchment craft takes time and patience but the results can be quite beautiful. It's best to practise the techniques on a scrap of parchment paper first.

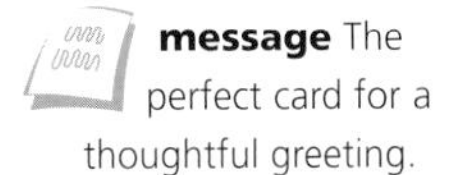

message The perfect card for a thoughtful greeting.

1 Fold the green sheet of paper in half to create the card blank. Trace or photocopy the design on page 221. Bearing in mind that the design is marked on the reverse side of the card, lay the A5 sheet of parchment over the design, fix in position with non-permanent adhesive tape and mark out the scalloped edge with a pencil.

2 Carefully remove the adhesive tape and use the sharp scissors to cut out the scalloped design.

3 Once again, lay the parchment over the design. If you traced the template, place a piece of white paper underneath the tracing so that you can see the design clearly. Use the embossing tool to mark out the double oval, then use a ruler to mark out the diagonal lines.

4 Place the parchment on the embossing pad. Decorate the oval border between the lines with the daisy tool, pressing the tool firmly into the paper.

continued ▸

5 Working on the reverse side of the parchment, use the embossing tool to score a line down the centre of the card at the edge of the design (line is indicated on design). Score another line 1.5mm (1/16in) away from the first line. This forms the spine of the card.

6 Turn the parchment back to the right side and decorate with gel pens. Colour the daisy petals white, the centres yellow and the stems green. Colour the yellow ribbon using the gel pen and the felt-tip pen.

7 Place the card on to a piece of scrap coloured paper (for additional clarity while working). Make four yellow dots at the intersections of the diagonal lines. Decorate around the edge of the card with yellow and green gel pens. Finally, apply glue to the inside of the spine and insert the green folded card.

speckled eggs

A sheet of pale green handmade paper reminiscent of the colour and patterning of wild birds' egg shells was the inspiration for this textured spring greetings card. Egg shapes have been cut from scraps of green and gold paper and embellished with gold outliner, birds' feathers and stars. As this card is not a standard size, you will need to make a matching envelope.

continued ▶

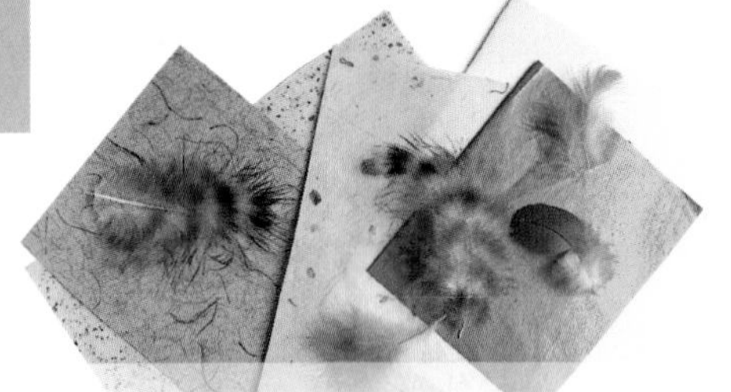

you will need

- Pencil and metal ruler
- Craft knife
- Cutting board
- A3 sheet of textured white card
- A4 sheet of pale green speckled handmade paper
- Glue stick
- Gold outliner
- Tracing paper
- Scissors
- Scraps of gold paper
- Piece of scrap paper
- Gold sparkle embossing powder
- Tweezers
- Gold stars
- A few small feathers

timing Making this card will take you some time but the effect is well worth it.

message A wonderful card to send as an Easter greeting.

1 Measure and cut out a 30 x 15cm (12 x 6in) rectangle of textured white card. Fold in half to create the card blank. Measure out a 13cm (5in) square on the pale green paper and tear out the shape. Glue it centrally on the white card.

2 Measure and cut out an 8cm (3¼in) square from the textured white card and glue centrally on top of the pale green paper. Decorate the edge of the white card with gold outliner. Leave to harden.

3 To make the eggs, trace the template on page 222 and cut out a number of egg shapes from scraps of speckled green and gold paper. The eggs can be decorated in a number of ways.

4 Make patterns on the eggs using gold outliner. Lay the eggs on a piece of scrap paper and, before the outliner dries, sprinkle the embossing powder over them. Tip the excess powder back into the pot.

5 To attach gold stars, pick up a star with the tweezers, draw the back of it gently over the glue stick and then place in position on the egg.

6 Once the gold outlined border has hardened, arrange the egg shapes on the card. When you are happy with the arrangement, glue in place. Use glue to attach the feathers and, as a final touch, tiny gold stars to highlight your card.

7 If you wish, make a coordinating envelope from pale green speckled handmade paper and decorate it with more eggs.

Attach tags to tiny bunches of flowers.

spice rack

This card not only looks great, it smells wonderful as well. It would look good mounted in a simple wooden frame and hung on the kitchen wall.

you will need

- A4 sheet of buff handmade paper
- A4 sheet of white card
- Spray adhesive
- Set square
- Pencil and metal ruler
- Craft knife
- Cutting board
- A5 sheet of brown paper
- A5 sheet of terracotta honeycomb paper
- A5 sheet of cream textured paper
- Glue stick
- Tracing paper
- Non-permanent adhesive tape
- Clear adhesive
- Selection of interesting shaped herbs and spices

timing Set aside an evening to make this highly effective card.

message Send birthday greetings to your foody friends.

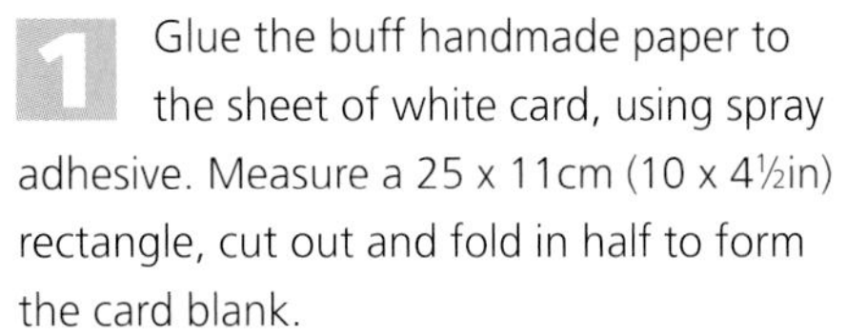

1 Glue the buff handmade paper to the sheet of white card, using spray adhesive. Measure a 25 x 11cm (10 x 4½in) rectangle, cut out and fold in half to form the card blank.

2 Measure a rectangle 10 x 8cm (4 x 3¼in) on the brown paper, a rectangle 9 x 7cm (3½ x 2¾in) on the terracotta honeycomb paper and a rectangle 8 x 6cm (3¼ x 2½in) on the cream paper and cut out. Using the glue stick, glue the rectangles one on top of the other on the front of the card.

3 Trace the template on page 222 on to tracing paper. Place the tracing on the remaining cream paper, fix in position with tape and cut out the basic shape and the nine windows. Glue on to the cream rectangle.

4 Squeeze some clear adhesive into each window and carefully place different herbs or spices into each one. Leave to dry.

A selection of spicy gift tags.

champagne celebration

An explosion of paper streamers and foil stars creates a stunning celebration card. The art of quilling was popular in the Victorian era. Narrow strips of paper were coiled and shaped into intricate patterns and used to decorate picture frames, boxes and even small pieces of furniture. This card and the next one provide two examples of quilling, one traditional and one more modern. Practise the basic techniques first, before you try your hand at creating a masterpiece of your own.

you will need

- A3 sheet of red card
- Pencil and metal ruler
- Set square
- Craft knife
- Cutting board
- A4 sheet of gold card
- A4 sheet of blue ribbed card
- Glue stick
- Tracing paper
- Scissors
- Natural corrugated card
- Quilling streamers in various colours
- Quilling tool
- PVA glue
- Small paint brush
- Foil stars
- Tweezers
- Gold outliner

timing Take a little time over this card for the best results.

message Time to celebrate – send with 18th or 21st birthday greetings.

Festive tags with which to address your gifts.

1 Measure a rectangle, 30 x 15cm (12 x 6in) on the red card. Cut out and fold in half. On the back of the gold card, mark a 12.5 x 12.5cm (5 x 5in) square. Mark out a 2cm (¾in) wide frame and use the craft knife to cut it out.

2 On the blue ribbed card, mark out a 11.5 x 11.5cm (4¼ x 4¼in) square and cut it out. Mark up a 1cm (⅓in) wide frame and cut out with the craft knife. Glue the layers one on top of the other, using a glue stick.

3 Trace the bottle template on page 222 and cut out. Trace around the template on natural corrugated card and cut out. Cut a label from gold card and use the glue stick to attach it to the bottle. Glue the bottle to the bottom right corner of the card.

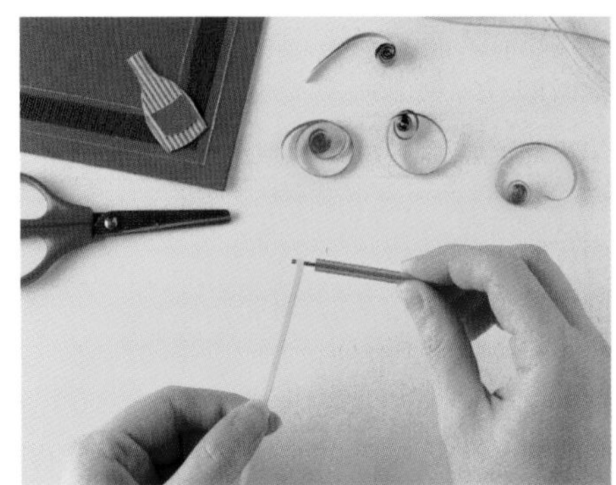

4 To begin quilling you need streamers 15cm (6in) long. Use the quilling tool to curl the ends by threading the streamer into the tool, winding around and then letting go. Repeat to make eight streamers.

5 Put a small blob of PVA glue on a scrap of card. Use the paint brush to apply the glue and carefully place the streamers on the card to create an explosive effect.

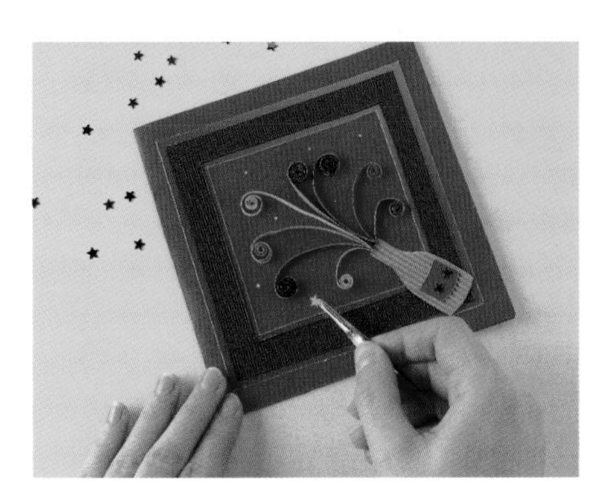

6 When all the streamers are in place, decorate the card with foil stars. Outline the top of the bottle and label with gold outliner.

vase of tulips

This vase of golden tulips makes a card just perfect for Mother's Day. Once you have mastered the quilling technique, try making different flower and leaf shapes.

you will need

- A5 sheet of yellow textured card
- Pencil and metal ruler
- Set square
- A5 sheet of red card
- Craft knife
- Cutting board
- Glue stick
- A4 sheet of white handmade paper
- Paint brush
- Quilling streamers in brown, yellow and green
- Quilling tool
- Scissors
- PVA glue

timing Quilling is an intricate craft so have plenty of time and patience when making the card.

message The ideal card for Mother's Day – just add a bunch of real tulips as an extra gift for a special person.

1 Create the card base by folding the yellow textured card in half. Measure a rectangle 9 x 7cm (3½ x 2¾in) on the red card and cut out.

2 Using the glue stick, glue the red card on to the yellow card base in a high central position.

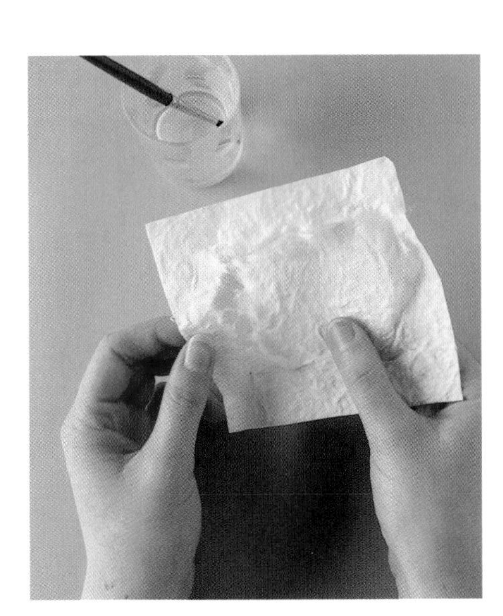

3 Measure a rectangle 8 x 6cm (3¼ x 2¼in) on the white handmade paper. Using the paint brush, paint a line of water around the rectangle, thoroughly soaking the paper. Carefully tear it out. Using the glue stick, glue it on top of the red card.

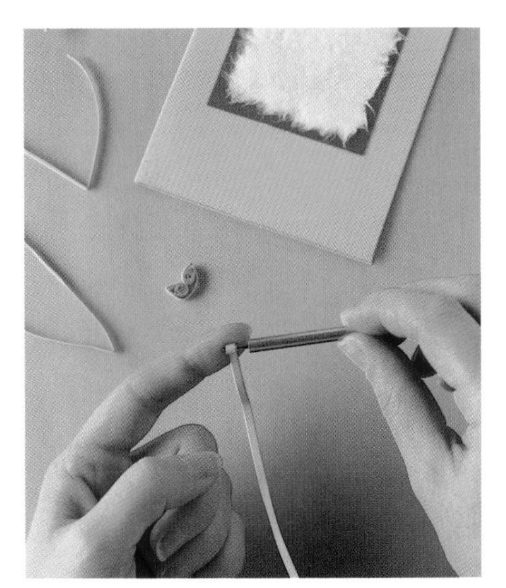

4 To make the flowers, fold a 15cm (6in) length of yellow quilling streamer in half. Using the quilling tool, coil one end of the streamer towards the fold.

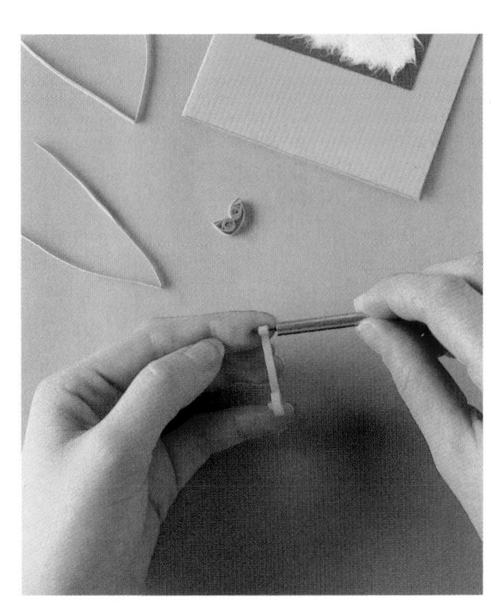

5 Release the coil from the tool, thread in the other end of the streamer and coil up towards the central fold.

continued ▶

Make simple quilled flowers to decorate gift tags.

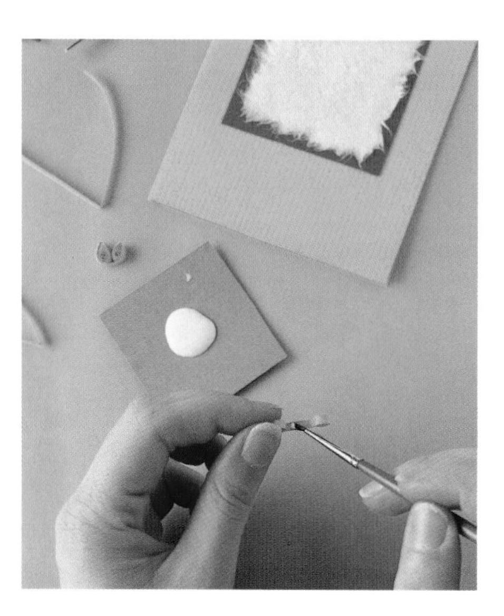

6 Place a small blob of PVA glue on a scrap of card. Allow the coils to unwind slightly, then glue the ends in place near the central fold.

7 Pinch the twin coils into a double teardrop shape to create the tulip flower. You need to make four flowers.

8 Coil three tiny bud shapes from yellow streamers and carefully glue the ends in place. Using the paint brush and PVA glue, stick the flowers and buds in position on the front of the card.

9 Each leaf needs a 15cm (6in) length of green streamer. Wind the streamer tightly around the quilling tool, release the streamer, then pinch into a scroll shape about 1cm (½in) long. Glue the ends in place.

10 The vase is made from three brown 20cm (8in) lengths of quilling streamer. Coil each length tightly around the quilling tool then release and pinch into a large eye shape. Glue the end in place and use PVA glue to attach to the card.

pop-up parrots

Pop-up cards can be quite difficult to make, but this one featuring bright and jolly parrots on a jungle background uses a simple movement.

continued ▶

you will need

- A4 sheets of heavy paper in dark olive green, red, lime green, apple green
- Pencil and metal ruler
- Set square
- Craft knife
- Cutting board
- Glue stick
- 2 A4 sheets of translucent sky blue paper
- Spray adhesive
- A4 sheet of white paper
- Tracing paper
- Scissors
- Yellow gel pen
- Paint brush
- Watercolour paints in yellow, dark and pale green, blue and red
- Black marker pen

1 Cut a piece of dark olive green heavy paper into a rectangle 24 x 12cm (9½ x 4¾in). Score and fold in half to create the card base. Cut a 10 x 10cm (4 x 4in) square of red heavy paper and stick on the front of the card. Cut a 9 x 9cm (3½ x 3½in) square of blue translucent paper. Using spray adhesive, back this with a square of white paper and, using the glue stick, glue on to the red paper.

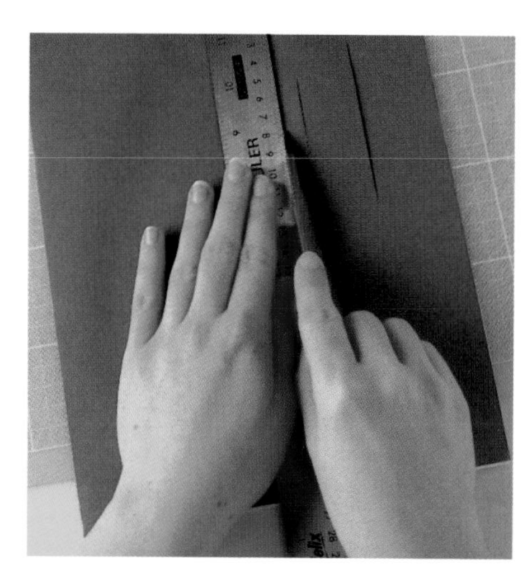

2 Using pencil trace the template on page 223 on to another sheet of translucent blue paper. Apply spray adhesive and attach it to the sheet of white paper and cut along the pencil outlines and cutting lines for the pop-up. Fold in half, with the white paper on the outside.

timing Pop-up cards take time to make, so set aside an hour or two.

message A fun greeting for a young child.

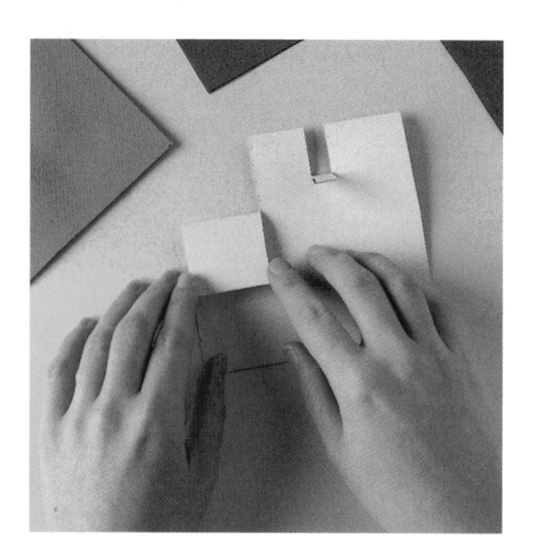

3 Fold back the first narrow tab and the large outer tab, then flatten down and open up the card.

4 Now pinch and pull these tabs outwards to create the structure of the pop-up. Apply glue to the areas of the white paper that will stick on the card base and glue inside the green card.

5 Using the templates on page 222, trace the foliage on to the various green cards and cut out. Trace and cut out the red flowers.

6 Using the glue stick, glue the various items in place inside the card. If any items overhang the sides, simply trim them.

7 Now attach the branch and flowers to the front of the card. Highlight the red flowers used on both the inside and outside of the card with yellow gel pen.

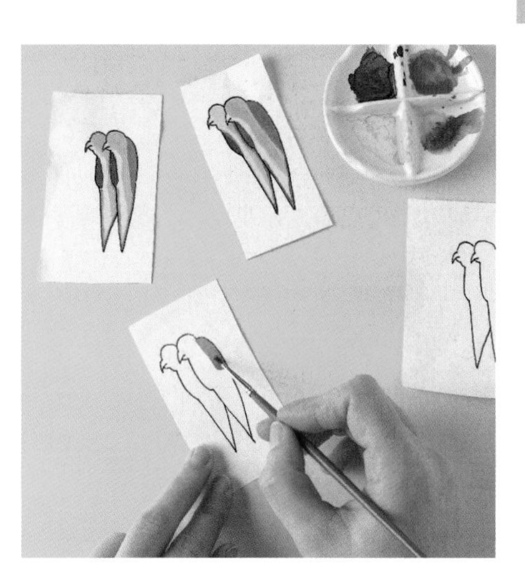

8 Trace the parrot template on page 222 and draw four pairs of parrots. Paint the parrots, copying the colours in the photo above.

9 Highlight and outline the parrots with black marker pen and add the eyes. Carefully cut out the parrots just outside the black outline.

10 Stick three pairs of parrots in position on the inside of the card, on the tabs. Make sure you position them so that the card can close without creasing the parrots.

11 Finally, using the glue stick, stick the fourth set of parrots in position on the front of the card.

ways with colour

projects

pretty daisies

He loves me, he loves me not, he loves me, he loves me not. White daisies with long, fragile stems, layered on lilac, green and white card, create this simply stylish birthday greeting.

you will need

- A5 sheet of lilac card
- Craft knife
- Pencil and metal ruler
- Set square
- Cutting board
- A5 sheet of green card
- A5 sheet of white textured card
- Glue stick
- Yellow watercolour paper
- Watercolour paints in white, green and orange
- Fine paint brush
- Scissors

timing Take your time when making this card and enjoy the painting.

message The spring colours of this card will brighten up a wintry day and bring a little sunshine into someone's home.

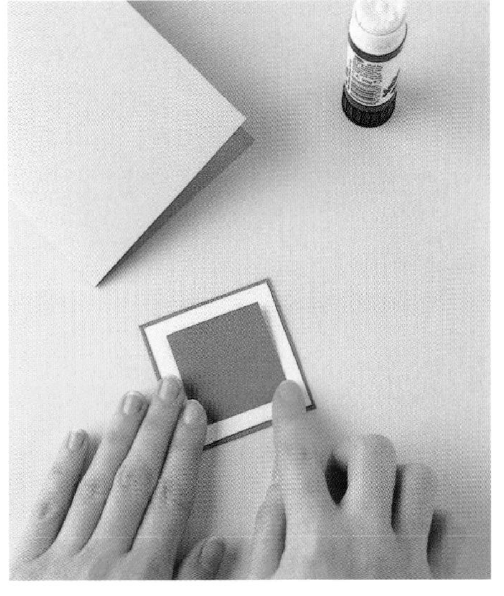

1 Fold the A5 sheet of lilac card in half to create the card blank. Next, create a layered effect by cutting the following: a 6.5 x 6.5cm (2½ x 2½in) square and a 4.5 x 4.5cm (1¼ x 1¼in) square of green card; 6 x 6cm (2¼ x 2¼in) square of white textured card. Layer as shown and glue on to the card base.

2 Paint the flowers on the yellow watercolour paper in groups of three, well spaced apart. Paint the white flowerheads first, followed by the green stems and leaves. It is a good idea to paint a few and choose the best one for your card. Spares can be used as gift tags.

Use any leftover daisies to decorate some gift tags.

3 When the white paint has dried, add orange centres to the daisies with a small dot of paint. Leave to dry.

4 When dry, use the set square and pencil to measure squares 4 x 4cm (1½ x 1½in) around the flowers and carefully cut out. Glue in place on the front of the card.

oriental flowers

Simply beautiful. The exquisite marble inlay work that decorates the Taj Mahal in India inspired this lovely card. You might want to create your own picture of flowers rather than use the template.

you will need

- A5 sheet of white textured paper
- Pencil and metal ruler
- Craft knife
- Cutting board
- Tracing paper
- Gel pens in gold, green, pale blue and pink

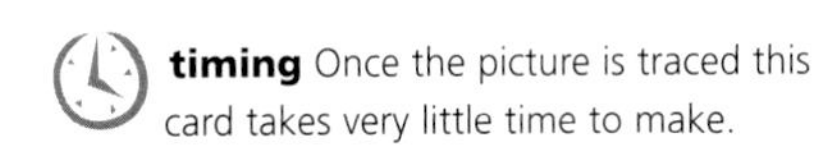

timing Once the picture is traced this card takes very little time to make.

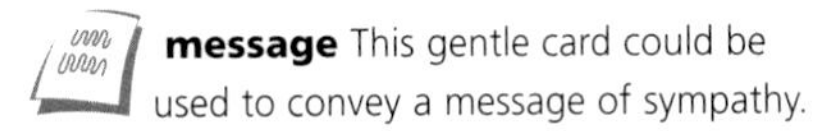

message This gentle card could be used to convey a message of sympathy.

1 Cut a 13.5 x 15cm (5¼ x 6in) piece from the sheet of white textured paper. Measure and mark the centre. Score the centre line and fold in half.

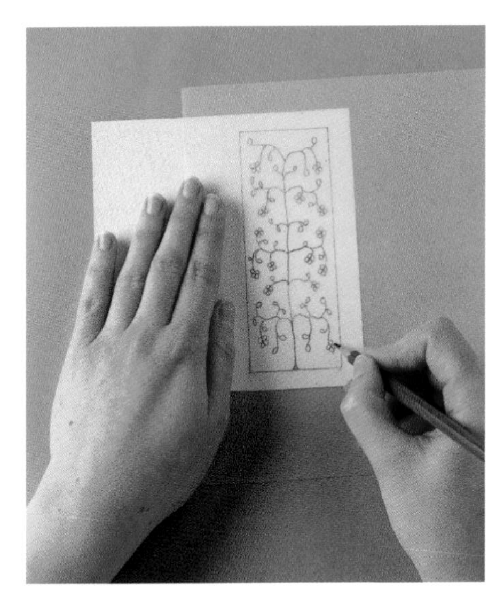

2 Open the card. Trace the template on page 224. Place the traced pattern over the front of the card and trace over the pattern again in pencil, to leave an impression in the textured paper.

3 Use the gold gel pen to create the border then, following the traced pattern, go over the stem, branches, leaves and flowers.

4 Looking closely at the photograph of the finished card, use the pink, green and blue pens to colour in the flowers and leaves.

Some freehand gilded swirls, petals and leaves turn plain gift tags into something quite special.

Christmas crib

I found this beautiful paper in a gift shop. It seems to change colour from spangled gold to peach to red, rather like an amazing sunset. I thought it made the ideal backdrop for a special Christmas card. To ring the changes make the card with a midnight blue sky or a golden yellow dawn.

you will need

- Suitable wrapping paper
- Pencil and metal ruler
- Set square
- Craft knife
- Cutting board
- Glue stick
- A5 sheet of white paper
- Tracing paper
- Non-permanent adhesive tape
- A5 sheet of stiff card, for template
- Scissors
- A5 sheet of black card
- Gold pen
- Gold outliner

timing Tracing the picture takes time, so settle down with a cup of tea to make this card.

message A lovely Christmas card to take pride of place on the mantelpiece.

1 Cut the wrapping paper to A5 size. Use the glue stick to attach the A5 sheet of white paper to the reverse side of the wrapping paper. Fold in half. This is your card blank.

2 To create the skyline, use a pencil and tracing paper to trace the template on page 224. Lightly stick the tracing paper template to a piece of stiff card and cut around the top and bottom outlines. Position this card template 1.5cm (¾in) from the bottom edge of the black card. Fix in position with non-permanent adhesive tape, then draw around the top and bottom outlines with a gold pen.

3 Fill in the rest of the detail with gold pen, then go over the lines with the gold outliner. You may need to practise a few lines and curves on a spare piece of paper before you begin to draw over the gold lines. Fill in all the decorative details, including the crib. Leave to dry.

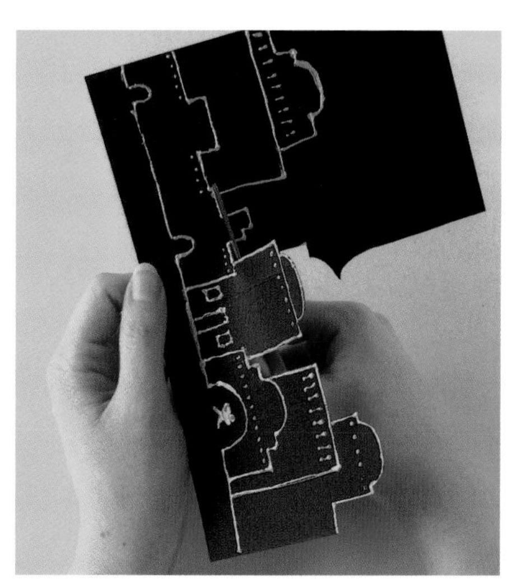

4 Once the gold outlines are dry, use scissors to cut out the picture along the top outline. Take care not to cut off the gold outliner.

5 Glue the black cut-out on to the 'sky'. Add the star of Bethlehem above the stable to complete the card.

glitz and glamour

To make a change from robins and Christmas trees, here silver birds and glitter glue are used to decorate this festive party card. The delicate stencilled bird can be printed on a variety of coloured tissue papers and glued on to silver card for a magical effect. You might like to mass-produce these cards as they are so quick and easy to make.

you will need

- Tracing paper
- Pencil and metal ruler
- Spray adhesive
- A4 sheet of thin card
- Craft knife
- Cutting board
- Silver acrylic paint
- Saucer
- Sponge
- Tissue paper
- A5 sheet of silver card
- Glue stick
- Green glitter glue
- Foil stars and glittery strips

timing Once set up, this card takes no time at all to make. A good card to mass produce.

message Suitable as a party invitation or seasonal greeting.

1 Trace the bird template on page 224. Spray a thin layer of spray adhesive on to the back of the tracing and attach it to the thin card. Use a craft knife to cut out a stencil from the card.

2 Pour a small quantity of silver paint on to the saucer and dip the sponge in it (do not put too much paint on to the sponge). Lay the stencil on the tissue paper and stencil silver birds on to it, dabbing with the sponge. Leave to dry.

3 Cut a piece of silver card 21 x 11cm (8½ x 4¼in). Fold in half to form the basic card. Use the ruler and pencil to draw a 7.5cm (3in) square around the motif and carefully cut it out. Use the glue stick to attach it centrally on the card.

4 Draw a glitter glue border around the design. Decorate the card with stars and glittery strips. It is easiest to pick up each strip or star with tweezers, pass it over the glue stick and then position on the card.

Experiment with different coloured papers and decorative elements.

robin red breast

Put your stencil to good use and make an interesting selection of cards.

Stencilling is an excellent technique to use when you need to make lots of greetings cards. Commercially produced stencils are available from art and craft shops, but they are also fairly simple to make yourself. Once you have the stencil, prints are quick to make.

you will need

- Pencil and metal ruler
- Tracing paper
- Glue stick
- Thin card
- Craft knife
- Cutting board
- Gold acrylic paint
- Saucer
- Sponge
- Black tissue paper
- Red glitter glue
- Black felt-tip pen
- A5 sheet of cream textured card
- Scissors
- Gold foil
- A5 sheet of red textured paper

timing This card is very quick to do and is great for children to make. A good card to mass produce.

message This cute little robin will send a delightful seasonal message to family and friends at Christmas. You could also create your own layered look in different colours.

1 Using a pencil and tracing paper, trace the robin template on page 225. Use the glue stick to attach it to the thin card. Cut out the stencil carefully with a craft knife. It is a good idea to prepare two or three stencils, especially if you want to make a lot of cards.

2 Pour a little gold paint on to a saucer and press the sponge into the paint. Do not use too much paint. Spread out the black tissue paper, hold the stencil firmly in place and dab the sponge on to the stencil. You might want to stencil more robins than you will need and use the best prints.

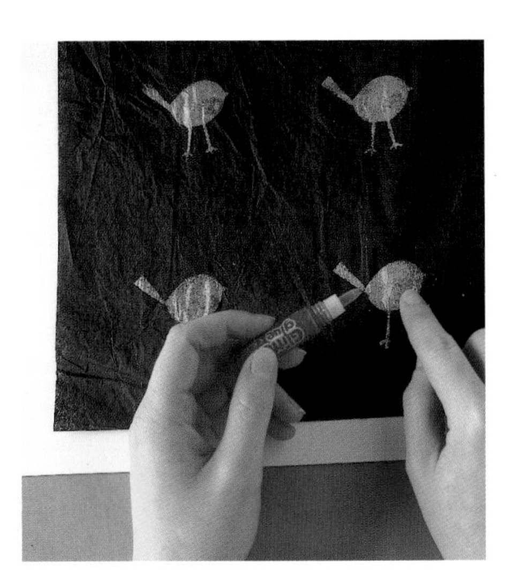

3 Once the gold paint is dry, dab the red glitter glue on to the robin's breast. Make a black dot for its eye with felt-tip pen. Now you are ready to put together the card.

4 Make a card base by folding the cream card in half. As this card has a naive feel to it, the layers are cut approximately to shape. The first layer is a rectangle of gold foil approximately 7.5 x 9.5cm (3 x 3¾in), glued on to the cream card. Glue in a high central position on the card base.

5 The second layer is a rectangle approximately 6.5 x 7.5cm (2¾ x 3in) cut from red textured paper. Glue it on top of the gold foil. Finally, cut out a rectangle around the robin motif, approximately 5 x 6cm (2 x 2½in) and glue it on top of the red paper.

Christmas candle

This glittery card shows how effective a repeat pattern can be. You could use this idea to create other card designs, such as Christmas trees, stars or holly leaves.

you will need

- A4 sheet of white textured card
- Pencil and metal ruler
- Set square
- Craft knife
- Cutting board
- Candle stamp
- Embossing stamp pad
- Scrap paper
- Red embossing powder
- Tweezers or metal tongs
- Precision heat tool
- Gold glitter embossing powder
- A5 sheet of red card
- Glue stick

timing This card is very simple to make; you could make a number of cards in an evening.

message A sophisticated festive greeting.

1 Mark out a rectangle 16 x 15cm (6¼ x 6in) in pencil on the white card, then cut out with the craft knife and metal ruler. With the longest edge at the top, score down the centre and fold. This is your card blank.

2 On the remaining white textured card, stamp a row of candles. You will barely be able to see the design as the ink is clear. Stamp more images than you need, as some may not be perfect.

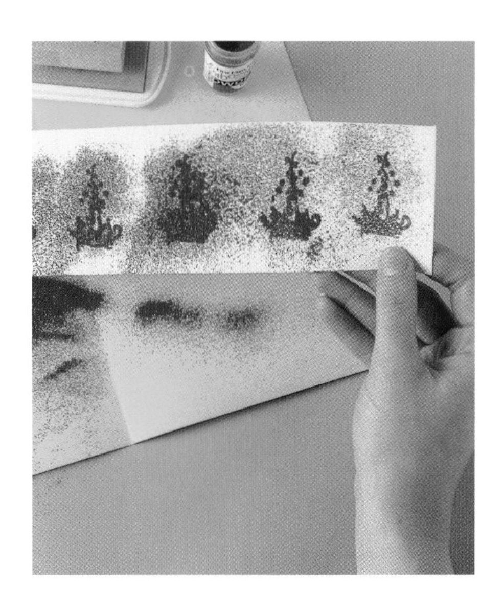

3 Working quickly, fold a sheet of scrap paper in half, then open it out. Holding the stamped card over the scrap paper, sprinkle over the red embossing powder (you need to do this before the ink dries). Shake the excess powder back on to the paper, then tip it back into the pot.

4 Holding the stamped card with tweezers or tongs, heat the embossing powder with the heat tool (see page 14) until melted. Mark a pencil rectangle 5 x 3.5cm (2 x 1¼in) around each stamp, keeping the design central, and cut out.

continued ▸

5 Sprinkle gold glitter embossing powder on to the scrap paper. Working quickly, press each edge of the design into the side of the embossing stamp pad (this is where there is most ink).

6 Dip the edges of the card rectangle into the gold powder. Melt with the heat tool as before.

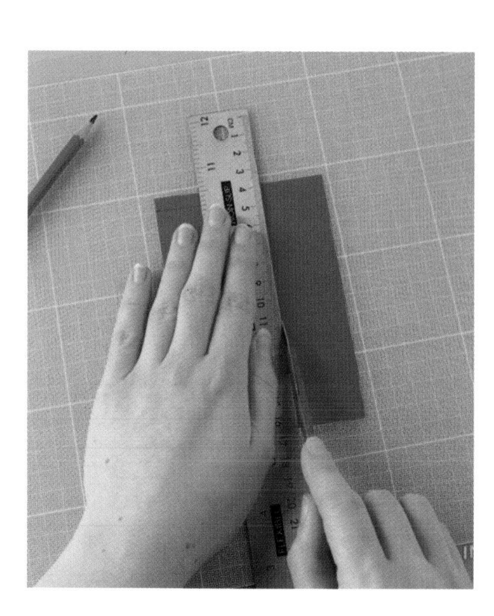

7 Measure out a rectangle 12 x 5.5cm (4¾ x 2¼in) on the sheet of red card and cut out.

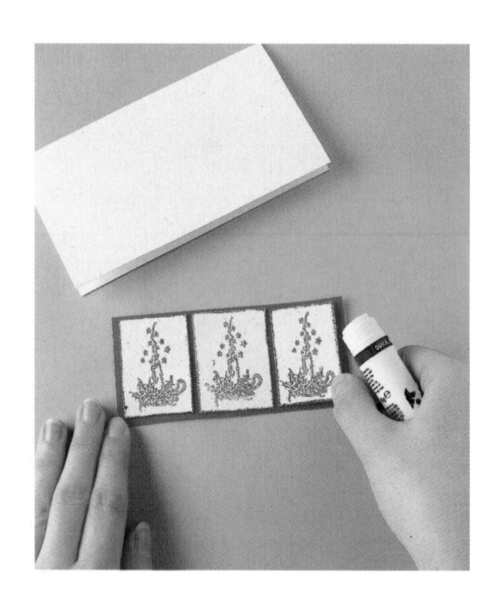

8 Glue three candle images on to the red card, then glue the red rectangle on to the white card blank.

Look around for other interesting stamps to use for cards and gift tags.

dolphin display

Leaping dolphins always make a fine picture. Glass paint works well on acetate, creating a stained glass effect. It can take up to 24 hours to dry so be sure to leave enough time to create this card.

continued ▶

you will need

- A5 sheet of white textured card
- Pencil and metal ruler
- Set square
- Pair of compasses
- Cutting board
- Craft knife
- A5 sheet of red paper
- Double-sided adhesive tape
- Tracing paper
- Black marker pen
- Acetate
- Non-permanent adhesive tape
- Glass paints in white, black, blue and green
- Palette
- Paint brush

timing Glass painting takes time, so this card is best made over a weekend to give the paint time to dry thoroughly.

message A good all-purpose greetings card. Send to friends about to go on holiday or as a birthday greeting.

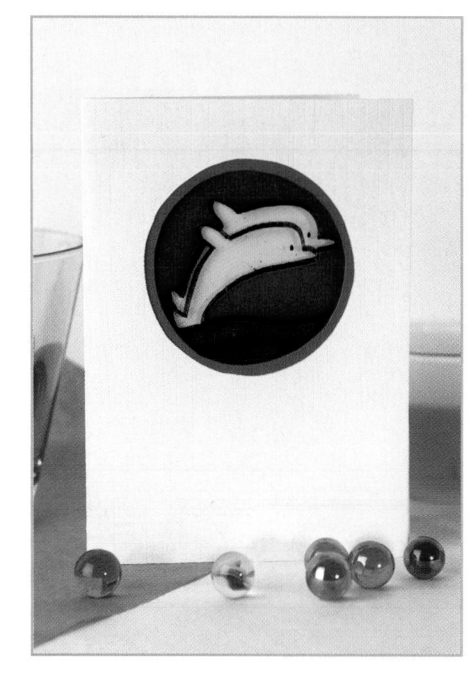

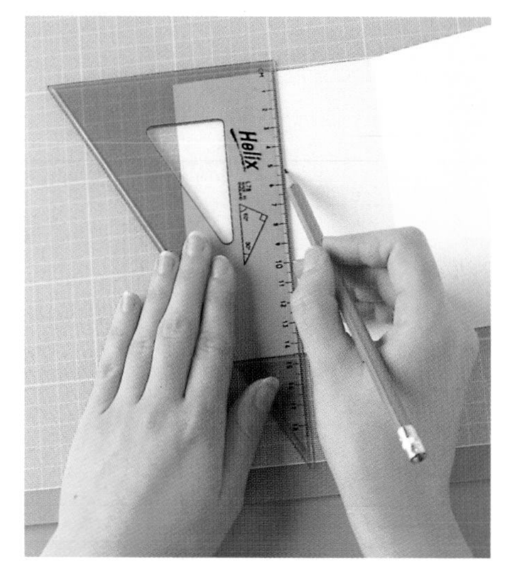

1 Fold the sheet of A5 paper in half to make the card blank. To create the circular window, open the card blank. The left-hand inside leaf of the card should measure 10.5cm (4¼in) across. Divide this in half and you have 5.25cm (2⅛in). Lightly rule a line down the card to mark the centre. Next, lie the set square down the ruled line and make a mark 5.25cm (2⅛in) down from the top of the card. This is the centre of the circle.

2 Place the point of the compasses on the centre mark and draw a circle with a 3.5cm (1⅓in) radius.

3 Place the card on the cutting board and carefully cut out the circle using the craft knife. This is not easy, so take your time.

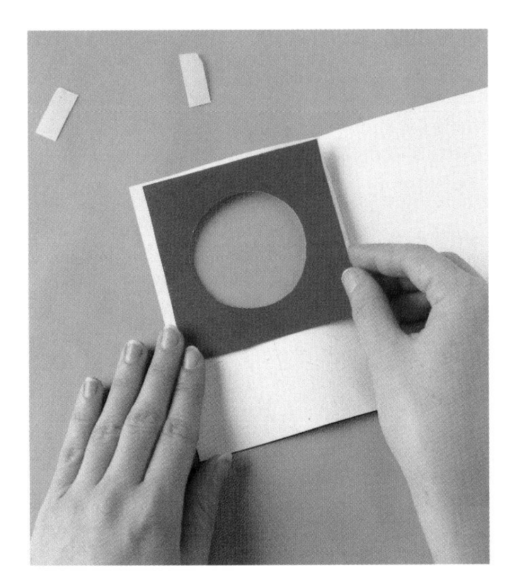

4 Cut a 10cm (4in) square from the red paper. Draw two diagonal pencil lines across the square to find the centre point, then draw a circle with a 3cm (1¼in) radius and, as in step 3, cut it out. Using double-sided tape, stick the red card inside the white card, to form a red border around the window. Before fixing firmly in place, look from the front of the card to ensure the red circle is displayed evenly.

5 Trace the dolphin template on page 225. Place this beneath the acetate and hold in place with non-permanent tape. Use a marker pen to trace the picture on to the acetate.

6 Colour in the dolphins with glass paint. Be sure not to go over the marker pen lines. You will need to leave the picture until quite dry – this may take several hours.

7 Once the paint has dried, you can put together the card. Use double-sided tape to attach the dolphin painting so that it is centred within the window.

Keep the shapes simple when creating your own designs.

fashioned in fabric

projects

cat on the mat

Brown paper, fabric scraps and a white felt cat with glowing green glitter glue eyes create this friendly greetings card. I have used squares of small print patchwork fabric to create a homely look. Use whatever fabric scraps you have to hand and simple felt animal shapes to create your own designs.

Scraps of fabric and sequins are useful when creating cards and tags.

you will need

- A5 sheet of mottled beige paper
- Metal ruler
- Craft knife
- Cutting board
- Blue fabric, 8.5 x 8.5cm (3¾ x 3¾in)
- Patterned fabric, 7.5 x 7.5cm (3 x 3in)
- Dotted fabric, 6 x 6cm (2½ x 2½in)
- Spray adhesive
- Scissors
- Tracing paper
- Pencil
- White felt
- Embroidery scissors
- White cotton thread
- Needle
- PVA glue
- Green glitter glue

timing Once you have cut out the shapes, it won't take long to make this card as all the elements are glued into place.

message A good card to send to friends settling into a new home.

1 Score and fold the sheet of mottled beige paper in half to create the card blank.

2 Prepare the fabric by spraying the backs of the squares with spray adhesive. Attach the blue piece of fabric to the card blank in an upper central position. Place the patterned fabric square centrally on top of the blue fabric and the dotted fabric square on top of that.

3 Trace the template on page 226 and cut out. Draw around the template on to the white felt and use embroidery scissors to cut out the cat shape.

4 The cat's whiskers are created using white cotton thread. Thread the needle and simply push it through the felt, pulling so that approximately 1cm (½in) of thread pokes out one side. Trim the other side so that it is even. Repeat three times.

5 Use PVA glue to stick the cat centrally on to the layered fabric. Finally, give the cat two green eyes by squeezing tiny green glitter glue dots on to the cat's face.

Christmas pudding

An embroidered motif on white silk on a white and gold card base makes up this extra special card with which to send Christmas greetings.

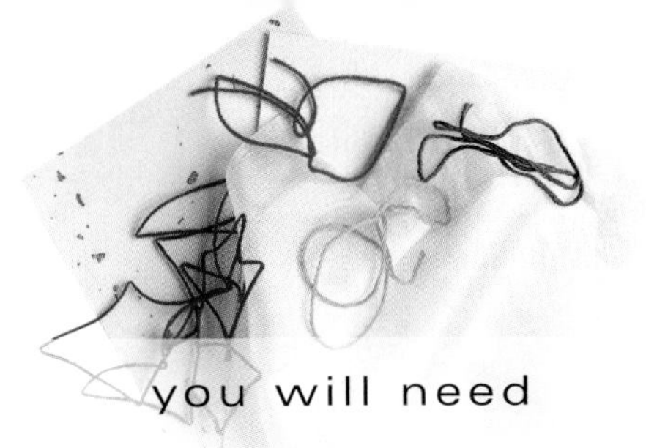

you will need

- A5 sheet of textured white card
- Pencil and metal ruler
- Craft knife
- Cutting board
- White paper with gold speckles
- Tracing paper
- Scissors
- Scrap paper
- Gold glitter embossing powder
- Embossing pad
- Precision heat tool
- Glue stick
- Gold pen
- White silk, 8 x 8cm (3¼ x 3¼in)
- Thin polyester wadding, 8 x 8cm (3¼ x 3¼in)
- Pins
- Embroidery thread in golden yellow, rich brown, green and red
- Needle
- Double-sided tape

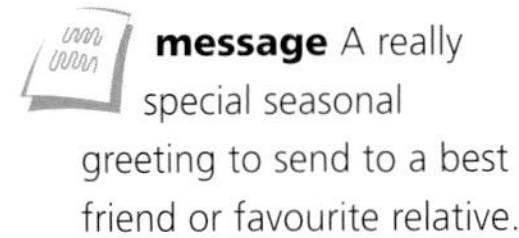

timing Completing the embroidery for this card will take a little time but the finished product will be worth it.

message A really special seasonal greeting to send to a best friend or favourite relative.

1 Fold the card in half. Measure in 3cm (1¼in) from each side and from the top and draw a 4.5cm (1¾in) square. Use a craft knife to cut out the square.

2 Trace the border template on page 225. Position on the white and gold paper and cut out the centre square with a craft knife. Cut out the shape with scissors.

3 Fold the scrap paper in half, open out and tip the embossing powder on to it. Press the edges of the border into the pad, then dip into the powder. Use the heat tool (see page 14) to fix.

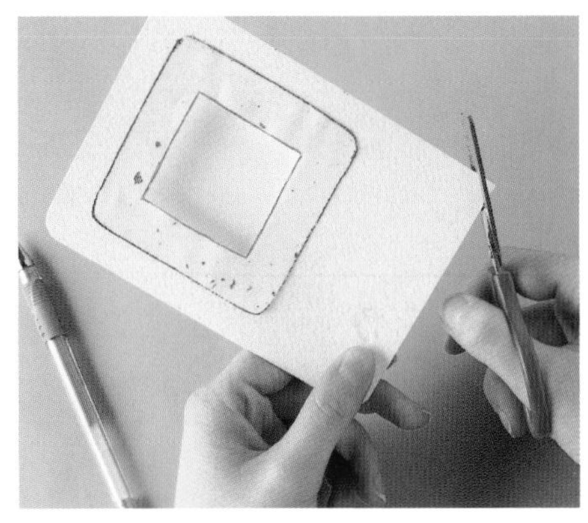

4 Glue this frame on to the card base. Draw a thin border around the central square with the gold pen. Carefully round the corners of the card base.

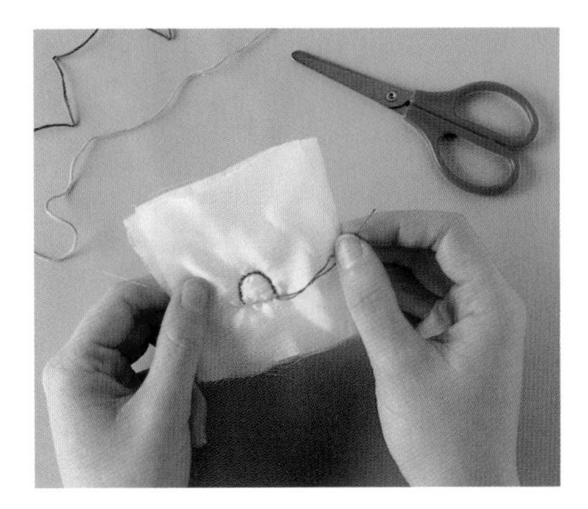

5 Pin the silk square to the wadding. Embroider a line of backstitch in yellow. Embroider the outline of the pudding in brown thread, then fill in the centre. Embroider the leaves in green and the holly berries in red. An outline of the pudding shape is included on page 225.

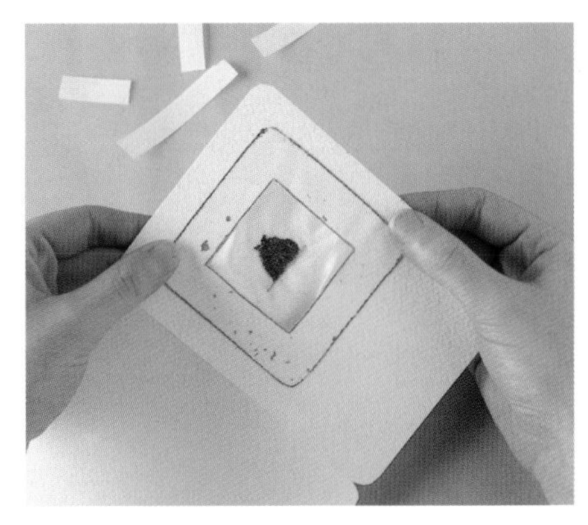

6 Using double-sided tape, position the embroidered picture behind the window and stick it in place.

scented lavender

Lavender, muslin and a little simple embroidery set on handmade paper make the perfect birthday card. Harvesting aromatic lavender flowers is a seasonal pastime I look forward to every year. Pick them in the morning when the dew has dried. Hang bunches in a shady, airy spot for a few weeks. Packed away in paper bags, lavender will hold its fragrance for many years.

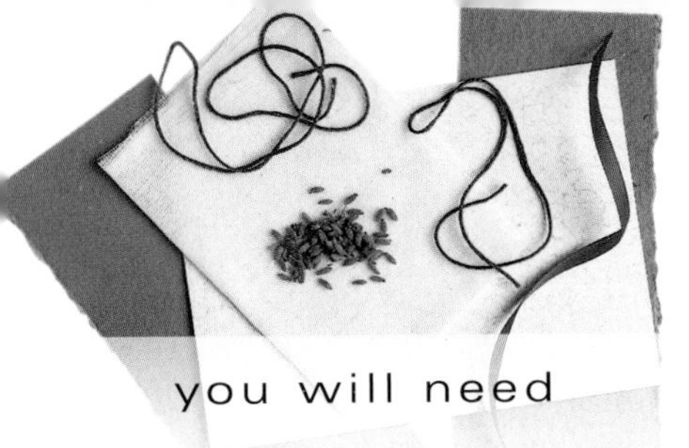

you will need

- Muslin, 22 x 16cm (8½ x 6½in)
- Scissors
- Needle
- White thread
- Small handful of lavender
- Teaspoon
- Lavender-coloured narrow ribbon
- Embroidery threads in green and lavender
- A5 sheet of white patterned paper
- Glue stick
- Blue handmade paper, 8 x 11cm (3¼ x 4½in) with torn edges
- PVA glue
- Paint brush

timing A lavender harvest, embroidery and a little crafting make this a more time-consuming card but the result is a memory that will last for years.

message Send to a friend who needs a little cheering up.

1 Fold the muslin in half. The fold will become the upper edge of the bag.

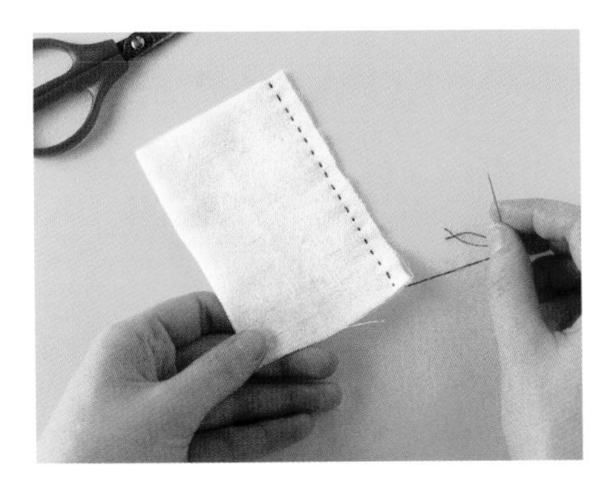

2 Fold in half again the other way. Keeping the folded edge at the top, bring the raw edges together and sew a line of running stitch from top to bottom on the longest side. (The stitching is best done in white thread – I've used blue here so that it can be clearly seen.)

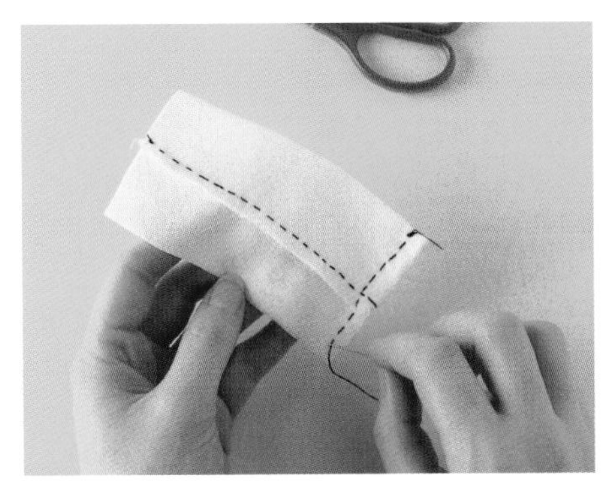

3 Open the partly made bag to make the seam you have just sewn form the centre back of the bag. Sew a seam across the bottom of the bag. Turn the bag right side out.

4 Fill loosely with lavender. Tie a ribbon bow tightly around the top to hold it in place.

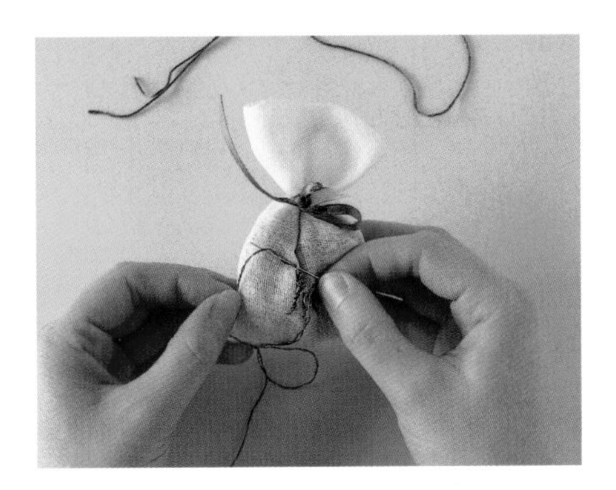

5 Neatly sew violet French knots and green backstitch stems to the bag to make a bunch of lavender (see pattern on page 226).

6 To make the card base, fold the sheet of A5 white patterned card in half. Use the glue stick to centrally attach a torn piece of lavender blue handmade paper. Use PVA glue to attach the lavender bag (use just a little glue so that the bag can be detached from the card and used to scent a drawer or wardrobe).

woven ribbon

This woven ribbon heart in delicate creams, pinks and greens is bordered with a cotton lace frill and set in heavy watercolour paper. Ribbon weaving was a popular pastime amongst the nimble-fingered middle classes of Victorian and Regency England. Modern spray adhesives and the wide range of ribbons available make this an extremely accessible hobby.

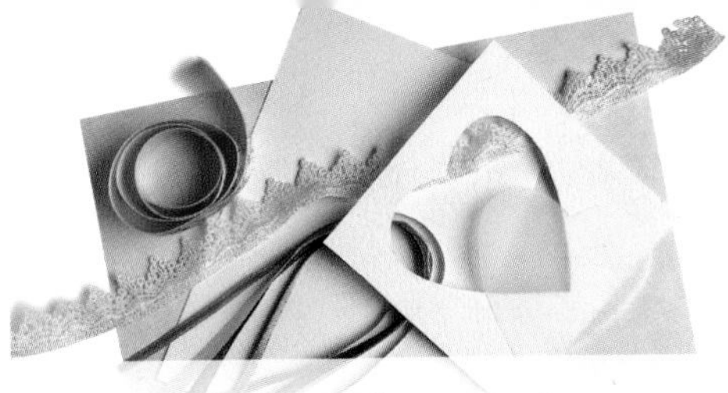

you will need

- A5 sheet of pink card
- Pencil and metal ruler
- Set square
- Craft knife
- Cutting board
- Sheet of lightweight paper
- Spray adhesive
- Selection of narrow ribbons in pink, green and cream
- Scissors
- Heavy watercolour paper
- Tracing paper
- 35cm (14in) length of narrow cotton lace
- Glue stick
- Needle
- White thread

timing The craft of ribbon weaving requires patience and time, so set aside a few hours of solitude to make this pretty greetings card.

message A wonderful birthday card or romantic Valentine.

1 The card blank is made from pink card. Use the ruler, set square and pencil to mark up a rectangular shape 10.5 x 21cm (4¼ x 8½in). Cut out and fold in half.

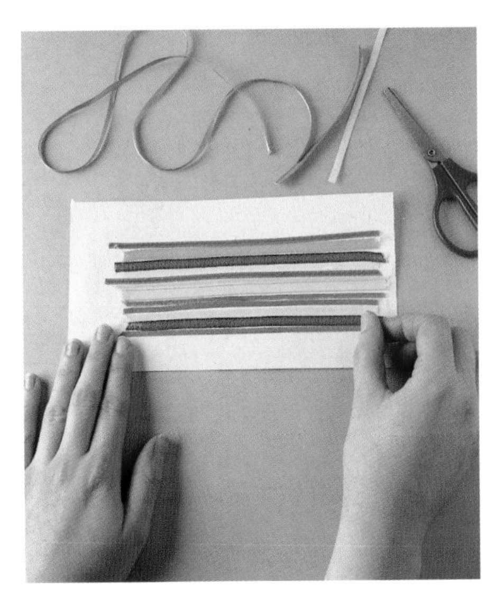

2 Next take a sheet of lightweight paper and spray a 20 x 10cm (8 x 4in) area with spray adhesive. Allow it to become tacky. Place 15cm (6in) lengths of ribbon, one beside the other, across the paper to a depth of 9cm (3½in).

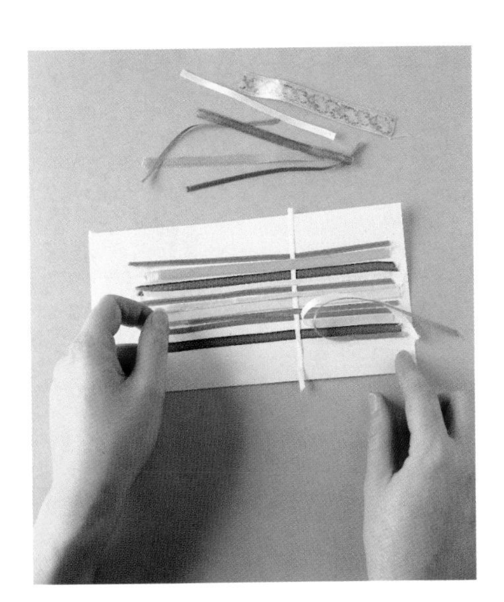

3 Lift up every other length of ribbon, starting with the second strip, and fold it back. Place a length of ribbon vertically then lie the horizontal ribbons back in place.

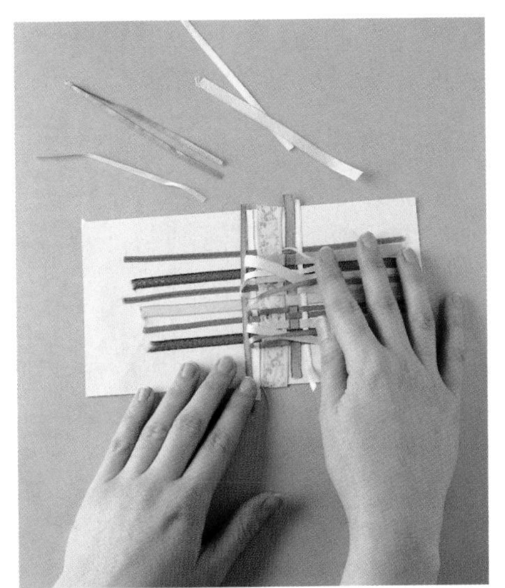

4 Now lift up every other length of ribbon, this time starting with the first strip, and repeat the process with another vertical length of ribbon. Continue until you have covered an area at least 9cm (3½in) square.

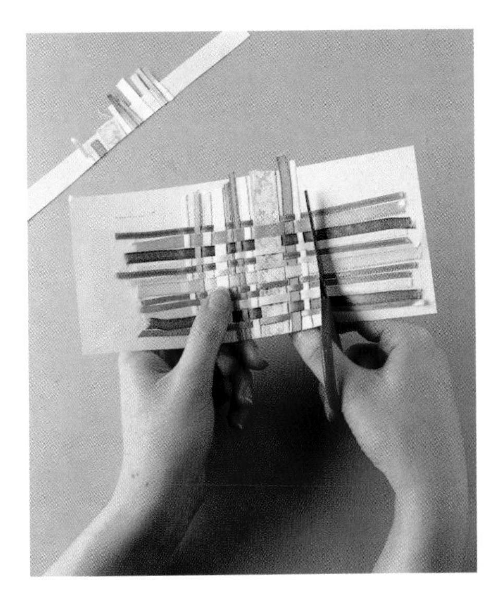

5 When you have made a woven square of ribbon, press the ribbons down firmly on the card so they don't lift up, then trim the card to a square 9 x 9cm (3½ x 3½in).

continued ▸

6 Cut a 9 x 9cm (3½ x 3½in) square of watercolour paper. Trace the heart template on page 226 and cut it out. Place the heart shape centrally on the square of watercolour paper and draw around it.

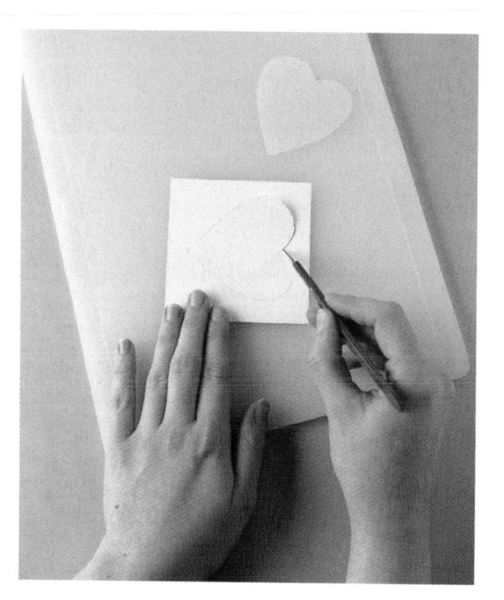

7 Cut out the heart shape using the craft knife.

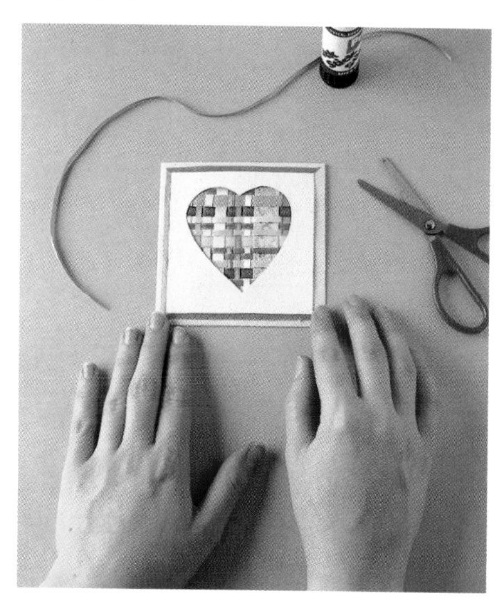

8 Glue the square of ribbon weaving centrally on to the card blank and glue the heart frame on top of that. Glue a dusky pink ribbon border to the watercolour paper.

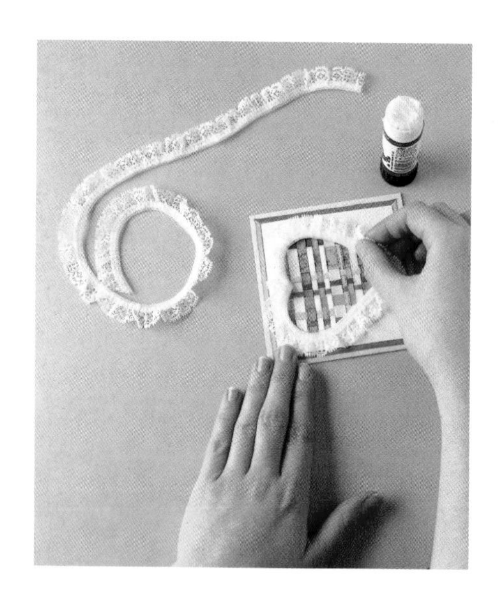

9 Finally, sew a running stitch along the length of lace, gently pull the thread to gather up the lace and attach as a border around the ribbon heart with the glue stick.

Use any excess woven ribbon to create interesting gift tags.

card for cooks

This unusual card uses a variety of materials – gingham fabric, beads, modelling clay and craft foil – all of the useful bits and pieces that you will have stashed away in your card-making box!

continued ▶

you will need

- A5 sheet of turquoise card
- Pencil and metal ruler
- Red gingham fabric
- Fabric scissors
- Spray adhesive
- A5 sheet of white textured card
- Paper scissors
- Set square
- Glue stick
- Scrap of thin craft wood (or beige card)
- Emery board
- Small sheet of craft foil
- Pen
- Modelling clay in light brown
- Two small red beads
- Tracing paper
- Pin
- Scrap of white fabric
- Red cord

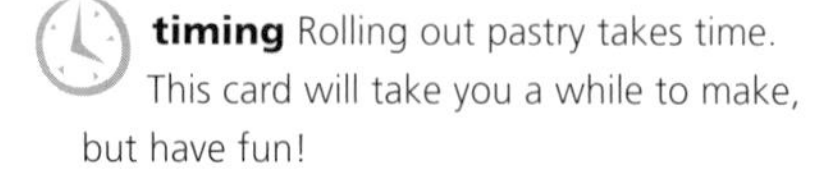

timing Rolling out pastry takes time. This card will take you a while to make, but have fun!

message Send to a young home baker.

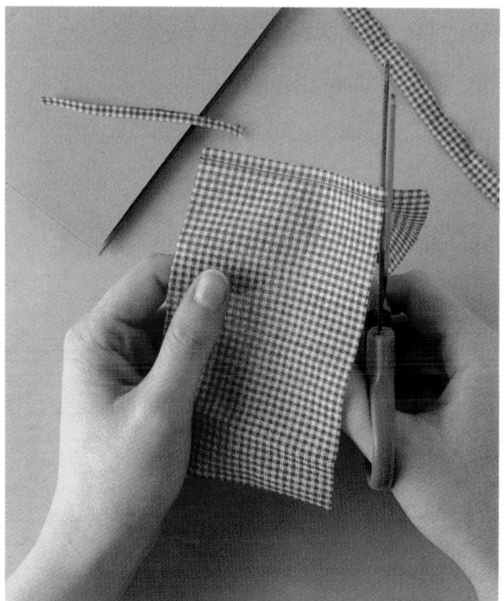

1 Fold the turquoise card in half to make the card blank. Measure and cut out a piece of red gingham fabric 8.5 x 13cm (3½ x 5in). Coat the back with spray adhesive and stick centrally on the card.

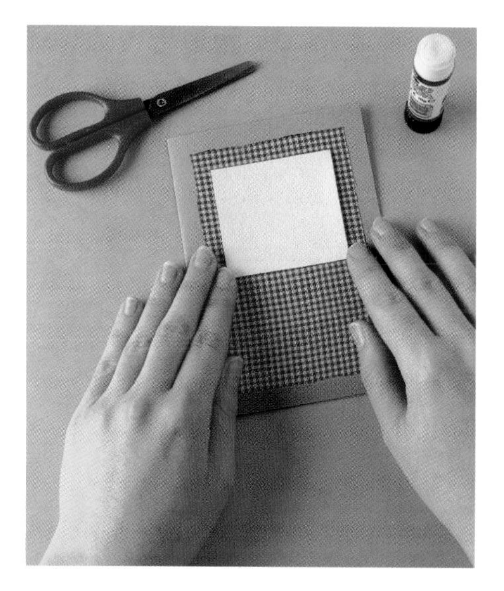

2 Measure and cut out a 6.5 x 6cm (2¾ x 2½in) piece of white textured card and stick on to the gingham in a high central position using the glue stick.

3 Cut a 2.5 x 4cm (1 x 1½in) piece of craft wood, round the corners with an emery board and glue into position on the white card. Cut out a 2.5 x 3cm (1 x 1¼in) piece of craft foil, rounding the corners. Make an impression around the edge of the foil 'tray' with a pen. Glue in position with the glue stick.

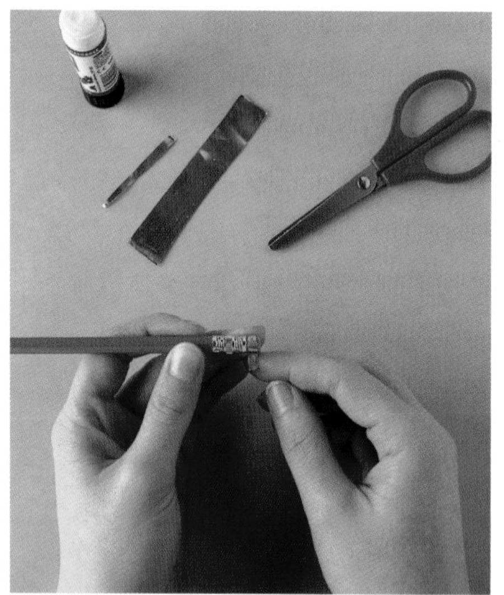

4 Wind a short length of 5mm (¼in) wide craft foil around the end of a pencil to make a cookie cutter shape. Glue the ends together.

5 Work a small ball of modelling clay between your hands to soften it. Make a rolling pin shape and roll out two small balls of clay (use the body of a smooth pen as a miniature rolling pin).

6 Cut out five biscuit shapes from one round of clay. Using the end of a pencil with the eraser removed, make impressions in the second round of clay. Bake the clay according to the manufacturer's instructions.

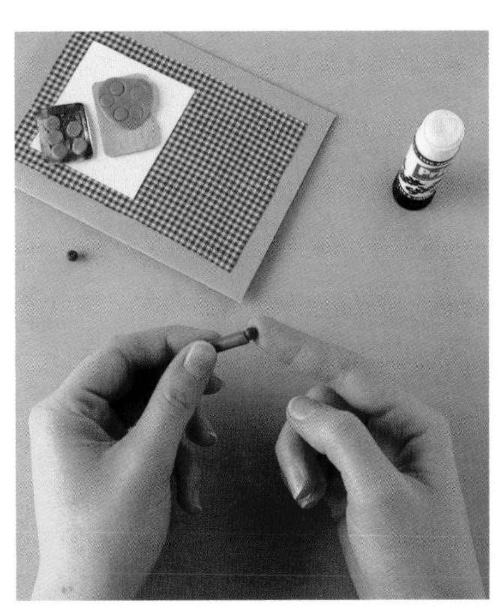

7 When baked and cooled, attach the clay to the card using the glue stick. Glue a red bead to each end of the rolling pin and then glue the rolling pin to the card. Glue on the cookie cutter.

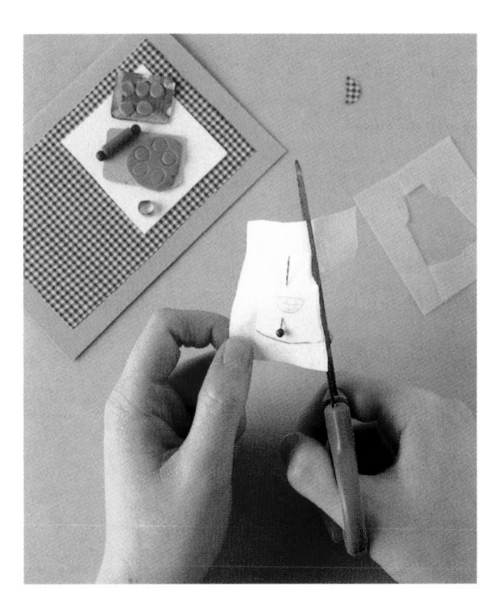

8 Trace the apron template from page 227 and cut out. Pin the template to a scrap of white fabric and cut out. Cut out a small pocket shape from gingham.

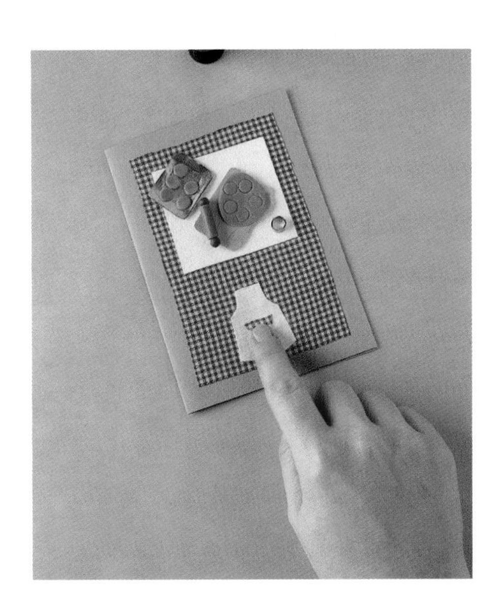

9 Spray the back of the apron with spray adhesive and attach to the card. Attach the pocket with glue stick.

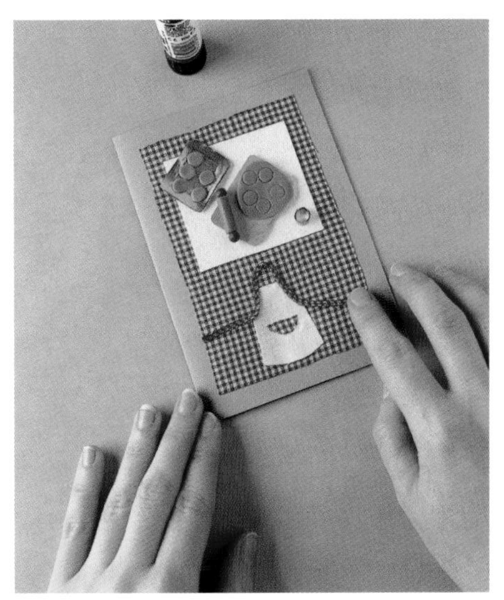

10 Cut an 11cm (4½in) length of red cord or ribbon to form the apron strings and glue in place.

memories of India

This picture made from richly patterned fabric, decorated gold thread and gilded mirrors was inspired by the richness of colour worn by the talented craftsmen and women who live in the desert state of Rajasthan, in the north-west of India. The silk used here comes from a scarf my grandmother used to wear, now damaged by age and use.

you will need

- A5 sheet of white textured card
- Patterned silk fabric
- Fabric scissors
- Spray adhesive
- A4 sheet of lightweight white paper
- Light coloured felt-tip pen
- Set square
- Scissors
- Glue stick
- Narrow gold ribbon
- Bindis or sequins for decoration
- Gold foil
- Pink glitter glue

timing Once you have collected all the materials this card should not take too long to produce.

message Good as a notelet, birthday greeting or thank-you card.

A hint of India is created in these gift tags with silks, bindis and gold foil.

1 Fold the A5 sheet of textured card in half to create the card blank. Cut a rectangle of silk slightly larger than the card front and use spray adhesive to attach it to a sheet of lightweight white paper.

2 Using a light coloured felt-tip pen and a set square, measure out a rectangle 8 x 12cm (3¼ x 4¾in) on the layered fabric and paper.

3 Using sharp scissors, cut out the rectangle of paper and silk. Apply glue to the paper and attach it centrally to the card blank.

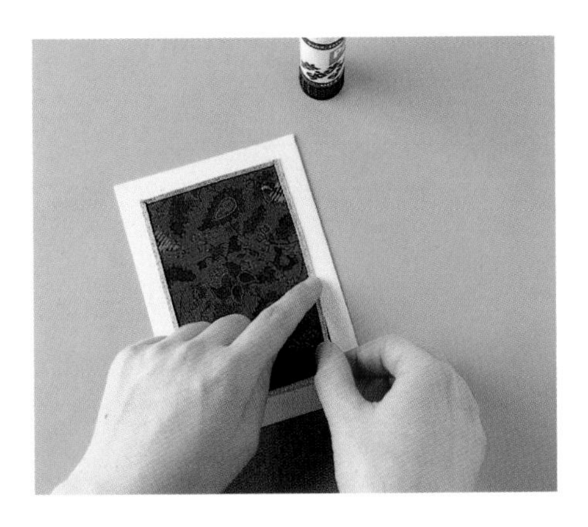

4 Your card is now ready for decoration. Glue a border of narrow gold ribbon around the fabric, carefully mitring the edges with sharp scissors.

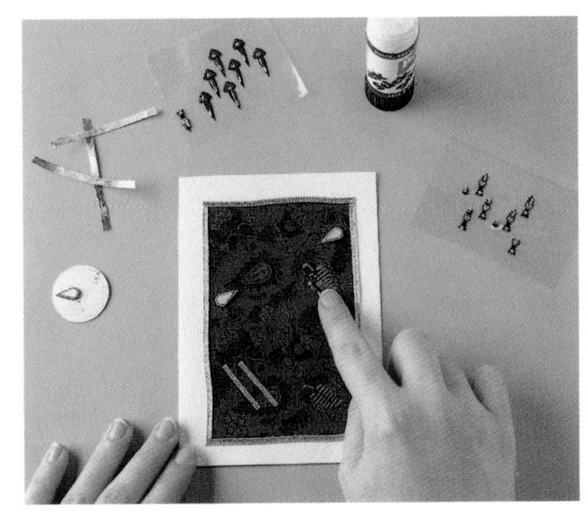

5 Use bindis or sequins and snippets of gold foil to embellish the silk. Attach them with the glue stick.

6 Finally squeeze a line of pink glitter glue along the ribbon border. Leave the glitter glue to dry overnight. You might like to decorate an envelope with a silk border for dramatic effect.

cross-stitch greeting

Tiny cross-stitch samplers to send to friends.

This card, carrying a romantic message in counted cross stitch, was created to send a message of future happiness to a newly engaged couple. Cross stitch can be used to sew simple messages for Mother's Day, weddings and special birthdays.

you will need

- Pencil and metal ruler
- A5 sheet of white textured card
- Craft knife
- Cutting board
- Sewing needle
- Embroidery thread in blue
- Scissors
- Cross-stitch fabric, 8 x 8cm (3¼ x 3¼in)
- Glue stick
- A5 sheet of blue handmade paper

timing This stitched card takes time to complete but the end result is a gift that the happy couple can frame and save forever.

message Send this card for an engagement, a wedding or as a housewarming gift.

1 Begin by creating the card blank. Using the ruler and pencil, mark out a rectangle 21 x 10.5cm (8½ x 4¼in) on the white textured card. Cut out and fold in half to create the card blank.

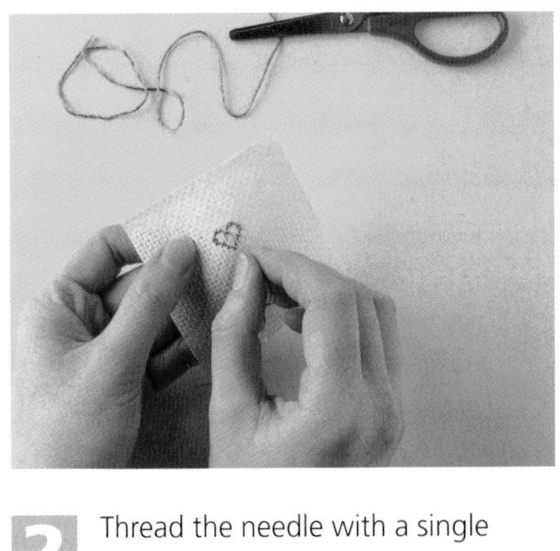

2 Thread the needle with a single strand of blue embroidery thread. Following the pattern on page 226, stitch the simple design. Start with the heart as this will give you a point of reference and makes counting out the pattern easier.

3 Stitch the house and the remainder of the pattern, completing the design with two initials of your choice.

4 Once you have completed the cross-stitch picture, carefully count out a frame around the cross stitch measuring 5 squares on each side. Cut it out.

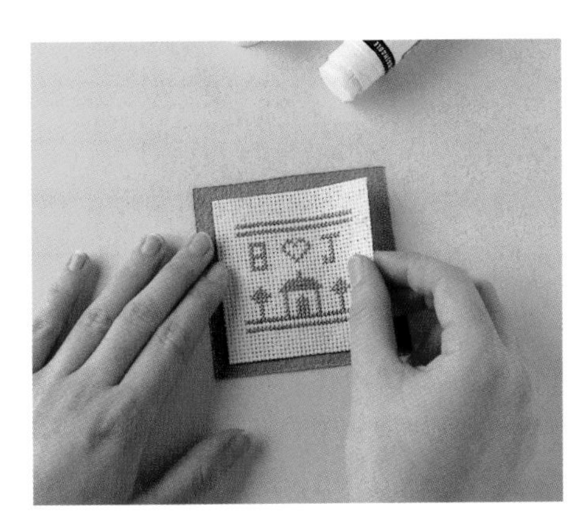

5 Use a glue stick to attach the embroidered fabric centrally to a 9 x 9cm (3½ x 3½in) square of blue handmade paper.

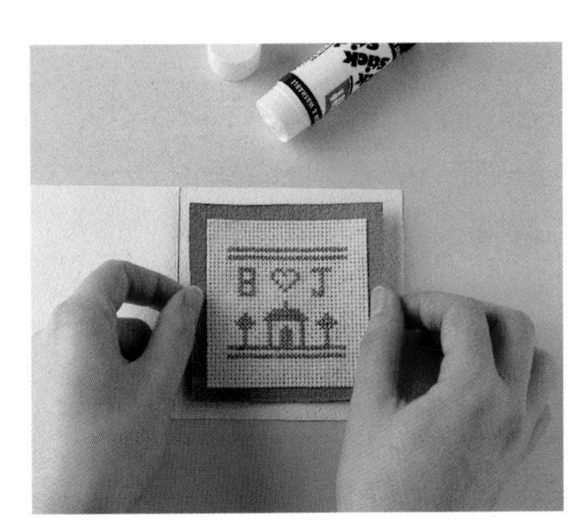

6 Use the glue stick to attach the framed cross stitch to the card blank. You may want to make a matching envelope in blue handmade paper to complete this delightful card.

more than a message

projects

welcome little stranger

What better way to share the joy of a new baby with grandparents and special friends? I used a computer to scan in the photograph, trimmed the picture and printed off a number of copies.

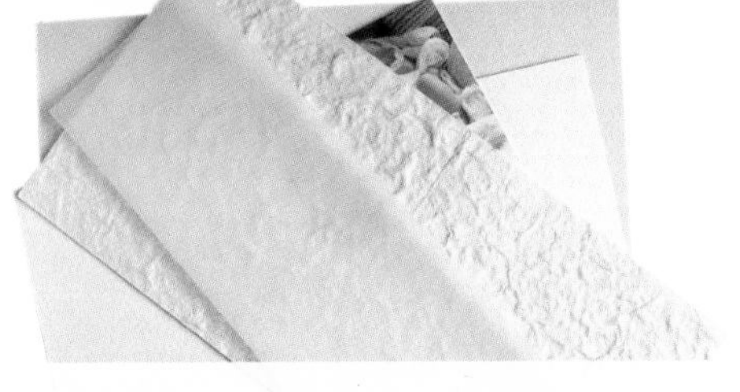

you will need

- White handmade paper, 23 x 11.5cm (9 x 4½in)
- Pencil and metal ruler
- Craft knife
- Cutting board
- Glue stick
- White textured card, 10 x 10cm (4 x 4in)
- Pale pink heavy textured card, 9 x 9cm (3½ x 3½in)
- Tracing paper
- Scissors
- Flower punch
- Silver pen
- Photograph of the baby

timing A little technical know-how, a touch of artistic talent and a little time will make this delightful card.

message Send to faraway grandparents and special friends to announce the new arrival.

1 Score and fold the piece of white handmade paper in half to create the card blank. Next glue the square of white textured card in a central position on the card base.

2 The image surround is cut from a square of pale pink textured card. Trace the template on page 227 or create a shape suitable for your photograph. Cut it out by first cutting a cross in the centre of the oval with a craft knife and then cutting around the oval with scissors.

3 Create a decorative frame by using the punch to cut out flowers from card offcuts. Use a glue stick to attach them around the oval shape. Mark a small silver dot in the centre of each flower.

4 Position the decorated frame centrally over the photograph and glue firmly in place.

5 Glue the framed photograph centrally on the card blank and decorate with a silver border and a flower on each corner.

photo frame

This elegant card comprises three-dimensional flowers on a white textured paper base. It's a wonderful gift and a greeting all-in-one.

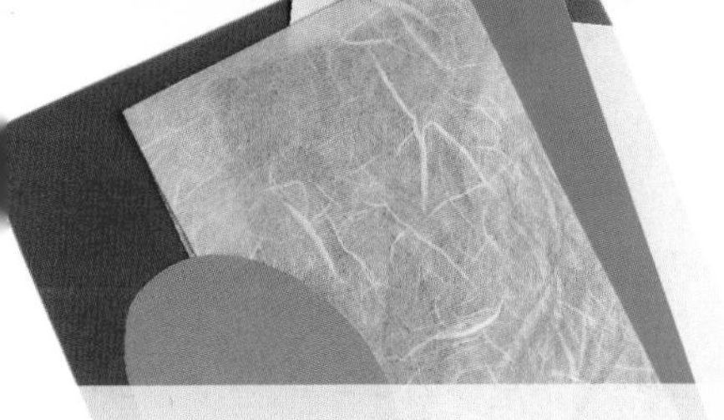

you will need

- 2 A5 sheets of slightly textured white paper
- Pencil and metal ruler
- Craft knife
- Cutting board
- Tracing paper
- Scissors
- White mulberry paper
- Spray adhesive
- Glue stick
- A5 sheet of green paper
- A5 sheet of red paper
- Piece of thick card

timing A very quick card to make – what takes the time is choosing which photograph to enclose.

message A great card to send as a greeting to a friend, particularly if the photograph holds special memories for you both.

1 Fold a sheet of A5 paper in half to create the blank. Trace and cut out the oval template on page 227, position centrally on the card and draw around it. Cut a cross in the oval with a craft knife and then cut around the oval with scissors.

2 Cut the sheet of mulberry paper to a rectangle 23 x 17cm (9 x 6¾in). Coat with spray adhesive and place the card blank on top of it. Mitre the corners, then fold over the overhanging sides and stick down.

3 Using the craft knife, cut a small oval out of the centre, then cut tabs in the remaining overhanging paper, turn in and stick down on the inside of the card.

4 Take the second sheet of A5 paper and trim 5mm (¼in) off all sides. Fold in half. Apply glue stick all over the paper apart from the top of the left-hand side, as this is where the photograph is inserted. Stick the white paper inside the mulberry paper card.

5 Trace the flower and leaf templates on page 227. Cut out eight leaves from green paper. Glue them in place as shown. To make the flowers, cut out four circles from red paper. Make a snip from the edge to the centre and twist the paper to make a shallow cone shape.

6 Glue the flowers to hold their shape. Glue one red cone in each corner of the card, then flatten the cones to make flower shapes – it is easiest to place a piece of thick card over the flowers and then press down. Trim your chosen photograph if necessary and insert.

romantic red rose

This is the perfect Valentine. Layers of handmade paper and a pressed rose create this deeply romantic card. You might be inspired to press other flowers, for example to create a pressed pansy birthday card. Flower presses are available from craft shops but you can also layer the flowers between cartridge paper, place inside a heavy book and place a weight on top of the book.

you will need

- Pencil and metal ruler
- A3 sheet of white handmade paper
- Set square
- Scissors
- A4 sheet of pink handmade paper
- Glue stick
- A5 sheet of cream textured card
- Pressed rose
- Gold marker pen

timing Pressing the flowers is what takes the time (about two weeks), but once they have dried you can put together a card in minutes. Choose flowers that aren't too 'fleshy' as they may go mouldy in the press.

message The perfect love greeting – ideal for Valentine's day or for sending a surprise romantic greeting to a loved one.

1 Measure and cut out a rectangle 22 x 26cm (8¾ x 10½in) from white handmade paper, fold in half, then in half again to make a double layer card base.

2 Next, measure and cut out a rectangle 10.5 x 8.5cm (4¼ x 3¼in) from the pink handmade paper. Use a glue stick to attach it in a central position on the card base.

3 Measure and cut out a rectangle 6 x 9cm (2½ x 3½in) from cream textured card. Glue it centrally on the pink handmade paper rectangle.

4 Use the glue stick to attach the pressed rose to the card. Handle the rose carefully as it will be very delicate.

5 Using a ruler, draw a gold border on the white handmade paper around the edge of the card and on the cream card around the rose.

memories of summer

A picnic tea enjoyed on the edge of a field of harvested corn inspired this card. The paper has dried grasses and golden summer flowers layered into it, which create a background for a selection of the grasses and seed heads I picked and pressed that sunny afternoon.

you will need

- Handmade paper impressed with leaves and flowers
- Pencil and metal ruler
- Set square
- Cutting board
- Craft knife
- A5 sheet of tan-coloured handmade paper
- Glue stick
- A5 sheet of cream card
- Selection of dried and pressed seed heads and grasses
- Scissors

timing This card is stylishly simple and easy to make.

message A suitable birthday greeting or thank-you card.

1 To make the base of the card measure out an area 23 x 20cm (9 x 8in) on the sheet of handmade paper. Place on the cutting board and use the steel ruler and craft knife to cut out the shape. Score and fold the card in half.

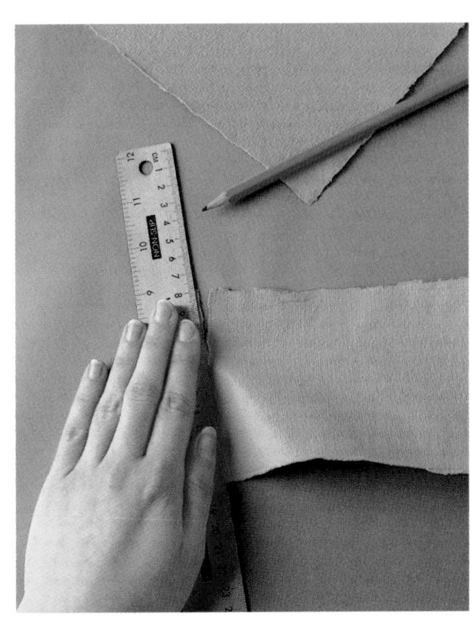

2 The first layer of the card is made from the tan-coloured paper, which forms a frame for the pressed grass picture. Measure a rectangle 10 x 17.5cm (4 x 6¾in) in size and tear the edges along the metal ruler. Apply glue and attach it in a central position on the front of the card base.

3 The final layer is cut from the cream card. Measure and cut out a rectangle 9 x 17cm (3½ x 6½in).

4 Using the glue stick attach the cream rectangle centrally on top of the tan paper.

5 Sort through your selection of grasses and seed heads and trim them as necessary. Choose some suitable pieces and lay them on the card. When you are happy with the arrangement, glue them to the card.

autumn walk

Take an autumn stroll through the park and make a collection of golden brown, red and green leaves. Once home, press them between the pages of a book for a week or so. When they are dry you will be ready to get to work.

you will need

- A5 sheet of cream card
- Pencil and metal ruler
- A4 sheet of speckled handmade paper
- Cutting board
- Craft knife
- Glue stick
- Selection of pressed leaves
- Black felt-tip pen
- Small hole punch
- Thin leather cord

timing This card won't take long to make and you have the added bonus of a walk through crunchy autumn leaves to collect your materials.

message Send a friend a magical autumn greeting.

1 Fold the A5 sheet of cream card in half to make the card base. Use the pencil and ruler to measure an area 14 x 20cm (5½ x 8in) on to the speckled handmade paper. Place the paper on to the cutting board and cut out the measured area using a metal ruler and craft knife.

2 Open out the card base. Apply glue to the speckled paper and attach it in a central position on the card base.

3 Lay a selection of pressed leaves across the card. Take care to choose sympathetic colours and shapes. Do not lay leaves over the central fold as the card will not close properly. When you are happy with the layout, apply glue to the leaves and position them on to the card.

4 Use the black felt-tip pen to draw a line of tiny footprints across the front and back of the card.

5 Measure a point halfway down each side of the card. Mark the points with a light pencil mark. Use the hole punch to make two small holes.

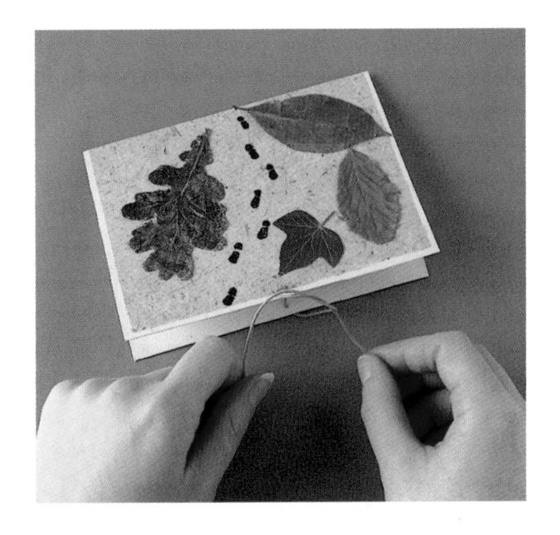

6 Thread the leather strip though the two holes and tie a neat bow.

photo wallet

A friend or relative will treasure this simple photo wallet greetings card, especially if it contains a special selection of photographs. It is very simple to make and with the handy ribbon tie has an heirloom feel about it. You might want to decorate the paper wallet using different punched motifs to suit it to your own style.

you will need

- Metal ruler
- Set square
- Pencil
- Large sheet of cream handmade paper
- Cutting board
- Craft knife
- A5 sheet of red paper
- Punch
- Glue stick
- 60cm (24in) red ribbon
- Scissors

timing This gift is very quick to make and will last a lifetime.

message A wonderful gift to send to a friend to remind them of old times.

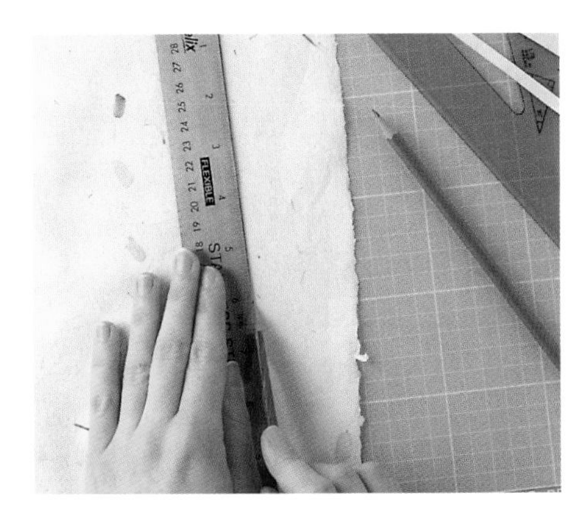

1 Use the ruler, set square and pencil to mark up a rectangle 25 x 40cm (10 x 15¾in) on the sheet of handmade paper. Cut out the rectangle using the craft knife.

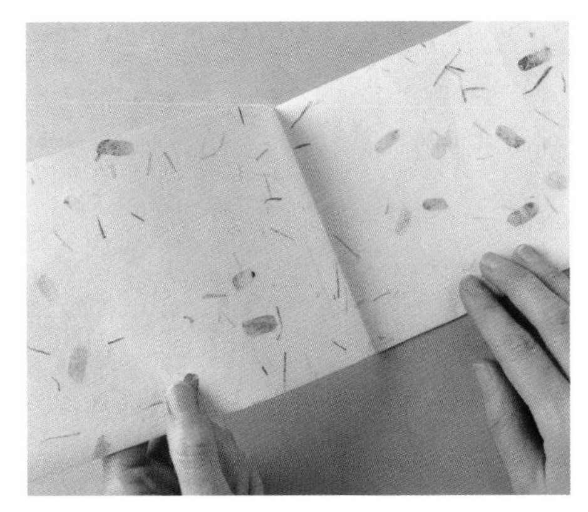

2 Fold the sheet in half lengthways and draw your thumb along the fold to create a sharp edge. Then fold the card in half widthways, press the fold firmly, then open out.

3 Turn the paper over and fold each end into the centre fold. You should now have four equal rectangles; these form the pages of the album.

4 Take the sheet of red paper and punch out six decorative edging shapes using your chosen punch. Unfold the card. Use the glue stick to attach a shape to alternate upper corners of each of the four pages closest to you. Then attach a shape to the top left and bottom right corners of the upper left page. This will become the front of the card.

5 Lay the card on the cutting board. Use the craft knife to cut two small slits in two opposing corners of each page. These slits will hold the photographs or pictures in place.

6 Finally fold the album back into shape and use the glue stick to attach the ribbon across the back of the card. Bring the ribbon ends around to the front and tie in a bow.

hanging star

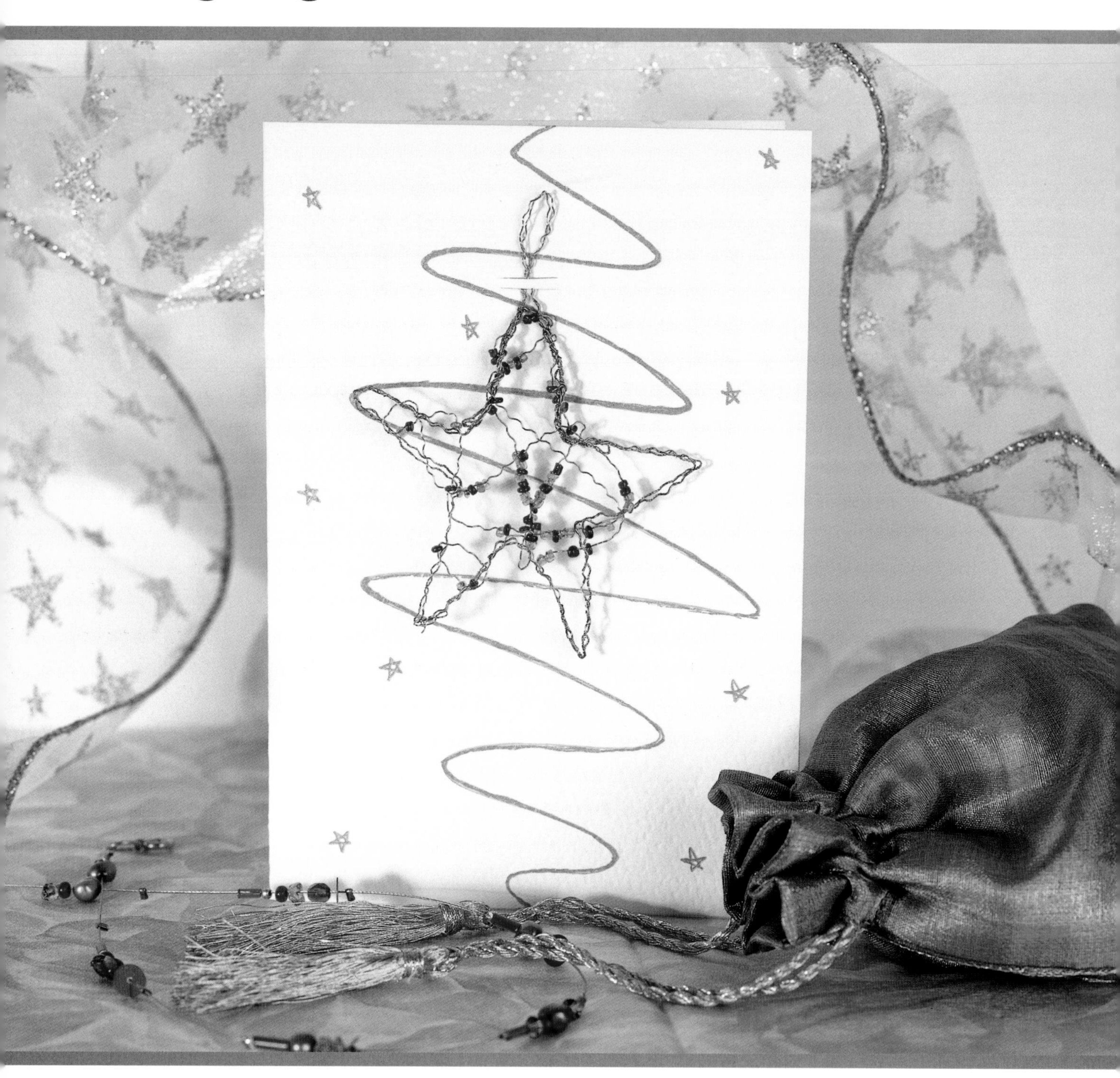

This Christmas card is a jewelled star decoration attached to a white card base decorated with a gold swirl. Even when the star is removed to be hung on the tree, the card is still very pretty.

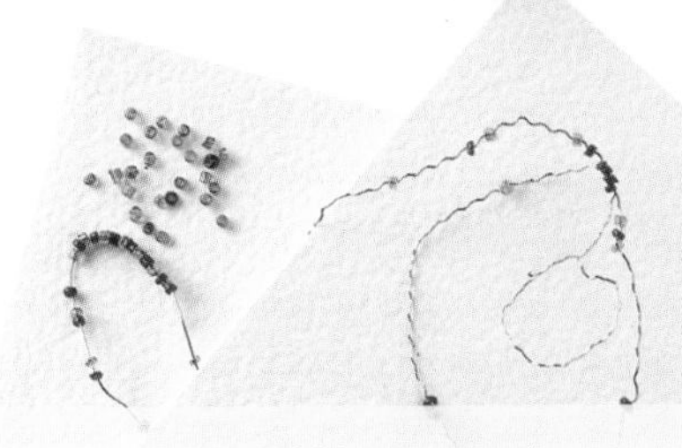

you will need

- Reel of decorative gold wire
- Scissors
- Metal ruler
- 15 small red beads
- 15 small gold beads
- A5 sheet of white textured card
- Gold pen
- Craft knife
- Cutting board

timing A simple card, but it does take a little time to make as the star decoration is delicate and quite intricate.

message A great card to send to a friend at Christmas time, as they can use the decoration again and again and will always be reminded of the sender.

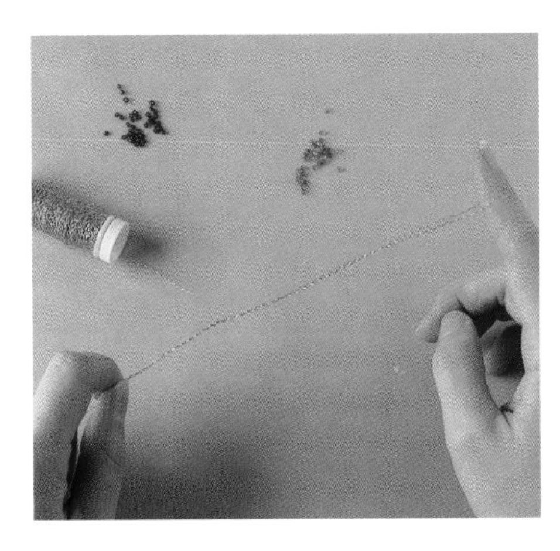

1 Cut a 60cm (24in) length of gold wire. Fold in half and twist the two strands together.

2 Bend the wire into a series of five points, with each side of the point 2cm (¾in) long, leaving a little wire spare at the beginning and end.

3 Form the zigzags into a five-pointed star. Coil the ends of the wire together to hold the star shape in place. Twist the end of the wire around to form a loop. Wrap around to secure and snip off the surplus wire.

4 Thread the beads on to a 20cm (8in) length of wire, alternating red and gold. Hold the bottom of the wire firmly, then attach the top to any point on the star and randomly weave the beaded wire around the star. Twist the end firmly around the star to hold.

5 Fold the sheet of card in half. Using the gold pen, draw a fluid zigzag on the front of the card. Draw small stars on either side.

6 Using the craft knife, make two small parallel slits near the top of the front of the card, 1cm (½in) long. Thread the loop of the star through the slit so it hangs freely.

dreamcatcher

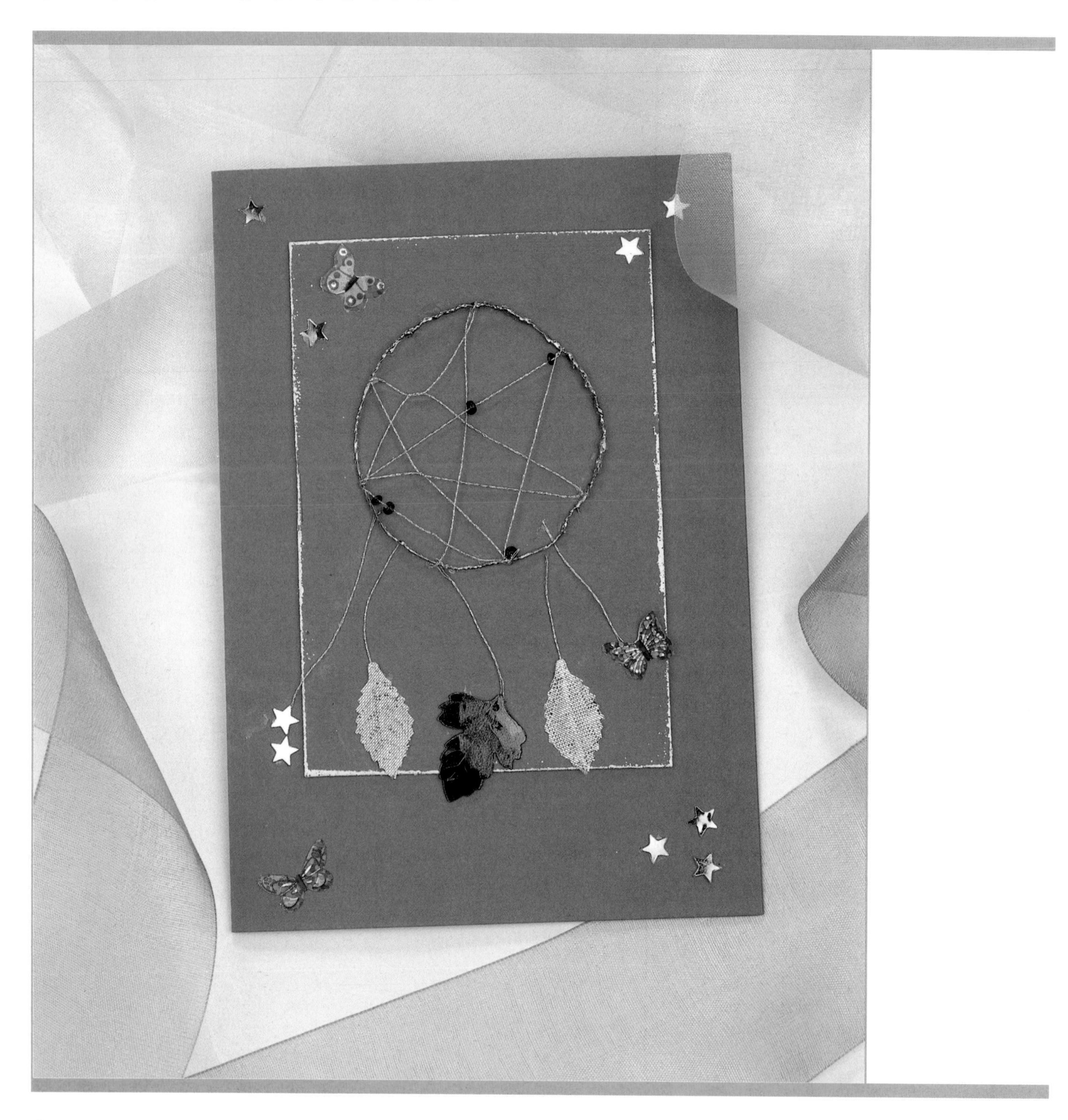

Send this dreamcatcher to a young friend to bring a little magic into his or her life and help slay the dragons that might be troubling their dreams. You could personalize the card by decorating the net with minature items that are significant to the recipient. If you cannot find a suitable bangle, shape a length of thin silver wire into a small circle.

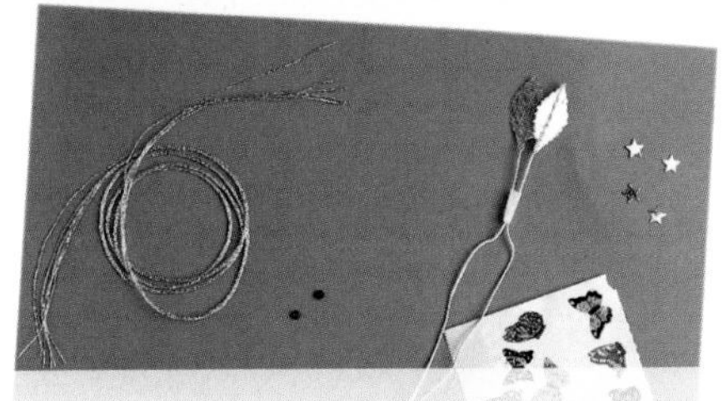

you will need

- 2 A5 sheets of violet card
- Craft knife
- Cutting board
- Metal ruler
- Set square
- Pencil
- Embossing stamp pad
- Silver-white embossing powder
- Precision heat tool
- Glue stick
- Silver thread
- Scissors
- Small silver bangle
- PVA glue
- Paint brush
- 5 small beads
- Selection of foil leaf shapes
- Butterfly stickers
- Silver stars

timing This card takes some time to make, so to ensure a good result, set aside an hour or two when you will not be disturbed.

message A magical card suitable for 'get well' greetings.

1 Score and fold an A5 sheet of violet card to create the card base. Cut a rectangle 7 x 10cm (2¾ x 4in) from the other sheet of violet card. Press the edges of the rectangle into the embossing pad and then dip into the embossing powder. Use the heat tool to set (see page 14).

2 Using the glue stick, cover the back of the decorated card with glue and attach it in an upper central position to the card base. Cut a length of silver thread and tie it to the silver bangle. Use a dab of PVA glue to hold the thread in place.

3 Loop and weave the thread around and across the bangle to create a net effect.

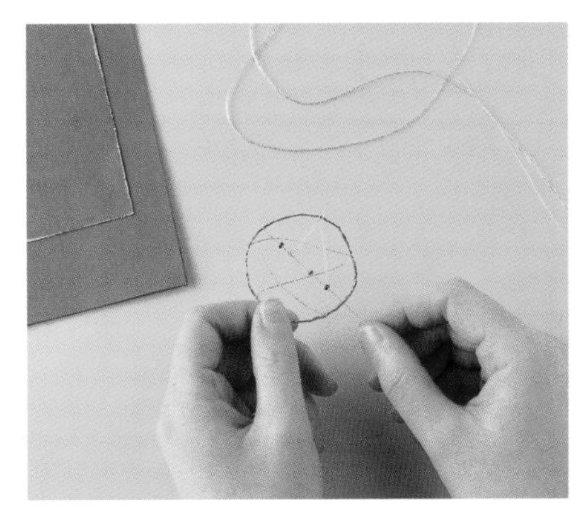

4 Take another short length of thread. Tie a knot in one end, thread on five beads and knot the other end. Tie on to the bangle and weave through the net.

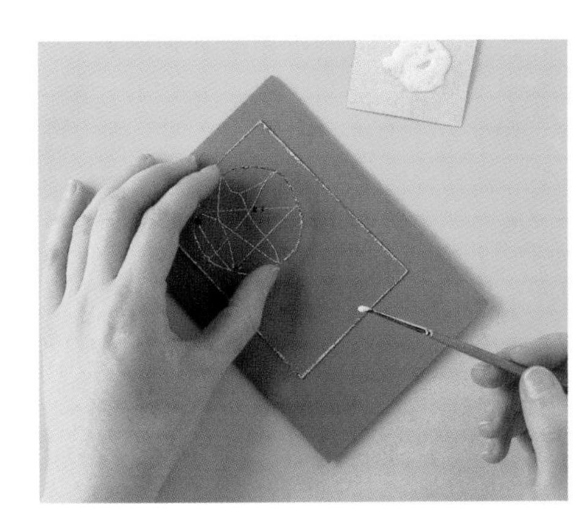

5 When you are happy with the appearance of your dreamcatcher use a little PVA glue to attach it to the card in a high central position.

6 Attach five lengths of thread to the bottom of the dreamcatcher. Place a leaf, star or butterfly at the end of each thread and decorate the corners of the card with butterflies and stars.

tic-tac-toe

A game of three-in-a-row played on this bright yellow gift card decorated with ladybirds and daisies should bring a smile to someone's face. The game board is marked out with green card strips and the ladybirds are stamped on to card, cut out and coloured in with felt-tip pen.

you will need

- A4 sheet of yellow card
- A4 sheet of white card
- Pencil and metal ruler
- Cutting board
- Craft knife
- Glue stick
- A5 sheet of green card
- Wavy-edged scissors
- Acetate, 2 x 8cm (¾ x 3¼in)
- Piece of white card, for the counters
- Fine black pen
- Orange and red felt-tip pens
- Scissors
- Ladybird stamp
- Black ink pad

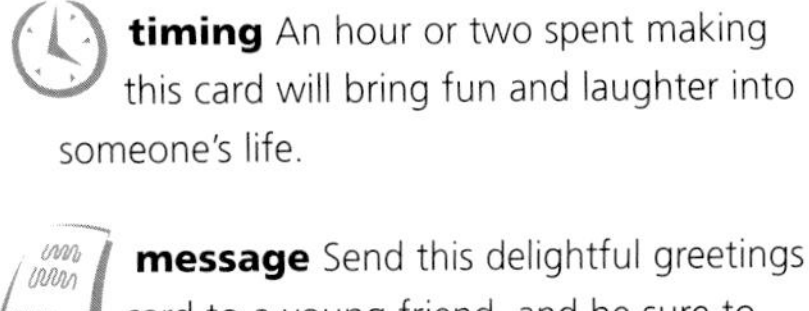

timing An hour or two spent making this card will bring fun and laughter into someone's life.

message Send this delightful greetings card to a young friend, and be sure to have a game when next visiting.

1 Cut the A4 sheet of yellow card in half. Fold one half in half; this is the card base. Cut out a piece of white card 7 x 7cm (2¾ x 2¾in) and a piece of yellow card 6.5 x 6.5cm (2½ x 2½in). Glue the white square diagonally at the top of the card then stick the yellow square on top.

2 Cut four narrow strips of green card, each approximately 7cm (2¾in) long. Using the photo for guidance, glue them across the square to create the game board.

3 Trace and cut out the pocket template on page 227. On the green card draw around the template and cut out the shape. Use wavy-edged scissors to decorate the outer edge.

4 Glue the pocket surround to the acetate and then glue the pocket to the bottom of the card. The pocket opening should face upwards.

5 The counters are made from white card. Using the fine black pen, draw seven simple daisy shapes and decorate with orange felt-tip pen.

continued ▶

6 Carefully cut out the daisy shapes, cutting just outside the black line.

Individual flowers and ladybirds make neat gift tags.

7 Use the ladybird stamp and the black ink pad to print five counters on the remaining piece of white card.

8 Neatly colour in the ladybirds using the red felt-tip pen. Carefully cut them out.

9 Glue two of the daisies at the top corners of the card and place the rest in the pocket with the ladybirds.

the big day

Romantic pastel colours, golden hearts and a gold embossed stamp neatly enfold a gift of flower petal confetti. This card would make a lovely wedding invitation or wedding gift card.

continued ▶

you will need

- A4 sheet of white textured card
- Pencil and metal ruler
- Craft knife
- Cutting board
- Handmade paper in pastel pink
- Paint brush and water
- Iron and ironing board
- Glue stick
- Stamp with a romantic image
- Embossing stamp pad
- Embossing powder in gold
- Precision heat tool
- Scissors
- Gold foil hearts
- Tweezers
- Gold outliner
- White mulberry paper, 12 x 10cm (4¾ x 4in)
- Hole punch
- Suitable dried flower petals
- Short length of narrow ribbon in palest pink

timing This card takes time and love to make but is well worth it, and once you have made one you might want to set up a production line and make them as wedding invitations.

message Send to newly-weds or as an anniversary card.

1 Cut the A4 sheet of paper in half and fold one half in half; this is the card blank. Using a ruler and the lightest of pencil marks measure a rectangle 13 x 9cm (5 x 3½in) on the handmade paper.

2 Using the paint brush generously dipped in water, paint a water line around the marked rectangle, thoroughly soaking the paper.

3 Carefully tear out the rectangle. Set an iron to medium heat and iron the paper dry. Allow the paper to cool, then use the glue stick to attach it centrally to the card blank.

4 Using your chosen stamp, print the image using an embossing stamp pad on to the white textured card. You may wish to print several images.

5 Sprinkle the gold embossing powder over the stamped image. Shake off the excess powder on to a piece of scrap paper and then return it to the pot.

6 Set the embossed image using the heat tool (see page 14). Cut out leaving a narrow border around the image.

7 Use the glue stick to attach the embossed picture to the card. Once the glue has set, decorate the card with gold foil hearts; pick them up with tweezers, dab them on to the glue stick and place on the card. Frame the embossed image with the gold outliner.

8 To make the bag of confetti, fold the two sides of the mulberry paper into the centre so they overlap slightly and fold up the base. Glue the edges in place.

9 Emboss the image on the front of the bag and use a hole punch to make two small holes for the ribbon tie. Fill the bag with flower petals. Thread the ribbon through the holes, tie a bow and use a small dab of glue to attach inside the card.

A matching envelope completes this elegant card.

general greetings

projects

ship ahoy

This card has a jaunty seaside theme and is decorated with rub-on transfers. Transfers are a quick and easy way to decorate gift pouches and gift-bags as well.

you will need

- A5 sheet white linen finish card
- Stylus
- Metal ruler
- Blue card
- Silver card
- Blue glitter paper
- Craft knife
- Cutting mat
- Pencil
- Double-sided tape
- Scissors
- Rub-on transfer
- Transfer stick

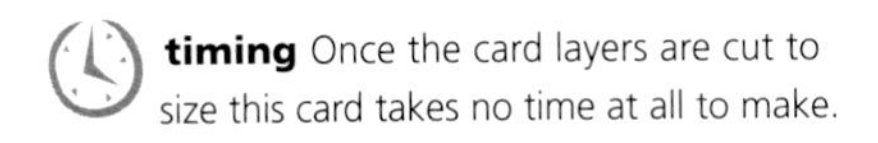

timing Once the card layers are cut to size this card takes no time at all to make.

alternative Use a flower transfer on a white background, layer it on to coordinating paper and attach to a pastel card base to create a Mother's Day card.

1 Score and fold the sheet of white card to create the card base. To create the layers cut a 5.5cm (2¼in) square from blue card, a 5cm (2in) square from silver card and a 4.5cm (1¾in) square from blue glitter paper. Use double-sided tape to attach the squares in an upper central position on the card.

2 Cut around the transfer you wish to use, leaving a 5mm (¼in) border. Remove the backing sheet. Place the transfer on the blue glitter paper and use the transfer stick to rub over the image. Gently peel off the plastic sheet.

There are literally hundreds of different transfer designs available.

3 Cut out the accent decorations and transfer first the sun, then the cloud to the top right-hand corner. Transfer the fish on the left beneath the motif.

4 Finally place a small transfer on the back of the card. This added extra gives your card a professional finish.

friendly frogs

Cheeky frog stickers and 3D paint on brightly decorated card create a great child's birthday card or simply a cheering message to a friend.

you will need

- A5 sheet navy blue card
- Metal ruler
- Stylus
- A5 sheet yellow translucent paper
- Craft knife
- Cutting mat
- Pencil
- Aerosol glue
- A4 sheet white card
- Double-sided tape
- Scissors
- Blue card
- Yellow card
- Black card
- Green card
- 3D adhesive tape
- Suitable frog stickers
- Green and blue 3D paint

timing Take your time when measuring and cutting the layers as they are the focus of the card.

alternative A row of robins on red, white and brown card layers would create a fun, seasonal card. For other animal-theme cards try three sheep with shades of pastel green, white and pink, or pink pigs on brown, white and cream.

1 Score and fold the sheet of dark blue card to create the card blank. Cut a 12.5 x 9cm (5 x 3½in) rectangle of yellow translucent paper. Spray it with aerosol glue and stick it to a piece of white card to back it. Cut away the excess white card.

2 Attach the backed yellow paper centrally to the front of the card blank with double-sided tape.

3 Cut a rectangle of blue card 7.5 x 4cm (3 x 1½in) and use double-sided tape to place it centrally on the yellow paper. Cut a piece of yellow card 6 x 2.5cm (2½ x 1in) and layer this on to the blue card.

4 Cut a 5.5 x 2cm (2¼ x ¾in) rectangle of white card and tape it to the black card. Cut a narrow frame. Tape the framed white card to a piece of green card and cut away all but a narrow frame.

5 Create a 3D effect on the final layer of your card. Place three pieces of 3D tape on the back of the framed white card and stick it on the central panel on the card.

6 Starting with the frog in the middle, place three stickers on the white card. Frame the motif with spots of blue 3D paint and finally squeeze a green spot of paint in each corner of the blue card. If you have a spare sticker attach it to the reverse of the card.

indigo blue

Turn your snapshots into mini masterpieces. Here, the deep blue decorated paper complements the bark and green ivy in the photograph.

you will need

- A4 sheet white card
- Craft knife
- Metal ruler
- Cutting mat
- Pencil
- Aerosol glue
- Sheet indigo blue decorative paper
- Chosen photograph
- Double-sided tape
- Scissors
- Dark blue card

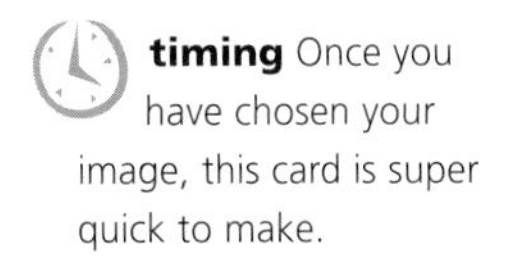

timing Once you have chosen your image, this card is super quick to make.

alternative You could use any photograph in this way – perhaps shots of holidays or family occasions. For a good result it is important to spend time choosing the paper that will frame your image.

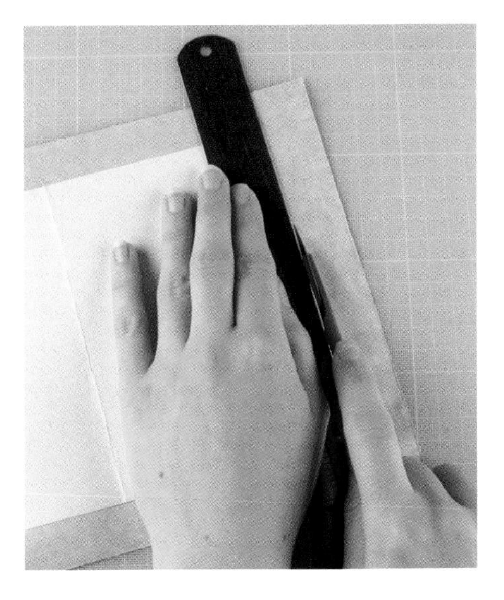

1 Cut the sheet of A4 card in half to create two A5 pieces. Score and fold one half to create the card base. Spray a layer of aerosol glue on the exterior of the card base. Lay it on the sheet of decorative paper and cut away the excess paper with a craft knife.

2 Draw a 6 x 4cm (2½ x 1½in) rectangle around an area of your chosen photograph and cut it out.

3 Use double-sided tape to attach the photograph to a small piece of dark blue card. Use scissors to cut away all but a 5mm (¼in) frame.

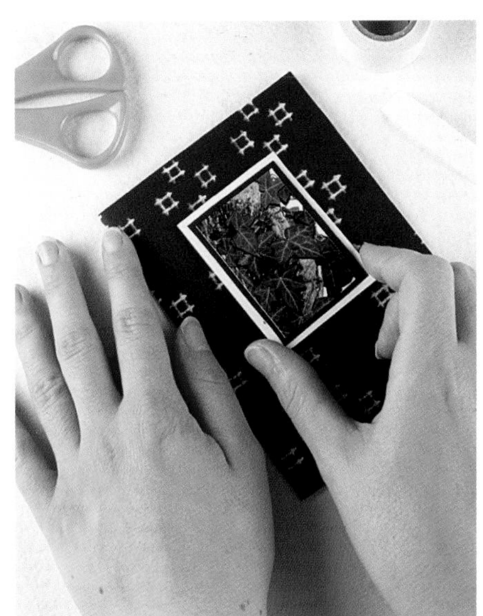

4 Use double-sided tape to attach the framed photograph to a small piece of white card and once again cut away all but a 5mm (¼in) frame. Attach the layered motif in an upper central position on the front of the card.

sew simple

Buttons, lace and workbox-themed paper create the perfect card for a crafty friend.

you will need

- A4 sheet blue card
- Craft knife
- Cutting mat
- Metal ruler
- Pencil
- Stylus
- Suitable decorative paper
- Double-sided tape
- Scissors
- A5 sheet white card
- Green translucent paper
- White ricrac
- 3 blue buttons

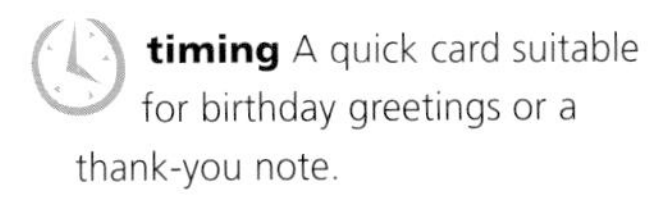

timing A quick card suitable for birthday greetings or a thank-you note.

alternative Themed paper is easy to find in craft shops. A sheet of romantically decorated paper and a framed row of pretty pearl buttons would make a lovely wedding card.

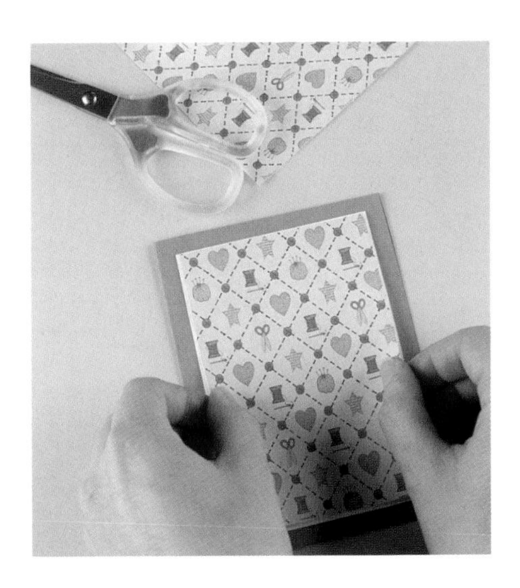

1 Cut the sheet of blue card in half to create two A5 pieces. Score and fold one half to make the card base. Cut out an 8.5 x 12.5cm (3½ x 5in) rectangle from the decorated paper. Use double-sided tape to attach it to the white card. Cut away all but a thin frame around the paper. Use double-sided tape to attach the framed picture centrally on the card front.

2 Cut a piece of white card, 2 x 5cm (¾ x 2in). Use double-sided tape to attach this to a piece of blue card. Cut away all but a narrow frame. Next, layer this up on green translucent paper using double-sided tape. Cut a narrow frame around the blue card.

variation *Make up this design in other colourways, using interesting buttons as a central feature.*

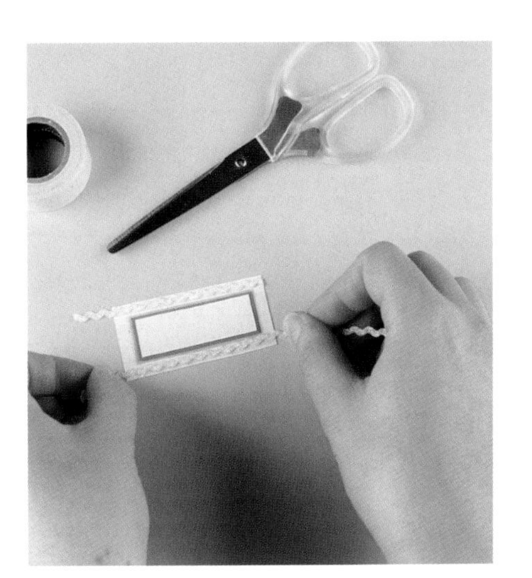

3 Use double-sided tape to attach the layered design to white card. Cut a 5mm (¼in) frame. Place thin strips of double-sided tape around the white frame. Lay the ricrac on the tape to stick it down firmly. Trim. Layer up on to blue card and cut a 5mm (¼in) border.

4 Use double-sided tape to attach the framed picture centrally on the card front. Tape the buttons on to the card layers. You might want to add a little decoration to the back of the card. Try using a motif cut from the decorative paper.

pastimes

Hobbies and pastimes make good starting points when designing a card for a friend or relative.

you will need

- A5 sheet olive green card
- Metal ruler
- Pencil
- Craft knife
- Cutting mat
- Stylus
- A5 sheet dark red card
- Double-sided tape
- Scissors
- A5 sheet dark green card
- A5 sheet cream card
- Suitable decorated ribbon
- Small piece black card
- Golf shoes and club (cake decorations)
- Super glue
- Hole punch
- PVA glue
- Small piece white card
- Gold 3D paint
- Flower sticker

timing This card is extremely quick to make.

alternative Both craft and cake decorating stores stock a wide variety of hobby-related decorative items, so you can create many different cards using this design as a base.

1 Cut out a 13.5 x 14cm (5¼ x 5½in) rectangle of olive green card. Score and fold in half to create the card base.

2 Cut out a 10.5 x 5.5cm (4¼ x 2¼in) rectangle of dark red card. Use double-sided tape to attach it in an upper central position on the front of the card.

3 Take the dark green card and cut out a 9.5 x 4.5cm (3¾ x 1¾in) rectangle. Use double-sided tape to attach it centrally on the dark red card. Measure and cut out a 9 x 4cm (3½ x 1½in) rectangle from cream card. Use double-sided tape to stick it on top of the dark green card.

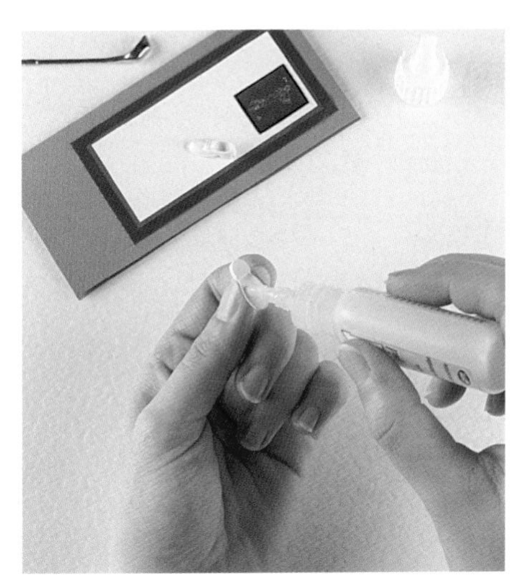

4 Your card is now ready to decorate. Cut a piece of ribbon so that the motif is in the centre and use double-sided tape to attach to a piece of black card. Cut away all but a narrow frame. Tape it in the upper right-hand corner of the cream card. Use super glue to stick the golf shoes and club in place.

5 Punch three small circles out of white card and use PVA glue to stick them in a row beneath the framed picture. Paint a gold 3D dot in the corners of the dark red card. Put the flower sticker in the bottom right-hand corner.

peacock feather

Clean whites and shimmer gold give this card an air of sophisticated understatement. Use this card as a party or wedding invitation, to say thank-you or to send birthday greetings. This versatile stamp can be used in so many colourways.

you will need

- A5 sheet cream textured card
- Stylus
- Metal ruler
- Craft knife
- Cutting mat
- Pencil
- Embossing pad
- Peacock feather stamp
- Sheet plain white card
- Scrap paper
- Gold embossing powder
- Precision heat tool
- Double-sided tape
- Scissors
- Sheet shimmer gold card
- Sheet white parchment
- Gold 3D paint

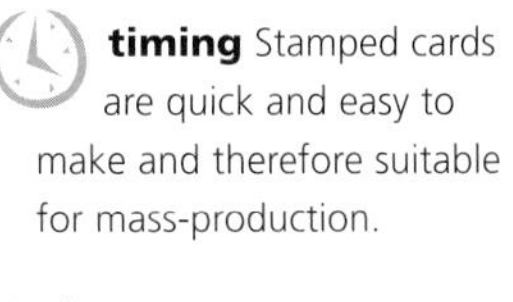

timing Stamped cards are quick and easy to make and therefore suitable for mass-production.

alternative Use a poppy stamp and emboss it in brilliant red and green to create a different, but still very stylish, card.

Create a decorative frame using a corner cutter and mount a wonderfully coloured feather in it.

1 Trim the cream textured card to 19cm (7½in) wide. Score and fold to create the card base. Using the embossing stamp pad, print a single peacock feather on a sheet of plain white card.

2 Fold a sheet of scrap paper in half. Hold the stamped white card over the paper and sprinkle with gold embossing powder. Shake off the excess powder and return it to the container.

3 Use the precision heat tool (see page 14) to set the embossed design.

4 Once the paper has cooled, measure a 10.5 x 5cm (4 x 2in) rectangle around the embossed design so that it is in the centre. Cut out.

5 Use double-sided tape to attach the design to a piece of gold card. Cut away all but a narrow frame.

6 Attach the framed design to a sheet of parchment. Cut away all but a 1cm (½in) frame. Attach with double-sided tape to the card front and decorate with four gold 3D paint dots; one in each corner of the parchment frame.

bead dolly

Plastic beads and bead boards have been a part of my life for as many years as I have had children. They can be used to create both simple and intricate designs.

you will need

- A5 sheet of plasma
- Stylus
- Metal ruler
- A5 sheet white paper
- Double-sided tape
- Scissors
- Paper napkin with suitable design
- Aerosol glue
- Red, flesh, blue and yellow heat seal beads and board

timing Bead art takes time and patience; have fun creating your own designs.

alternative A bead Christmas decoration would look good on a plasma base with a seasonal edging cut from a Christmas napkin. Make the decoration removable so that it can be used on the tree for years to come.

1 Score and fold the plasma in half. Score and fold the white paper in half and attach it inside the plasma using double-sided tape.

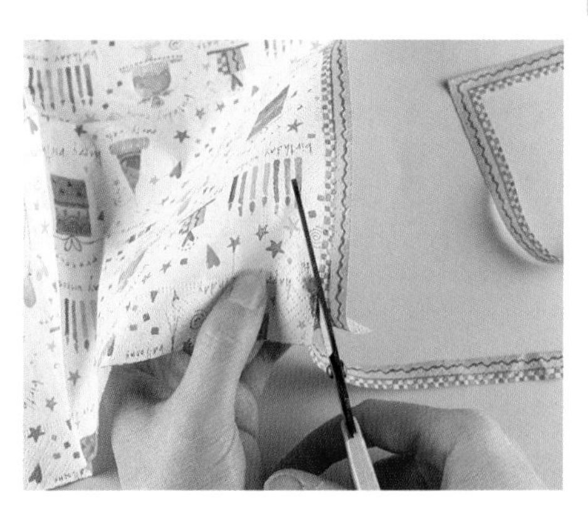

2 Cut out the border pattern from the paper napkin. Separate the patterned layer from the backing layers.

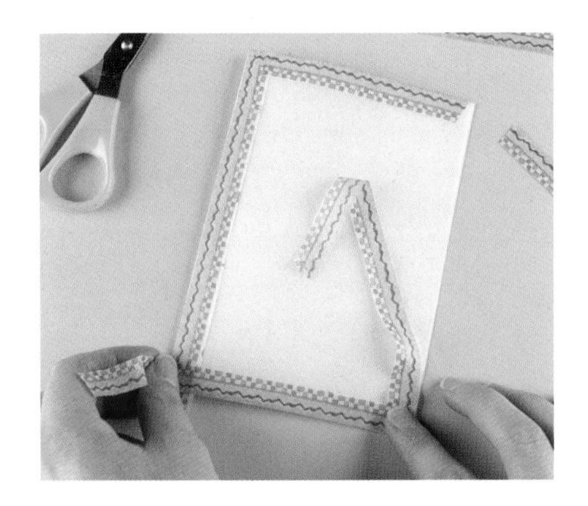

3 Use aerosol glue to attach the border around the edge of the plasma cover. Cut away any excess and be sure to mitre the corners.

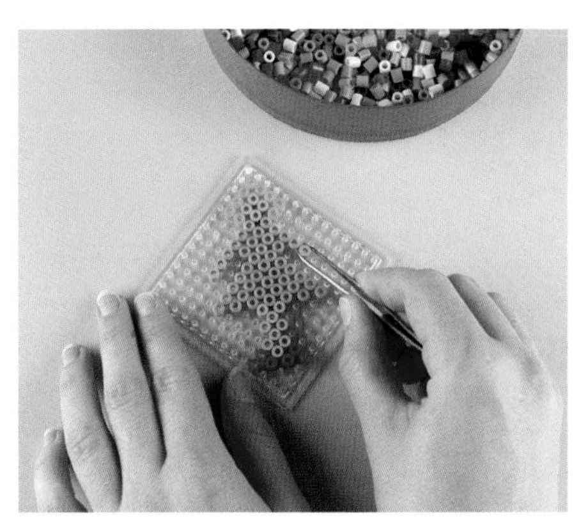

4 Use the pattern on page 228 to make up the dolly design using beads and the bead board. Heat seal the beads following the manufacturer's instructions. Use double-sided tape to attach the bead dolly centrally on the card.

variations *These cards were created by my children. Use beads to create simple designs, geometric patterns and pictures. You can make a card suitable for any occasion.*

olive branch

The dove of peace flies across a glittering sky holding an olive branch. For an alternative design create a sunny, rainbow-filled sky.

you will need

- Oval cutter, template and board
- A5 sheet blue card
- Scrap paper
- Aerosol glue
- Spangle glitter
- A5 sheet olive green card
- A5 sheet white textured card
- Double-sided tape
- Scissors
- Acetate
- Fine point black pen
- White card scrap
- Spring green card scrap
- PVA glue

timing This card takes a little time as you need to take care when cutting out the various elements.

alternative A red card base and gold oval could frame a winter backdrop featuring a chubby snowman with a carrot nose.

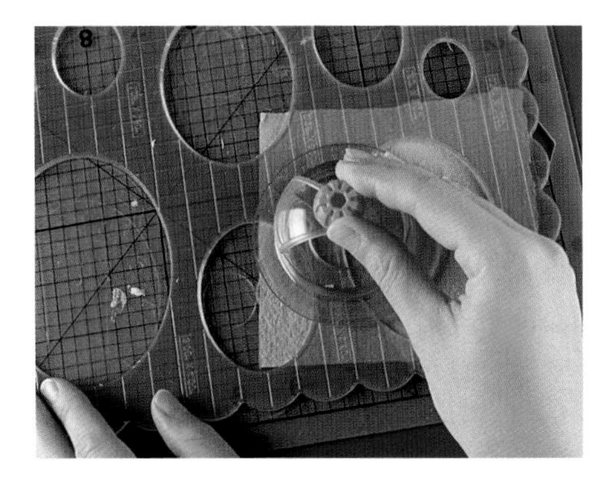

1 Use the oval cutter, template and board to cut out a 10 x 7.5cm (4 x 3in) oval in blue card. If you do not have an oval cutter use the template on page 229.

2 Fold a sheet of scrap paper in half and open it out. Coat the blue oval with aerosol glue and, holding it over the scrap paper, sprinkle it with spangle glitter. Shake off the excess glitter and return it to the container.

3 Using the oval cutter cut a 10 x 7.5cm (4 x 3in) oval from olive green card. Now cut a second, slightly smaller oval from the centre of the first. You now have a frame. If you do not have an oval cutter use the template on page 229.

4 Score and fold the sheet of white textured card to create the card blank. Use double-sided tape to attach the blue oval in a central position on the front of the card. Tape the green frame directly on top of the blue oval.

5 Trace the dove and olive branch templates on page 229. Cut the dove pieces out of white card and the olive branch from spring green card. Use PVA glue to attach the bird in a central position within the frame. First place a wing, then the body and finally the second wing.

6 Use a black fine point pen to draw around the edge of the bird's body and wings, and draw an eye. Use PVA glue to attach the olive branch so it looks as though the bird is carrying it in its beak.

bookmark

This card contains both a gift and a greeting. The bookmark can be removed and will be a wonderful reminder of a birthday or special occasion.

you will need

- Pattern cutting sheet
- Cutting mat
- Masking tape
- Scissors
- Mauve and pink two-tone paper
- Craft knife
- Metal ruler
- PVA glue
- Double-sided tape
- Black card
- Mauve card
- Corner cutter
- Purple dauber
- Mottled grey card
- Stylus
- Silver 3D paint
- 4 tiny green beads

timing Take your time when marking up and cutting the pattern for this card; it has to be precise.

alternative You could make a bookmark using an embossed, stamped design. Make up a base in sympathetic colours.

1 Secure the cutting sheet to a cutting mat with masking tape. Slide a 13 x 4cm (5¼ x 1½in) piece of two-tone paper under the chevron pattern and cut a line of chevrons 8.5cm (3½in) long. (If you do not have a pattern cutting sheet use the template on page 229. Trace on to acetate, then cut through the marked chevrons to create the folding areas.)

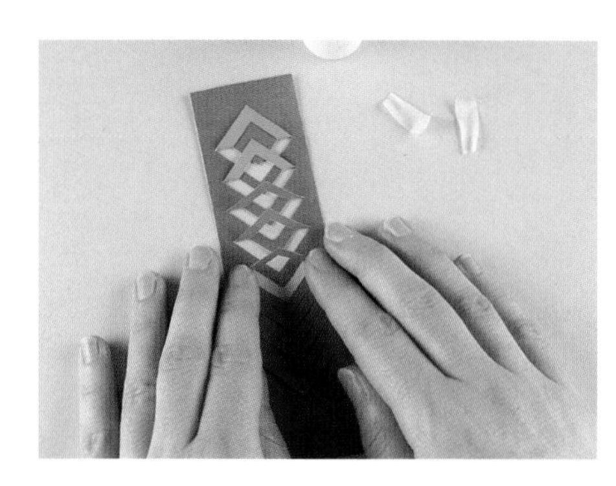

2 Fold the cut out chevrons to create the pattern and use PVA glue to hold them in place. Shape the top and bottom into points. Use double-sided tape to attach the chevron pattern centrally on a 13.5 x 4.75cm (5¼ x 1⅞in) rectangle of black card. Shape the top of the black card into a point and round the bottom corners.

3 Cut out a 14 x 6cm (5½ x 2½in) piece of mauve card. Use a corner cutter to cut out each corner. It must make a cut that will hold the bookmark in place.

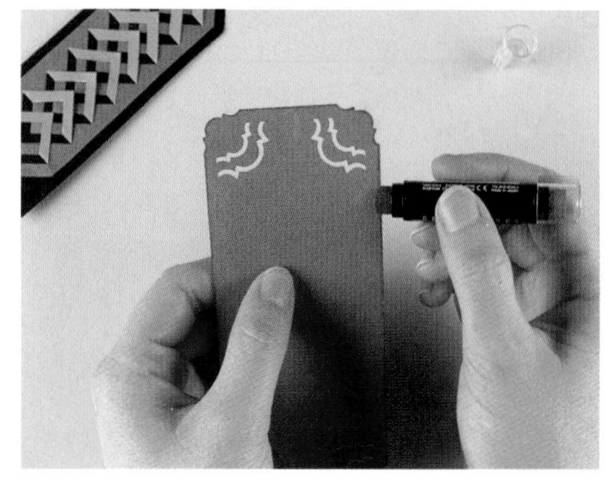

4 Press a dauber around the edge of the mauve card.

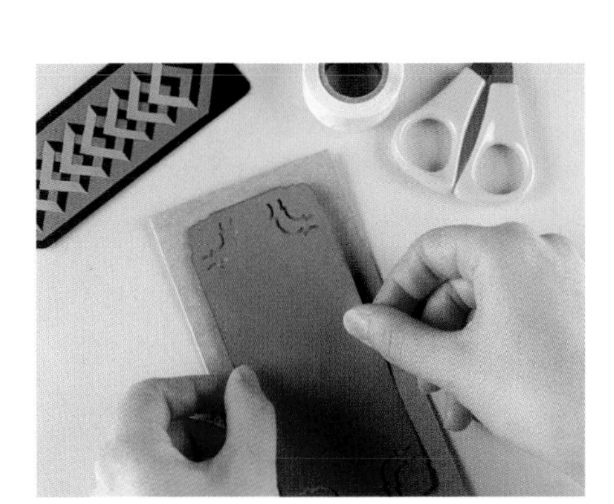

5 Cut out a 16.5 x 16cm (6½ x 6¼in) piece of mottled grey card. Score and fold it in half to create the base. Use double-sided tape to attach the bookmark holder centrally on the card base.

6 Slip the bookmark in place. Put tiny dots of silver 3D paint in each corner of the mauve bookmark holder. Place a bead on each paint dot.

memories

When searching for an idea for a Mother's Day card I came across this long-forgotten photograph.

I hope it inspires you to make something similar for someone special in your life.

you will need

- A4 sheet mottled brown card
- Craft knife
- Metal ruler
- Pencil
- Cutting mat
- Stylus
- Oval cutter, template and board
- A5 sheet textured cream card
- Suitable photograph
- Corner punch
- Double-sided tape
- Scissors
- A5 sheet cream paper

timing Take your time when making this card; it's a gift as well as a greeting.

alternative Try the card in more modern colours if you are using a recent photograph.

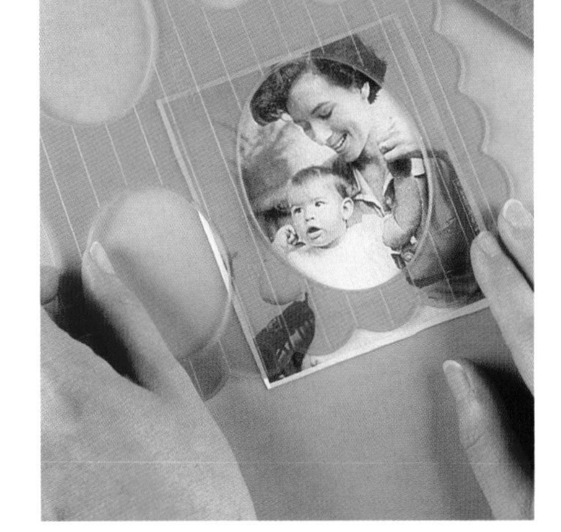

1 Cut a 21 x 13cm (8¼ x 5in) rectangle from the sheet of mottled brown card. Score and fold it in half to create the card base. Use the oval cutter, template and board to cut your photograph into a 10 x 7.5cm (4 x 3in) oval shape. If you do not have an oval cutter use the templates on page 230.

2 Cut a 10 x 12cm (4 x 4¾in) rectangle out of textured cream card. Cut a 9 x 6.5cm (3½ x 2½in) oval in a central position on the cream card. Cut a 10.5 x 7.5cm (4¼ x 3in) oval from mottled brown card and then cut a 9 x 6.5cm (3½ x 2½in) oval out of that. This will frame the photograph.

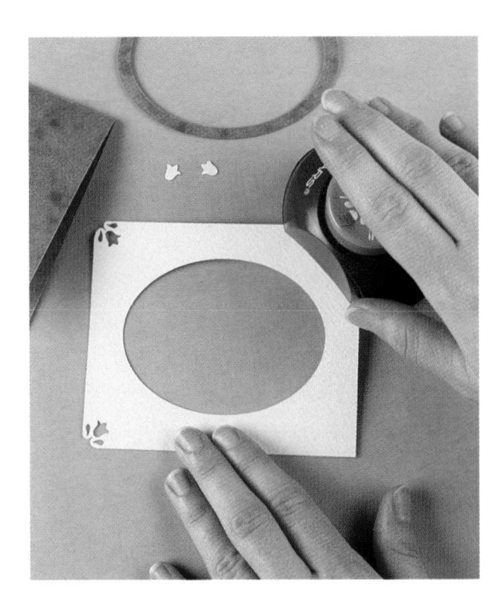

3 Use a punch to decorate each corner of the cream card. (If you do not have a corner punch you might want to trim the card with scissors and decorate it with dots of 3D paint).

4 Use double-sided tape to layer up the card. Tape the photograph in position beneath the decorated cream card and attach the frame. Stick the completed picture to the card front.

5 Cut a 20 x 11cm (8 x 4¼in) rectangle from cream paper. Fold it in half and fix in place inside the card with double-sided tape.

star surprise

No collection of cards is complete without a pop-up. This card would make a great birthday greeting for a young friend.

you will need

- A4 sheet red card
- Craft knife
- Metal ruler
- Cutting mat
- Pencil
- Stylus
- Rectangle cutter, template and board
- A5 sheet blue shimmer card
- Double-sided tape
- Scissors
- Birthday cake and parcel sequins
- Red 3D paint
- Glow-in-the-dark star
- Silver pen
- Sheet of plasma

timing Take your time over this card as it is important to get the construction right.

alternative Once you have mastered the art of pop-up, the sky's the limit. Use different background colours and replace the star with a flower, spaceship, buzzy bee, birthday cake – anything you want!

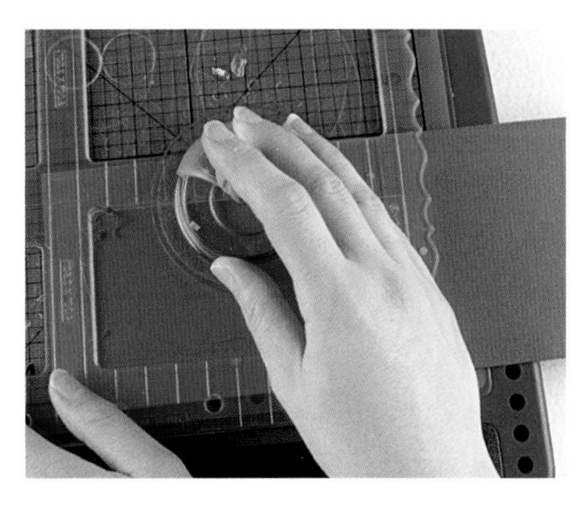

1 Cut the sheet of red card in half lengthwise. Take one piece and score and fold it in half to create the card base. Cut out a 6 x 10cm (2½ x 4in) rectangle from the front of base.

2 Cut out a 6 x 10cm (2½ x 4in) rectangle from the centre of the sheet of blue shimmer card. Cut a 1.25cm (½in) border around the rectangular hole to create a frame. Use double-sided tape to attach it to the front of the card to frame the window.

3 Use double-sided tape to attach birthday cake and parcel sequins around the frame.

4 Use 3D red paint to print a pattern of dots between the sequins. Leave to dry.

5 Tape the glow-in-the-dark star to the red card. Cut around it to leave a frame. Decorate the frame using a silver pen (see photo opposite) and embellish the star with red 3D paint.

6 When the paint is dry assemble the card. Cut a strip of plasma 0.5 x 14cm (¼ x 5½in). Tape one end to the interior of the card and stick the star to the other end.

balloon magic

A perfect birthday card. Use the balloon design to decorate gift-bags and boxes. If you do not have a suitable bow button, use a fabric or string bow.

you will need

- A5 sheet of violet card
- Stylus
- Ruler
- A5 sheet green card
- Craft knife
- Cutting mat
- Pencil
- Double-sided tape
- Scissors
- Sheet spotted paper
- White card scrap
- Yellow card scrap
- Blue, red and yellow craft wire
- Super glue
- Circle cutter, template and board
- Blue and red card scraps
- 3D tape
- Bow-shaped button
- 3 tiny beads – blue, red and yellow
- Purple 3D paint

timing This card takes a while as cutting out the circles is a delicate operation.

alternative Place a bunch of cut out or punched flowers on green craft wire stalks. Tie together with a button bow and set them against a background of buzzing bee stamped paper.

1 Score and fold the sheet of violet card to create the base. Cut a 12 x 7.5cm (4¾ x 3in) piece of green card. Use double-sided tape to attach it centrally on the base. Cut an 11 x 6.5cm (4½ x 2½in) piece of spotted paper. Tape this to the green card.

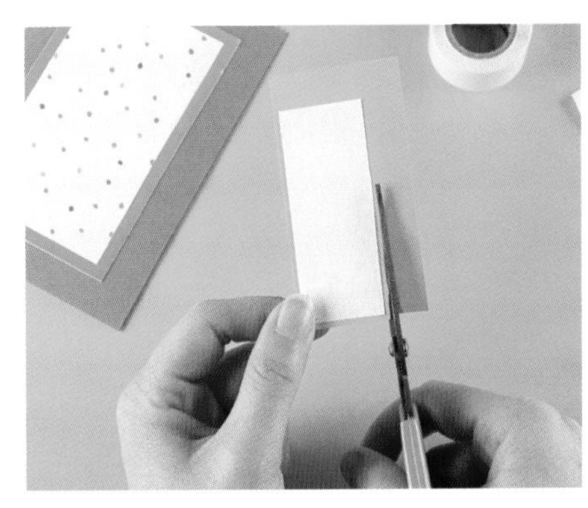

2 Cut a 3 x 7.5cm (1¼ x 3in) rectangle out of white card. Attach it to a piece of yellow card and cut away all but a narrow frame. Stick these layers centrally on the spotted paper.

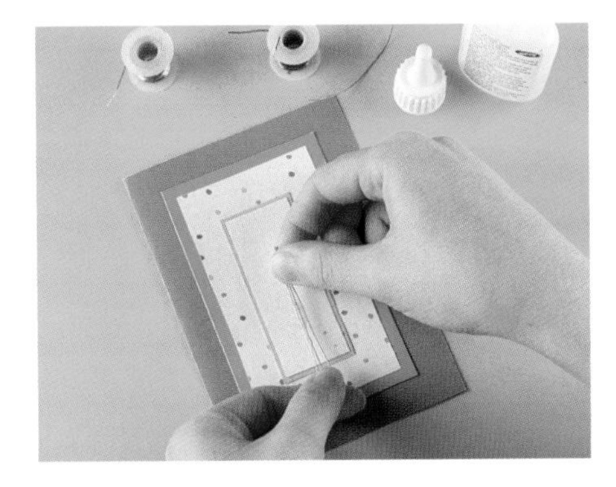

3 Cut 7cm (2¾in) of blue, red and yellow wire. Use super glue to attach a short section of the bunch of wire "strings" to the card. Allow to dry. Fan out the top and bottom of the wires.

4 Use the circle cutter, template and board to cut two 2.5cm (1in) circles each from blue, red and yellow card.

5 Using double-sided tape, position the bottom layer of each balloon on the card to correspond with the same colour wire. Place the circles underneath the wires. Put 3D tape on top of the wires then put the top layers of the balloons in place.

6 Use super glue to attach the bow and the beads, and paint 3D purple dots at each corner of the green card.

kaleidoscope

People have been folding paper to create patterns for generations. Teabag folding is an intricate system to create kaleidoscope-like effects.

you will need

- A5 sheet blue card
- Craft knife
- Metal ruler
- Pencil
- Cutting mat
- Stylus
- A5 sheet white card
- Double-sided tape
- Scissors
- A5 sheet orange card
- Sheet of decorative paper (suitable for folding)

timing You should spend some time practising your paper folding.

alternative The pattern created depends on the colours of the paper squares you use.

1 Cut a 21 x 10cm (8¼ x 4in) rectangle out of the blue card. Score and fold in half to create the card base. Cut a piece of white card 7cm (2¾in) square. Use double-sided tape to attach it to the orange card. Cut away all but a narrow frame around the white card. Use double-sided tape to attach it to the card front.

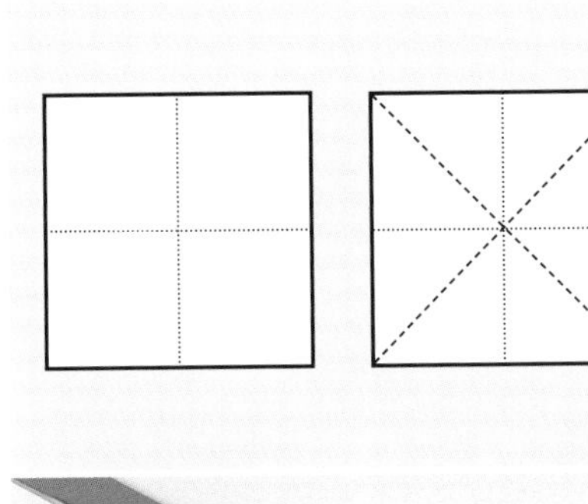

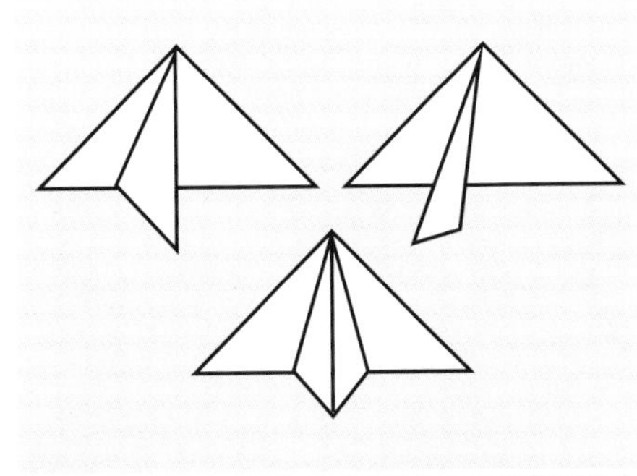

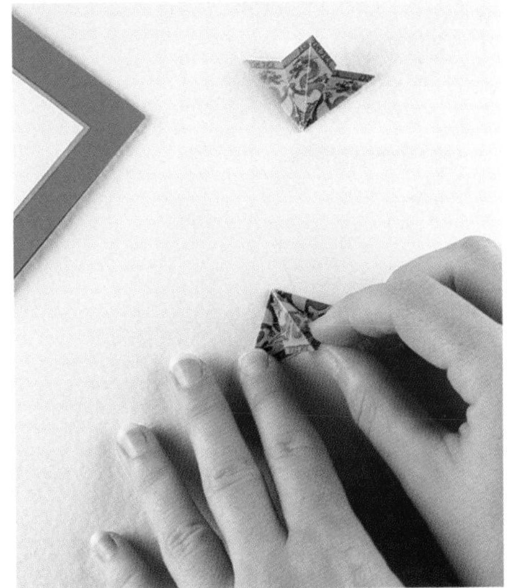

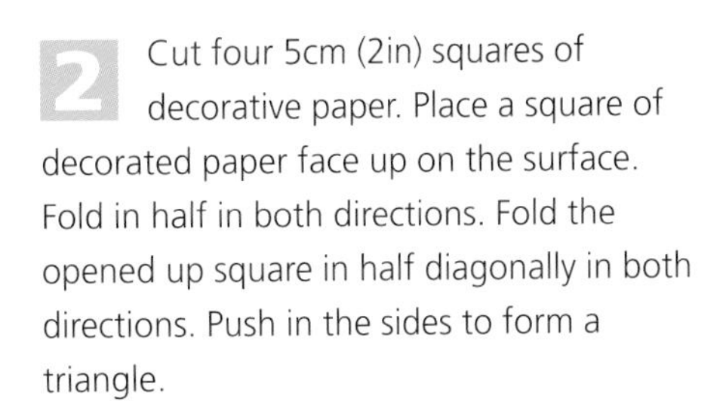

2 Cut four 5cm (2in) squares of decorative paper. Place a square of decorated paper face up on the surface. Fold in half in both directions. Fold the opened up square in half diagonally in both directions. Push in the sides to form a triangle.

3 Fold one corner towards the central fold line. Fold the corner back on itself. Make the same fold on the other side of the triangle. Open out both folds and flatten them to make the shape. Repeat with the other three squares.

4 Use double-sided tape to attach the four folded shapes to the card.

elephant trails

A wealth of history and craftsmanship has gone into creating this card. The stamp is one of many commercially available stamps handcrafted in India using traditional skills, local wood and handtools.

you will need

- A4 sheet white card
- Craft knife
- Metal ruler
- Cutting mat
- Stylus
- Aerosol glue
- Embroidered paper
- Suitable elephant stamp
- Red stamp pad
- Scrap paper
- Red sparkle embossing powder
- Tweezers or tongs
- Precision heat tool
- Pencil
- Gold pen
- Card in green, yellow, blue, red and gold
- Double-sided tape
- Scissors
- 3D double-sided tape

1 Cut the sheet of white card in half. Score and fold one half to create the card base. Spray a layer of aerosol glue on the exterior of the card base and set it aside for a minute or two to become tacky. Then lay the card base on to the reverse side of the embroidered paper. Smooth into place and cut away any excess.

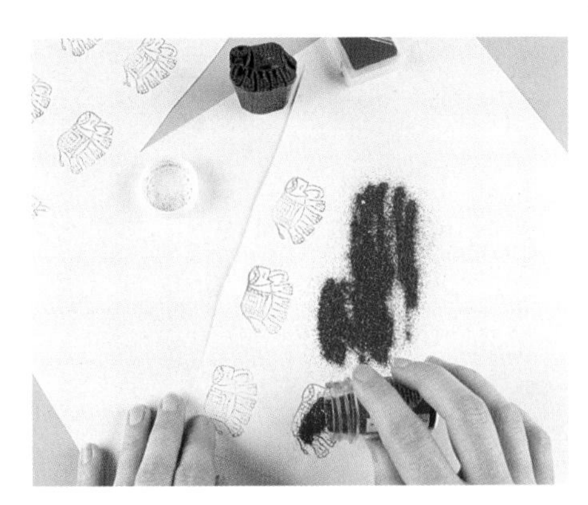

2 Using your chosen stamp and the red stamp pad print a selection of images across the white card. Fold a sheet of scrap paper in half and open it out. Place the white card on to the scrap paper and sprinkle the embossing powder over the images. Shake off the excess powder and return it to the pot.

3 Holding the stamped card with tweezers or tongs, seal the embossing powder with the precision heat tool (see page 14). Select the best image and use the ruler and pencil to mark up a 4 x 3cm (1½ x 1¼in) rectangle around it. Cut it out. Highlight the image with the gold pen.

4 Cut out the layers: 6.25 x 5.25cm (2½ x 2in) rectangle of red card; 5.5 x 4.5cm (2¼ x 1¾in) rectangle of blue card; 5 x 4cm (2 x 1½in) rectangle of yellow card and 4.5 x 3.5cm (1¾ x 1¼in) rectangle of green card. Use double-sided tape to attach them one on top of the other (in the order in which you cut them out) on the card base.

5 Use double-sided tape to attach the stamped and embossed elephant to a piece of gold card. Cut a narrow border around the image. Use 3D double-sided tape to attach it to the layers.

timing Take your time stamping and embossing the feature design.

alternative Traditional wooden stamps come in all shapes and sizes. Enjoy creating your own designs with handmade stamps.

coordinating items
A sheet of beautifully crafted wrapping paper can be used to make a gift-bag or to cover a gift pouch (see pages 20–21).

say it with flowers

projects

flower power

This display of paper flowers strewn across a violet card will bring a little summer magic into someone's life.

you will need

- A5 sheet violet card
- Metal ruler
- Stylus
- Craft knife
- Cutting mat
- Pencil
- Large flower punch
- Small flower punch
- Yellow, pink, red, orange, green and blue sugar paper
- Tweezers
- PVA glue
- Pale green gel pen
- Yellow 3D paint

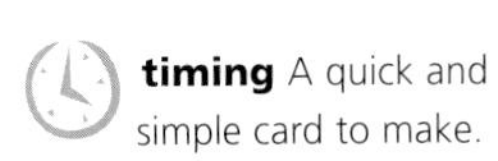

timing A quick and simple card to make.

alternative Decorate a sky-blue card with punched butterflies. Replace the gel pen dots with tiny stamped daisies.

1 Score and fold the violet card to create the card base. Use the metal ruler and craft knife to trim the folded card to a height of 11cm (4½in).

2 Use the punches to cut out a selection of large and small flowers from sugar paper. Use PVA glue to attach small flowers centrally on large flowers.

Coordinating items

Vary the background colour and try your hand at decorating a gift-box or tag using punched paper flowers. Use a flower stamp to decorate tissue paper. You might want to use embossing powder to highlight the flower petals or centres.

3 Attach the prepared flowers across the card in an attractive pattern using PVA glue.

4 Use the pale green gel pen to draw small spots between the flowers. Finally, decorate each flower with a centrally placed dot of yellow 3D paint.

pink gingham

Gingham and daisies come together to create this delightfully pretty card. Cover gift-boxes with daisy-stamped gingham paper and make coordinating gift-tags.

you will need

- A5 sheet white card
- Metal ruler
- Stylus
- Aerosol glue
- Pink gingham paper
- Craft knife
- Cutting mat
- Small piece white card
- Pencil
- Four small flower rubber stamps
- Pink stamp pad
- Sheet of scrap paper
- Pink embossing powder
- Precision heat tool
- Double-sided tape
- Scissors
- Small piece dark pink card
- Pink 3D paint

timing This card is easy to make, but take care when using the embossing powder. Make sure that you cover your work surface with scrap paper.

alternative Try this design in blue or green gingham with a stamped flower feature. How about red gingham with red hearts?

1 Score and fold the sheet of white card to create the card base. Spray aerosol glue over the exterior of the card. Lay the gingham paper on to the sticky card base and smooth it down, removing any air bubbles. Trim away any excess.

2 Cut a piece of white card measuring 5.5cm (2¼in) square. Using the rubber stamps and a pink ink pad, stamp four different flowers on to the square.

3 Fold a sheet of scrap paper in half and open out. Holding the printed white square over the paper, sprinkle pink embossing powder over it. Shake off the excess powder and return to the pot.

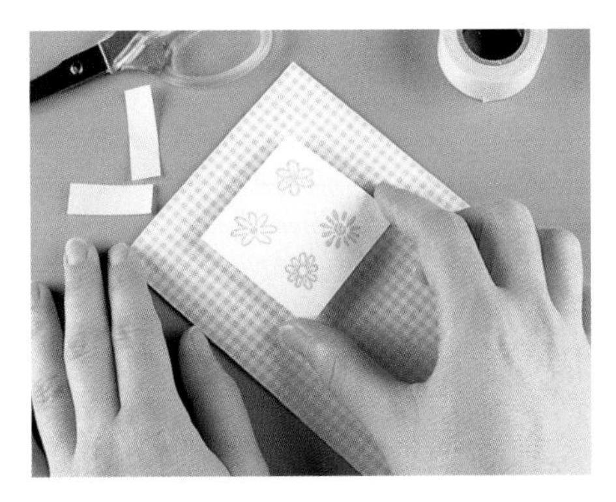

4 Seal the embossing powder with the precision heat tool (see page 14). Use double-sided tape to attach the prepared flower picture in an upper central position on the front of the card.

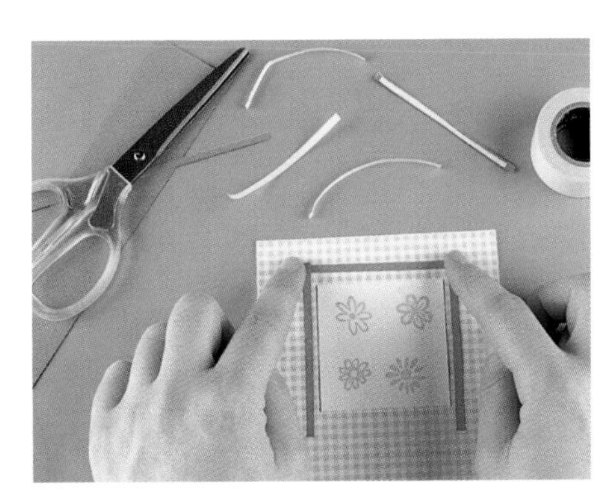

5 Cut out four narrow 8cm (3¼in) long ribbons from the dark pink card. Use double-sided tape to attach them to the card to create a frame. The ribbons should overlap.

6 Print four pink 3D paint dots, one in each corner of the frame, to give the card a professional finished look.

paper roses

As soon as I saw this lovely gift-wrap I had loads of great ideas for using it to make beautiful cards, bags and tags.

you will need

- A5 sheet pink card
- Craft knife
- Cutting mat
- Metal ruler
- Pencil
- Stylus
- Rose-patterned wrapping paper
- Double-sided tape
- Scissors
- Silver card
- Sheet of plasma
- Pink 3D paint

timing This card can be made in a matter of minutes, making it ideal to mass-produce for wedding invitations or thank-you notes.

alternative Gift-wrap with a nautical theme would be fun to use. Cut out a picture of a ship and set it against a blue backdrop.

1 Cut the card base out of the pink card; it should measure 21 x 10cm (8¼ x 4in). Score and fold in half. Cut an 8.75 x 8.5cm (3½ x 3¼in) rectangle from the wrapping paper. Attach it in a central position on the card base using double-sided tape.

2 Cut out a piece of silver card 7.5 x 7.25cm (3 x 2⅞in). Use double-sided tape to attach it in a central position on the rose-patterned square. Cut a piece of plasma 7 x 6.75cm (2¾ x 2⅝in) and stick this on top of the silver card.

Coordinating items *Use tissue paper to make unusual gift-bag handles: spray a thin layer of aerosol glue across a sheet of tissue paper, crinkle and roll the paper, pressing to make a length of "rope".*

3 Draw a box 5.5 x 5.25cm (2¼ x 2in) around a rose on the patterned paper. Cut out. Use double-sided tape to attach it centrally on the plasma.

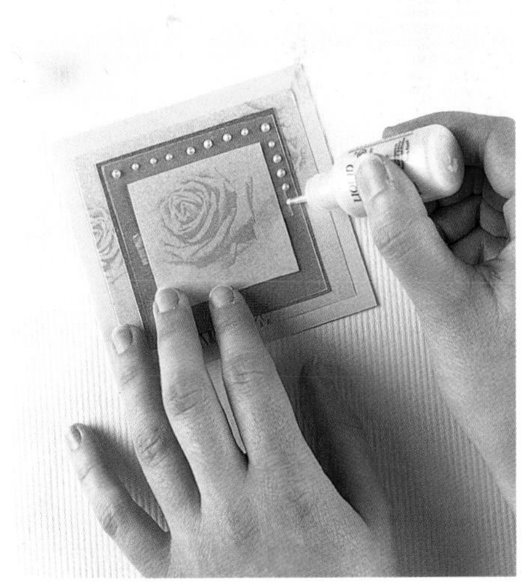

4 Use pink 3D paint to print dots around the edge of the plasma to frame the rose.

daisy rainbow

A rainbow of daisies decorates this bright yellow card, with highlights in green and gold.

you will need

- A5 sheet yellow card
- Craft knife
- Cutting mat
- Metal ruler
- Stylus
- Gold and green pens
- Daisy punch
- Blue, red, pink and white paper
- PVA glue
- Tweezers
- Purple 3D paint

timing This card is very effective, yet extremely easy to make. Using a punch is a quick way of working.

alternative A line of randomly placed punched dragonflies set against a dark blue base would make a stunning card.

1 Cut a rectangle 21 x 10cm (8¼ x 4in) from the yellow card. Score and fold to create the card base. Open it out. Use a ruler and the green and gold pens to draw lines down the card; front and back.

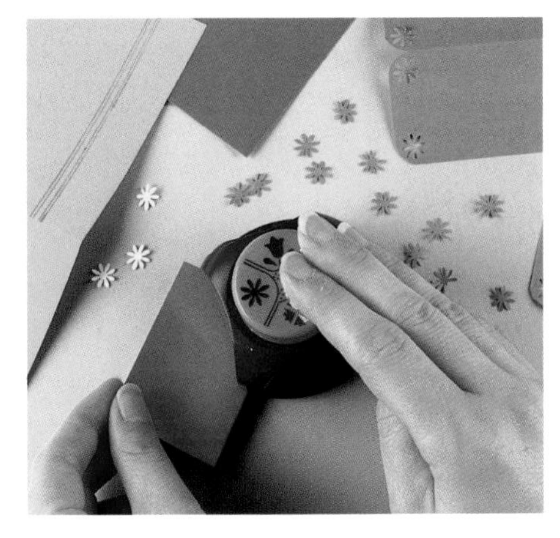

2 Punch around 20 daisies out of the coloured papers.

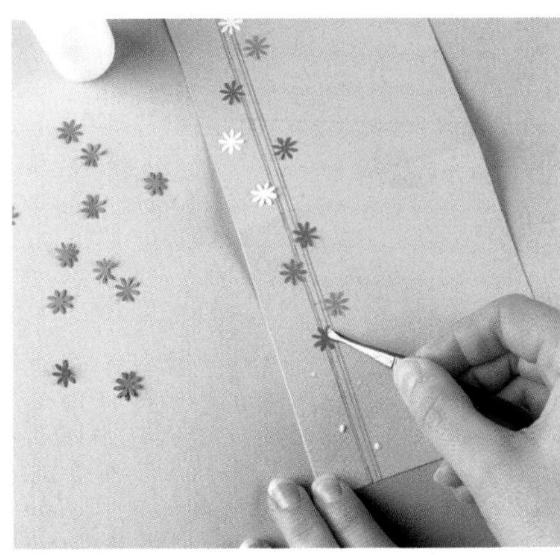

3 Place dots of PVA glue on and around the ruled lines. Position the daisies on the glue dots.

4 Squeeze a spot of purple 3D paint in the centre of each flower and also groups of three dots between the flowers.

Coordinating items *Have fun with your daisy punch. Use it to create wrapping paper, gift-tags, boxes and pouches.*

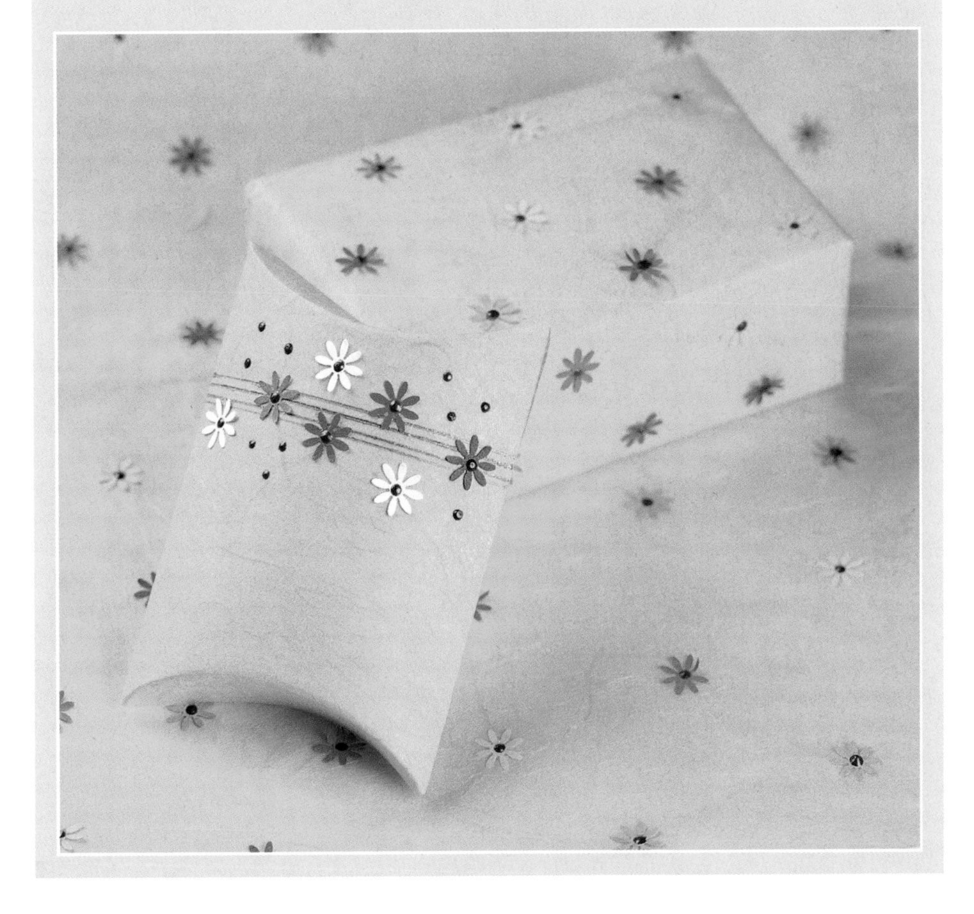

funky foam flowers

This stylish card is made from foam sheets that come in a wonderful array of colours and are easy to shape, cut and stick.

you will need

- A4 sheet spring green card
- Pencil
- Craft knife
- Cutting mat
- Metal ruler
- Stylus
- Scrap paper
- Scissors
- A5 sheet blue card
- Green, blue, pink and purple foam sheets
- Double-sided tape
- Pink and purple 3D paint

timing This card takes a little time to make as you need to cut the foam carefully.

alternative Make a Valentine's card with red, white and hot pink layers decorated with red hearts. Embellish with silver 3D paint.

1 Cut a rectangle 22 x 11cm (8½ x 4¼in) from the sheet of green card. Score and fold to create the card base. Trace and cut out the templates on page 231. Draw around the largest square shape on to the blue card and cut out the shape.

2 Cut the medium size square out of green foam and the small square from the blue foam. Cut out two large flowers from the pink foam, one large and one small flower from the purple foam and three leaves from the green foam.

3 Take the green card base and, using double-sided tape, attach the blue card layer, followed by the green foam layer and the blue foam layer.

4 Use double-sided tape to attach the flower and leaf shapes. Refer to the photograph opposite for their positioning.

coordinating items

Cut out a selection of flowers and leaves from the foam sheets and use them to decorate gift-boxes and cards. You might want to try the design in a different colour scheme.

5 Decorate the card with 3D paint using pink on the purple flowers and purple on the pink flowers and corners of the blue card.

topiary

Use rub-off transfers to create this lovely country garden scene. Once you have made the card, try decorating a gift-box or pouch using the same motif.

you will need

- A5 sheet pink card
- Metal ruler
- Stylus
- Rectangle cutter, template and board
- Lacy pattern vellum paper
- Scissors
- Double-sided tape
- Garden motif rub-on transfers
- Transfer stick
- Green, pink and violet gel pens

timing Putting together the elements of this card takes a little time, but the finished result will bring pleasure to the recipient.

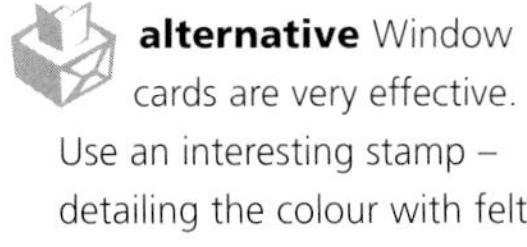

alternative Window cards are very effective. Use an interesting stamp – detailing the colour with felt-tip pens – in place of the transfer.

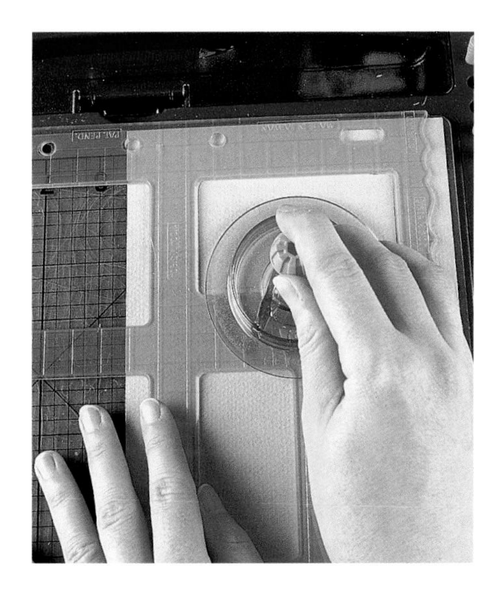

1 Score and fold the pink card to create the card base. Use the shape cutter, template and board to cut out a centrally placed 5 x 9cm (2 x 3½in) rectangle on the card front.

2 Cut two 10cm (4in) strips of vellum. Use double-sided tape to attach the strips to the interior of the card on either side of the window to give it a thin, lace border.

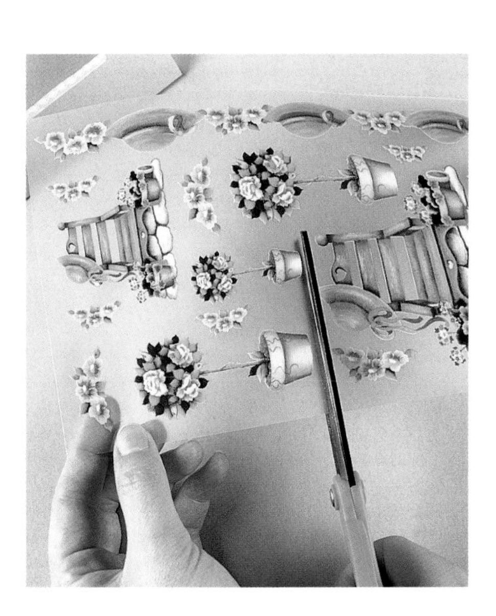

3 Cut out a suitable transfer and, following the manufacturer's instructions, transfer the design on to the interior of the card. The motif should be placed centrally so that it can be seen through the window.

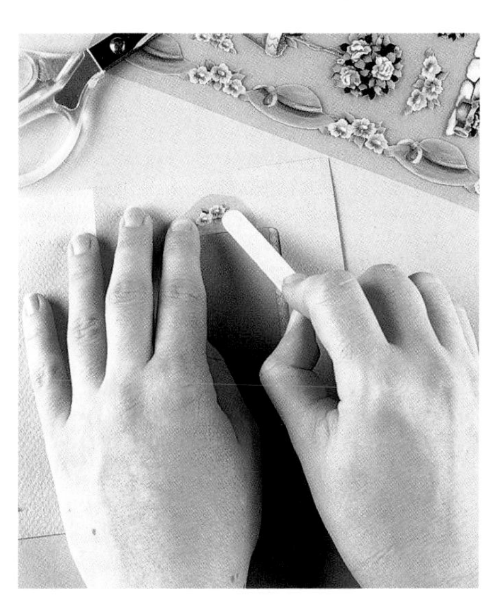

4 Apply a second transfer to the front of the card; place it centrally above the window. Use a third transfer to decorate the back of the card.

5 Frame the window with two borders using the green and pink gel pens. These can be drawn using a ruler or freehand. Complete the card by drawing little flower buds.

cherry blossom

Flower punches are so versatile. I use them all the time. This cherry blossom covered card was inspired by pictures of spring.

- A5 sheet grey card
- Metal ruler
- Stylus
- Scissors
- Pencil
- A5 sheet silver card
- A5 sheet black card
- A5 sheet turquoise blue paper
- Double-sided tape
- Small flower punch
- Pink paper
- Marker pen
- Small piece of acetate
- Small piece brown card
- PVA glue
- Tweezers
- Silver and green 3D paints

timing Set aside an hour to make this card as there are a number of elements to prepare.

alternative Use this technique to create a Christmas card. Use a brightly coloured base and a silver frame; attach Christmas decorations to the branch.

1 Score and fold the grey card to create the card base. Cut out an 8cm (3¼in) square from silver card, a 7cm (2¾in) square from black card and a 6.5cm (2½in) square from turquoise blue card. Use double-sided tape to attach the silver square in a high central position, then stick the black and blue squares on top.

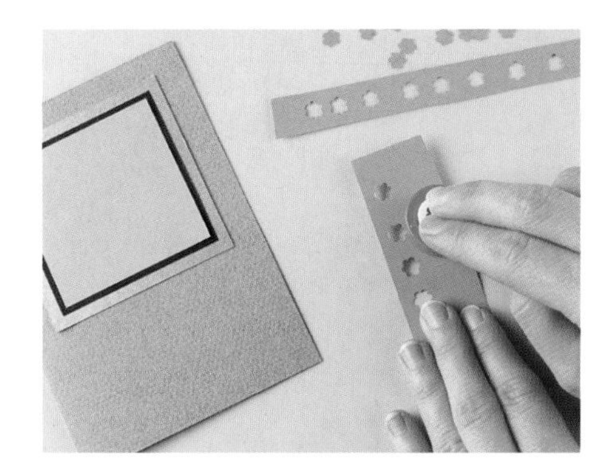

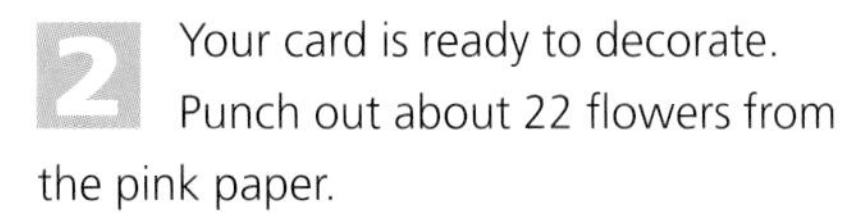

2 Your card is ready to decorate. Punch out about 22 flowers from the pink paper.

variation *This card base is gold and black gift-wrap, and the flowers punched from gold paper set against black. Use gold gel pen to draw on stems and leaves.*

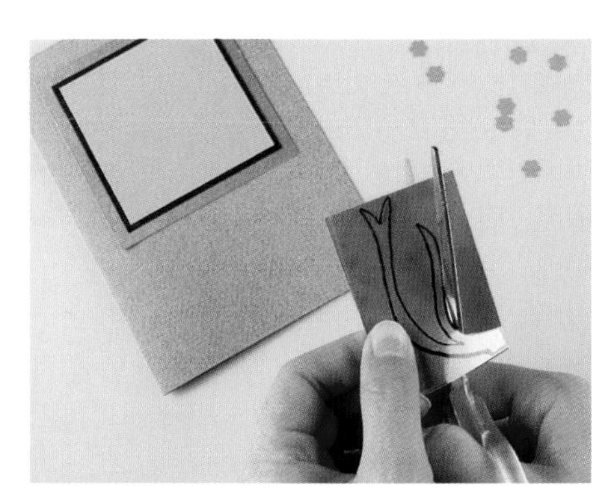

3 Use the marker pen to trace the branch template on page 232 on to acetate. Cut the shape out of brown card and attach it to the front of the card using double-sided tape. The branch should look as though it is growing out of the bottom left-hand corner of the blue square.

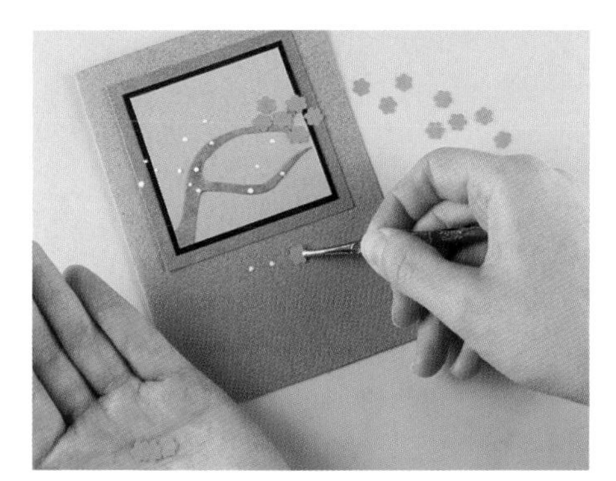

4 Squeeze 22 dots of PVA glue where the flowers will be placed. Cherry blossom grows in clusters of three or four blooms, so bear this in mind. Place a flower on each glue dot. Attach three flowers in a row beneath the picture.

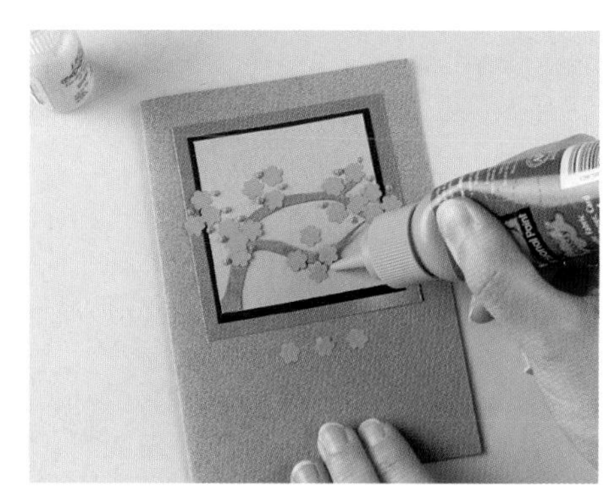

5 Place dots of green 3D paint between the flowers to resemble leaves (three or four leaves per cluster of flowers). Squeeze a dot of silver 3D paint in the centre of each flower. Don't forget to print leaves and flower centres on the flowers beneath the picture.

green blossoms

Hot orange and bright green blossoms decorate this versatile card.

Experiment with colours and produce your own designs using flower sequins.

you will need

- A5 sheet bright yellow textured card
- Metal ruler
- Stylus
- A5 sheet white card
- Craft knife
- Cutting mat
- Sheet of vellum
- Double-sided tape
- Scissors
- 3 green flower sequins
- A5 sheet orange card
- 3D adhesive tape
- Yellow 3D paint
- PVA glue
- 4 tiny green beads

timing Flower sequins are quick and easy to use.

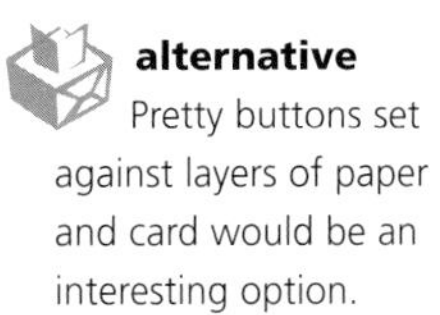

alternative Pretty buttons set against layers of paper and card would be an interesting option.

1 Score and fold the sheet of yellow card to make the base. Cut a piece of white card 2.5 x 5.5cm (1 x 2¼in). Use double-sided tape to attach it to a vellum sheet. Use scissors to cut away all but a narrow frame around the white card.

2 Turn the white card and vellum, vellum side up and use double-sided tape to attach three green flower sequins along the length of the white card.

3 Attach the sequin picture to a small piece of orange card using 3D tape. Cut away all but a 4mm (3⁄16in) edge around the picture.

4 Use double-sided tape to attach the layers you have just assembled to white card. Cut away all but a 5mm (⅛in) frame. Then attach this to a vellum sheet; cut a 5mm (⅛in) border.

5 Use double-sided tape to attach the multi-layered picture to the orange card and cut away yet another frame of 4mm (3⁄16in). Finally stick the layered, framed picture in an upper central position on the front of the card using double-sided tape.

6 Put a yellow 3D paint dot in the centre of each flower. Use PVA glue to attach a green bead in each corner of the white card.

bead magic

Wirework and flower beads are framed in mint green and white to create this pretty card. Use bead and wire designs to coordinate bags and gift-tags.

you will need

- A5 sheet of white line-embossed card
- Craft knife
- Metal ruler
- Cutting mat
- Stylus
- Pencil
- Rectangle cutter, template and board
- Small piece pale green card
- Double-sided tape
- Selection of pastel coloured beads
- Silver wire
- Wire cutters
- PVA glue
- Pink 3D paint

timing Threading and glueing the bead design for this card takes a little while.

alternative To create a Christmas card make a red frame and thread the wire with silver and clear beads and tiny stars. Scatter stars across the front of the card.

1 Cut a rectangle 16 x 15cm (6¼ x 6in) from the white card. Score and fold to make the card base. Mark up the horizontal centre of the card front, about one third of the way down.

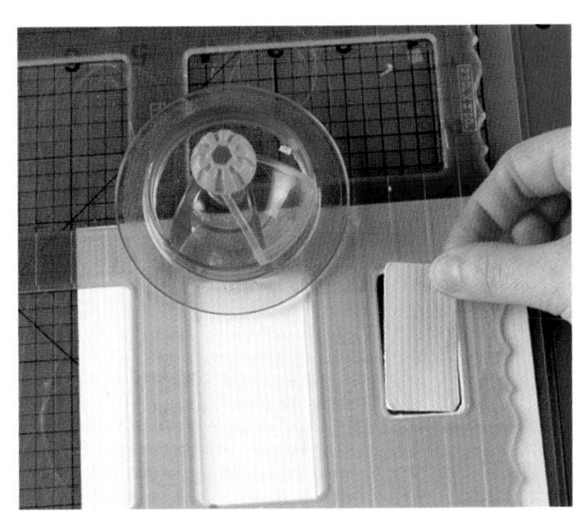

2 Using the point you have just marked as a guide, cut a 5 x 2.5cm (2 x 1in) window from the front of the card using the rectangle cutter.

3 Cut the same sized window from green card. Measure a 5mm (⅛in) border around the window and cut out.

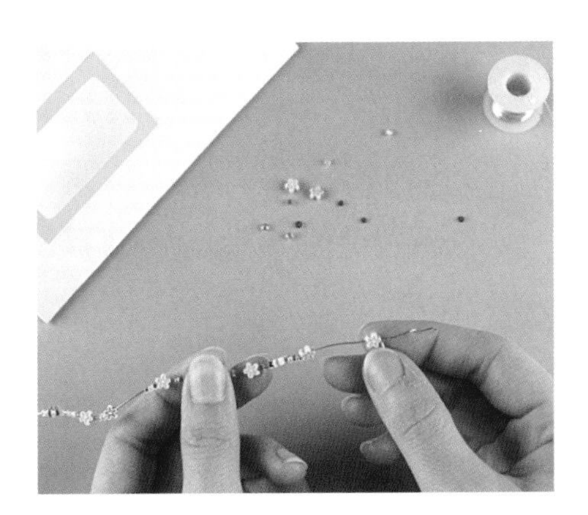

4 Use double-sided tape to attach the green frame around the window in the front of the card. Thread beads on to a length of silver wire 21cm (8¼in) long. Pinch the ends of the wire over so that the beads do not fall off.

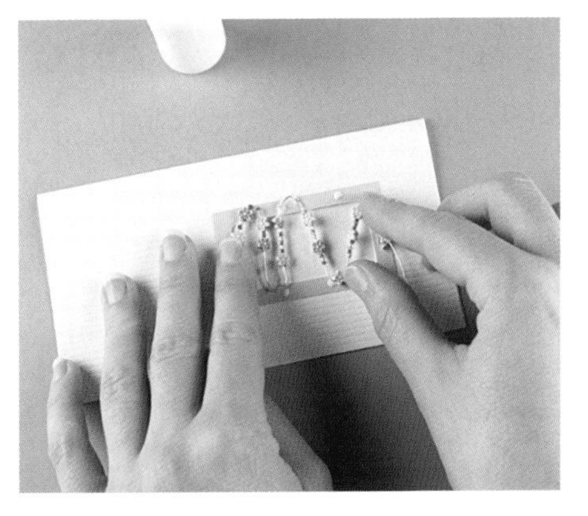

5 Shape the beaded wire into 3.5cm (1½in) zigzags. Use PVA glue to attach it to the card.

6 Mark dots in pink 3D paint along the frame. Use PVA glue to attach a single bead 5mm (⅛in) below the window.

pretty peonies

When I found these beautifully decorated paper napkins I just had to have them. Paper napkins decorated with flowers are so inspirational and pictures of peonies or roses make the most romantic greetings cards.

Use the peony napkins as gift-wrap and to decorate boxes and tags.

you will need

- 2 decorative paper napkins
- A4 sheet white card
- Craft knife
- Metal ruler
- Cutting mat
- Stylus
- Aerosol glue
- A4 white paper
- Pencil
- Small piece green card
- Small piece pink card
- Small piece white card
- Double-sided tape

timing Once you have mastered the method this card is quick and simple to make; a good design for mass-production.

alternative Make up this card in yellow and white daisies for a country feel.

1 Take the table napkins and separate the patterned layer from the remaining tissue layers. You will use the patterned layer to decorate your card. Discard the other layers.

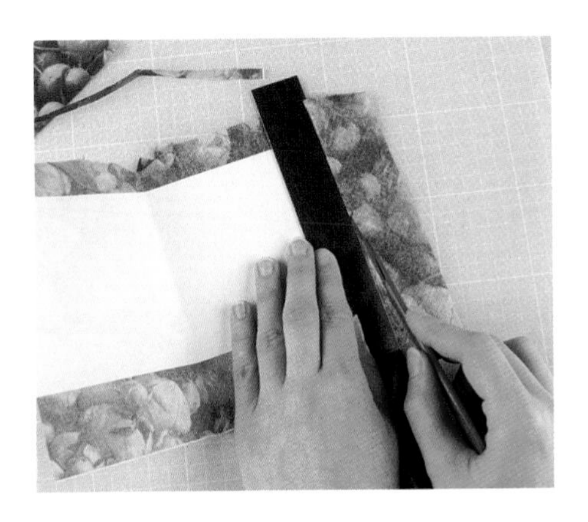

2 Cut out a 21 x 10cm (8¼ x 4in) rectangle from white card. Score and fold to make the card base. Spray the card base with aerosol glue and position it on the back of the patterned tissue layer. Turn over and carefully smooth the tissue on to the card base. Trim away the excess tissue paper.

3 Spray the A4 sheet of white paper with aerosol glue. Smooth the second patterned tissue layer over it to attach firmly.

4 Take the decorated paper sheet and use a pencil and ruler to mark up a 4.5cm (1¾in) square. Cut out with a craft knife.

5 Cut a 6cm (2½in) square from green card, a 5.5cm (2¼in) square from pink card and a 5cm (2in) square from white card. Use double-sided tape to attach the peony decorated square centrally on the white square.

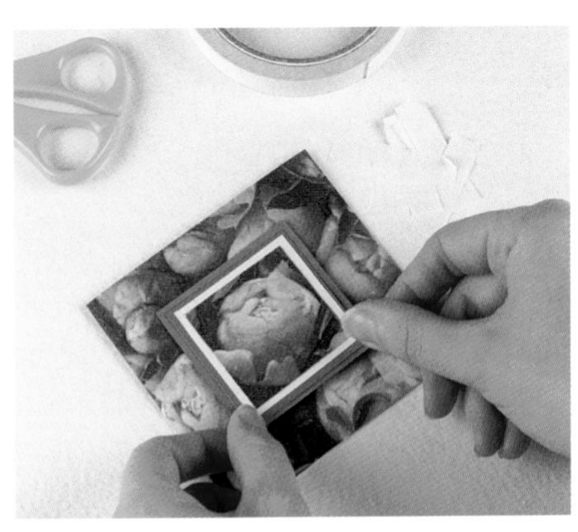

6 Layer this on to the pink square and then finally the green square. Use double-sided tape to attach the layered design centrally on the card.

special occasions

projects

patchwork house

This heart-warming little card is made from scraps of floral patchwork fabric. A perfect way to wish friends good luck in their new home.

you will need

- A5 sheet pink textured card
- Metal ruler
- Craft knife
- Cutting mat
- Pencil
- Stylus
- Tracing paper
- 4 scraps of patchwork fabric
- Scissors
- Aerosol glue
- Green gel pen
- 3D pink paint

timing Once you've gathered together the scraps of fabric, this card is quick to make.

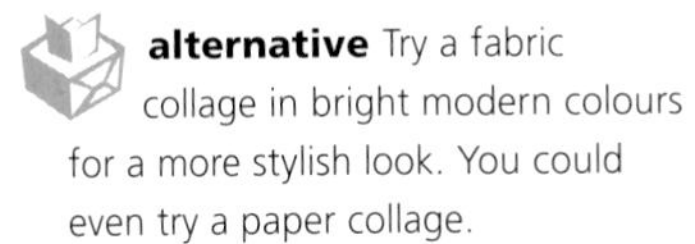

alternative Try a fabric collage in bright modern colours for a more stylish look. You could even try a paper collage.

1 Measure and cut out a rectangle 16 x 12cm (6¼ x 4¾in) from the pink card. Score and fold in half to create the base.

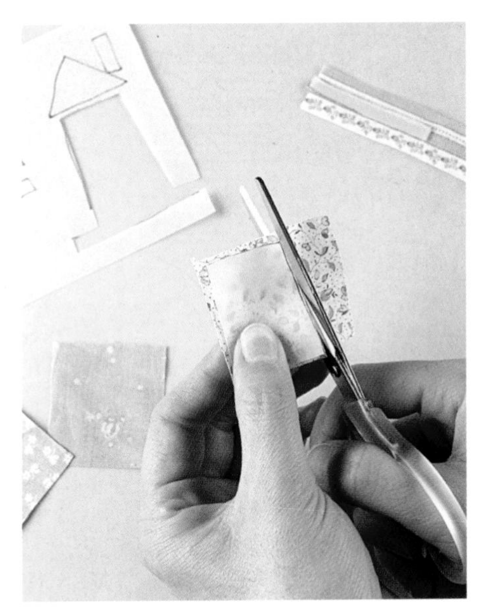

2 Trace the house template on page 232 and cut out the various shapes from your chosen fabrics.

coordinating items *Construct a gift-bag using suitable wrapping paper. Decorate it with a fabric collage to coordinate with your card, along with a gift-tag.*

3 Use aerosol glue to attach the fabric pieces on the card to form the house. The house should be in a lower central position.

4 Add details to the windows and door using the green gel pen. Complete the card by painting five pink 3D paint dots coming out of the chimney.

girl's best friend

Craft gems look great on cards. Here I have combined faux diamonds with silver thread and red hearts to create a modern yet romantic look, perfect for Valentine's Day or an anniversary.

you will need

- Red oven-bake clay
- Mini rolling pin
- Board
- Clingfilm
- Heart cutter
- Baking tray
- Stylus
- Ruler
- A5 sheet white textured card
- Double-sided tape
- Scissors
- Silver thread
- A5 white paper
- Super glue
- Tweezers
- Faux diamond

timing This card is very easy to make but you will need to set aside a little time as you have to bake the clay.

alternative Tiny stars and a faux jewel would create a stunning card to send best wishes to someone or even for a Christmas greeting.

1 Soften a small piece of red oven-bake clay and roll out between two layers of clingfilm. Cut out a dozen or so tiny red hearts and bake according to the manufacturer's instructions.

2 Score and fold the white card to create the card base. Place three strips of double-sided tape horizontally on the inside of the card front. One at the top, one in the middle and one at the bottom.

3 Wind silver thread around the card making sure it has a firm grip on the double-sided tape. Check the silver thread pattern you are creating on the card front as you go.

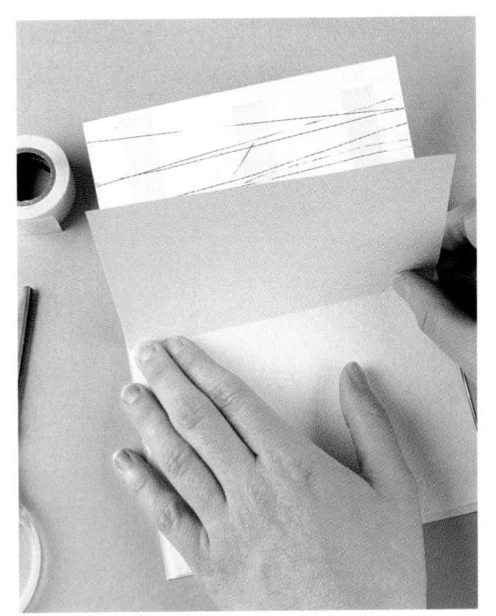

4 Attach with double-sided tape an insert of white paper cut slightly smaller than the card.

5 Use super glue to attach the red hearts to the card. Use double-sided tape to stick the faux diamond in place.

bunch of hearts

Wirework can be very effective. I have framed the wire design with tissue paper. Decorate bright pink tissue paper with gold dots to make gift-wrap and use the card design to make gift-tags.

you will need

- A5 sheet cream textured card
- Metal ruler
- Craft knife
- Cutting mat
- Stylus
- Pink tissue paper
- Aerosol glue
- Yellow paper
- Blue paper
- Double-sided tape
- Scissors
- Red, yellow, blue and pink craft wire
- Wooden dowel
- Super glue
- Gold 3D paint

timing This card takes a little time to make but is well worth the effort.

alternative Cut snowflakes out of tissue paper. Use aerosol glue to attach them to a card base then embellish with 3D paint.

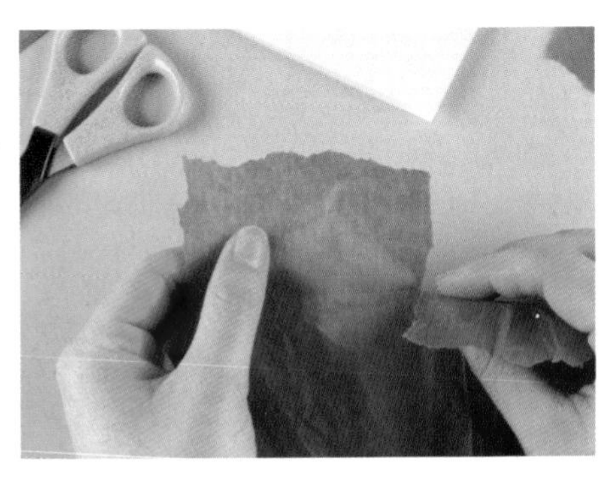

1 Use a craft knife to cut a 10.5 x 21cm (4 x 8¼in) rectangle from the cream card. Score and fold to form the base. Tear a piece of bright pink tissue paper approximately 8.5cm (3½in) square. Use aerosol glue to attach it in a central position on the front of the card.

2 Cut and assemble the layers (using double-sided tape) for the central motif in this order: a 5.5cm (2¼in) square of yellow paper; a 5cm (2in) square of blue paper and a 4.5cm (1¾in) square of cream card. Attach the layers centrally on the pink square.

3 Wind a length of red wire around a dowel three times and then stretch out a length of 10cm (4in). Cut off. Slide the wire off the dowel and press the coils together.

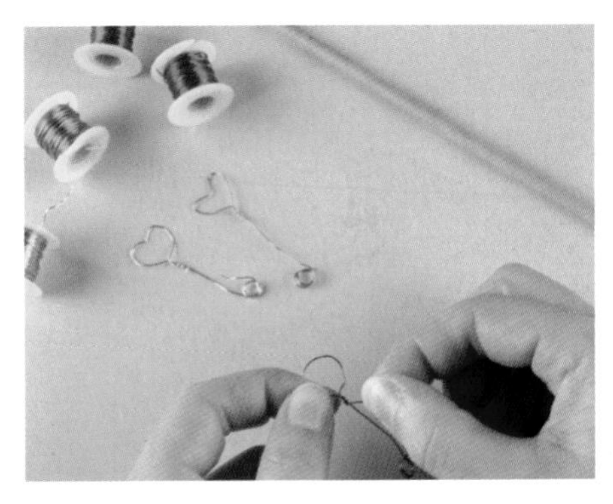

4 Measure 3cm (1¼in) up from the coils and make a circle of wire 1cm (½in) in diameter. Wind the excess wire around the stem. Press the top of the circle in to create a heart shape. Trim excess wire. Make hearts in blue and yellow wire as well. Use super glue to attach the hearts on the cream card.

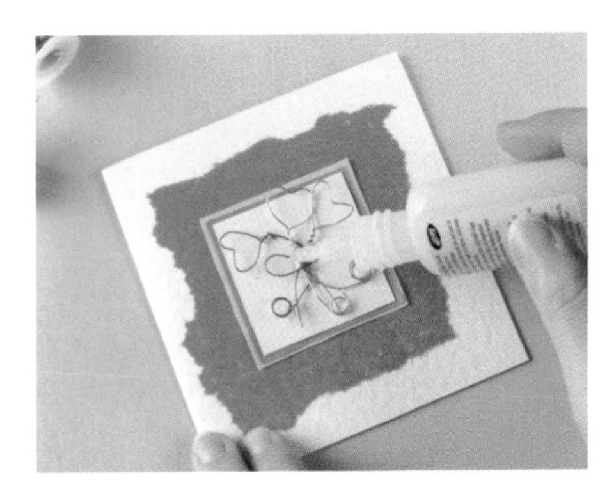

5 Cut a 6cm (2½in) length of pink wire. Make two loops then twist into a bow shape. Trim and fix in position with super glue.

6 Use 3D gold paint to outline and decorate the pink tissue paper. You could put a pink tissue paper or wire heart on the back of the card for an extra touch.

sparkling hearts

This is a romantic card perfect for sending Christmas wishes to a loved one. These glittery hearts would look good on gift-wrap and tags too.

you will need

- Sheet cream handmade textured paper
- Craft knife
- Metal ruler
- Cutting mat
- Pencil
- Stylus
- Sheet red handmade paper
- Double-sided tape
- Scissors
- Sheet white textured card
- Sheet white line-embossed paper
- Gold glitter glue
- Acetate
- Glue stick
- Sheet pink glitter paper

timing Set aside half an hour to make this card.

alternative A single heart would look good layered on a selection of handmade papers and set in the centre of a square card base.

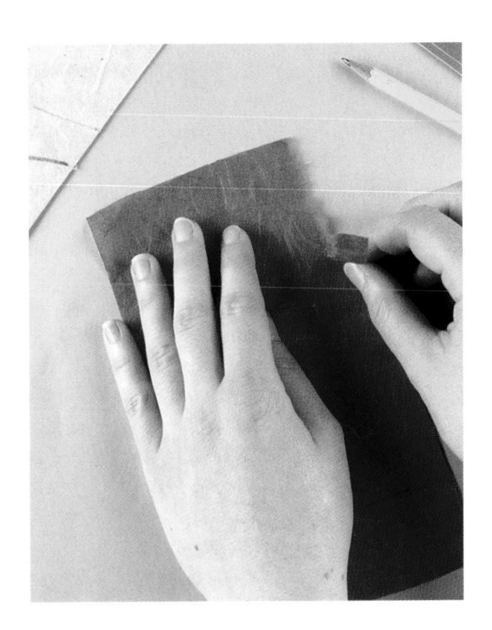

1 Cut a 17 x 18cm (6¾ x 7in) shape from the cream paper. Score and fold in half to make the card base. Tear a rectangle 16.5 x 7cm (6½ x 2¾in) from the red paper. Use double-sided tape to attach it in a central position to the card front.

2 Cut a 15 x 6cm (6 x 2½in) rectangle from the white textured card. Attach it in a central position on the red paper with double-sided tape.

3 Tear out three 4.5 x 5cm (1¾ x 2in) pieces of white line-embossed paper. Edge the torn pieces with gold glitter glue and set aside to dry.

4 Trace the template on page 232. Use it to cut three heart shapes from the red paper. Use a glue stick to attach them to the pink glitter paper. Cut around each heart shape leaving a narrow border of pink glitter paper.

5 Glue the hearts on to the gold-edged torn white paper pieces to create the motifs. Using double-sided tape, attach the central motif to the card, then position the other two.

roses are red

A sheet of angel hair paper and a bunch of red paper rosebuds were used to create this beautiful card. To make a wonderful birthday card use pink roses and pink paper instead.

you will need

- A5 sheet pink card
- Metal ruler
- Stylus
- Sheet white translucent paper
- Sheet angel hair paper
- Craft knife
- Cutting mat
- Double-sided tape
- Scissors
- Sheet red handmade paper
- Small piece green card
- Small piece white card
- 2 paper rosebuds
- Gold yarn
- PVA glue
- 2 red heart sequins

timing Once the shapes are cut out this card takes no time at all to make.

alternative To make a simple but unique card, attach a small bunch of silk lily of the valley to a sage green card base.

1 Score and fold the sheet of pink card to create the card base. Measure and cut out rectangles of white translucent and angel hair paper, 10.5 x 5.5cm (4¼ x 2¼in). Use double-sided tape to attach the white translucent paper in a central position on the card base. Stick the angel hair paper on top.

2 Tear an 8 x 4.5cm (3¼ x 1¾in) rectangle from the red handmade paper. Cut a 7 x 3.5cm (2¾ x 1½in) rectangle from the green card and a 6.5 x 3cm (2½ x 1¼in) rectangle from the white card. Using double-sided tape, layer the red paper, the green card and finally the white card on to the angel hair paper.

3 Tie the two rosebud stems together with a 10cm (4in) length of gold yarn. Use PVA glue to attach firmly in place on the card.

4 Trim the ends of the yarn to about 2cm (¾in) in length. Use double-sided tape to attach the red heart sequins to the ends of the yarn.

coordinating items
Gift-tags decorated with paper flowers look lovely attached to a birthday posy. Get hold of a bunch of paper flowers and experiment with backgrounds and layers.

wedding cake

A confection in candy pink, crisp white and subtle silver with which to send wedding or anniversary greetings. Use the cake motif to decorate boxes and pouches. These could be used for wedding favours.

you will need

- Sheet A4 white textured card
- Craft knife
- Metal ruler
- Cutting mat
- Stylus
- A5 sheet pink card
- Double-sided tape
- Scissors
- Sheet of plasma
- Silver and white 3D paint
- Acetate
- Marker pen
- Pink gel pen
- Silver pen
- Silver card
- Silver wire
- Pencil
- Silver heart sequin
- PVA glue
- Hole punch
- Thin white ribbon

timing The sophisticated simplicity of this card takes a little while to achieve.

alternative Make this card up in lemon yellow and replace the cake with a silver stork peel-off to make a delightful newborn baby card.

1 Cut out a 16 x 15cm (6½ x 6in) piece of white textured card. Score and fold in half to create the card base. Measure and cut out a 14 x 6cm (5½ x 2½in) rectangle from the pink card. Use double-sided tape to attach it in a central position on the card base.

2 Cut a rectangle of plasma measuring 5.5 x 12.5cm (2¼ x 5in). Use double-sided tape to attach it in a central position. Ensure that the tape is centrally placed on the plasma so it remains invisible on the finished card. Place a silver 3D paint spot in each corner of the plasma.

3 Trace the templates on page 232 on to acetate. Cut out of white textured card. Draw a pink scallop pattern along the upper edges of the cake layers. Use silver pen to colour in the cake boards along the lower edges of the cake layers.

4 Cut four narrow ribbons of silver card, 1cm (½in) in length. These will make the cake stands. Cut two lengths of silver wire 8cm (3¼in) long. Make a curl in the end of each length of wire by wrapping them around a pencil.

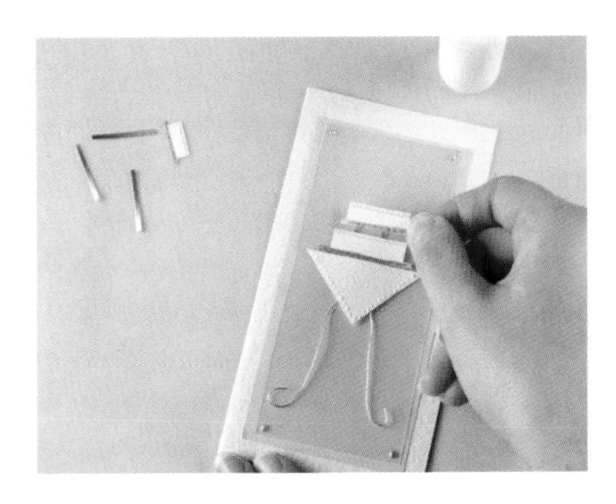

5 Use double-sided tape to assemble the card. Begin by laying the wire table legs in place. Attach the remaining pieces from the bottom up. Glue the heart sequin in place and decorate the tablecloth with a border of white 3D dots.

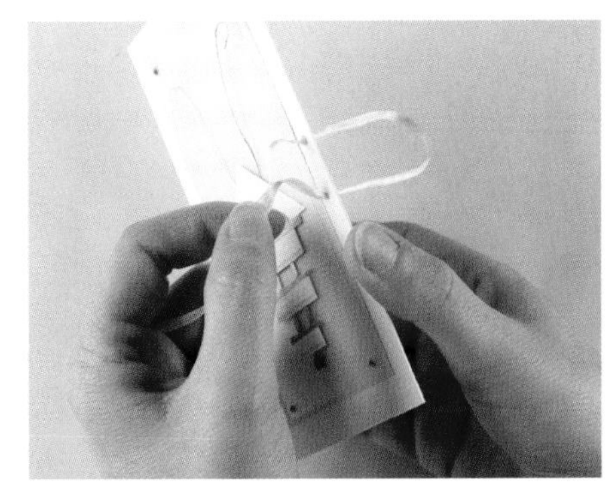

6 Use a hole punch to make two holes on the left side of the card. Thread white ribbon through the holes and tie a bow.

turtle-doves

Pretty cake ribbon is used to decorate this wedding card. Visit your local cake decorating store; you'll find plenty to inspire your greetings card creativity.

you will need

- A4 sheet white card
- Stylus
- Metal ruler
- Craft knife
- Cutting mat
- Aerosol glue
- White heart-decorated mulberry paper
- A5 sheet gold card
- Double-sided tape
- Scissors
- Decorative ribbon 5 cm (2in) wide

timing This card is easy to make and can be quickly mass-produced, making it an ideal wedding invitation.

alternative Make up this card in bright colours and use a length of nursery ribbon for an unusual birthday greeting.

variation *The mulberry paper used for this card makes a great base for a variety of cards and tags. The double hearts were purchased from a cake decorating shop.*

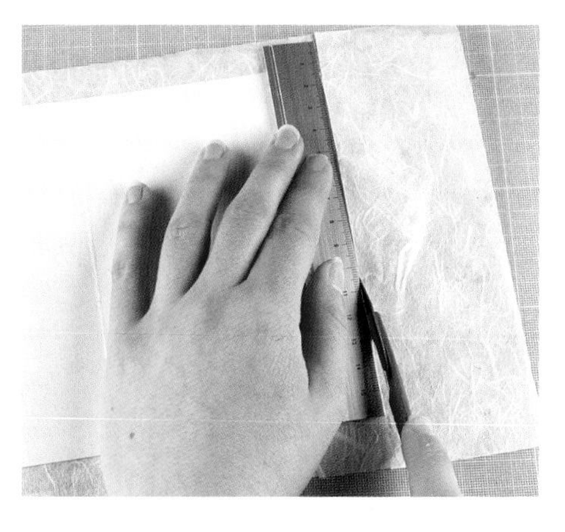

1 Cut the sheet of white card in half. Score and fold one half to create the base. Spray aerosol glue on the outside of the card base. Lay this on top of the mulberry paper. Smooth the paper over the card and use a craft knife to cut away the excess from around the card blank.

2 Cut a piece of gold card, 10 x 6cm (4 x 2½in) and a piece of white card, 9.5 x 5.5cm (3¾ x 2¼in). Use double-sided tape to layer them centrally on the card base.

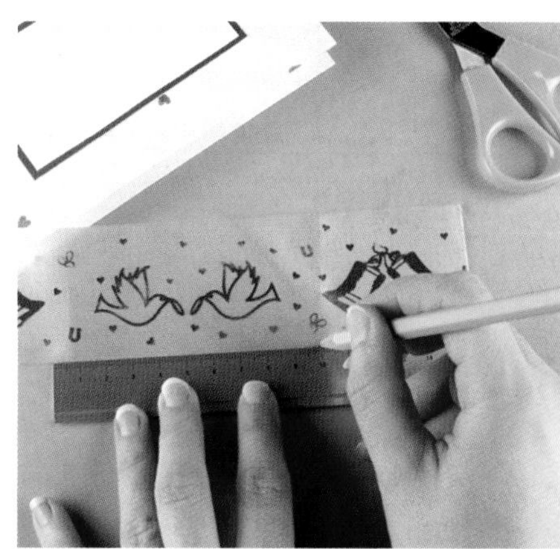

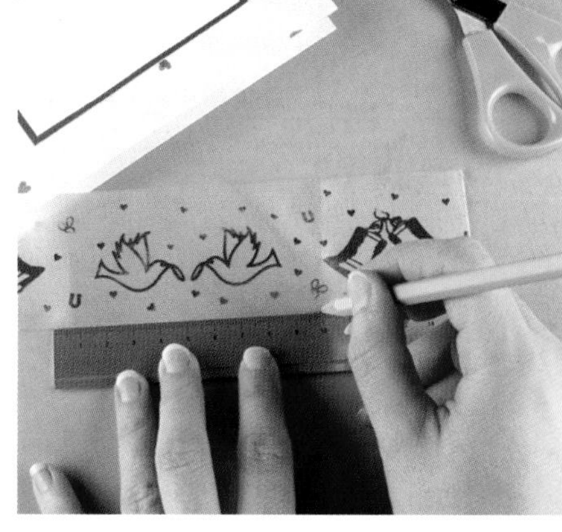

3 Measure and cut a 9cm (3½in) length of ribbon. Be sure to cut it so that the image is in the centre of the piece of ribbon.

4 Use aerosol glue to attach the ribbon centrally on the white card creating a framed picture.

tiny togs

I love this card. To me it is everything a new arrival card should be – simple, pretty and unbelievably cute.

you will need

- Small piece white textured card
- Deckle-edge scissors
- Pencil
- Metal ruler
- Blue and yellow 3D paint
- Suitable cut-out of baby outfit
- Acetate
- Marker pen
- Blue foam sheet scrap
- Scissors
- Small length of gold craft wire
- Double-sided tape
- 3D tape
- A5 sheet baby blue card
- A5 sheet white card
- A5 sheet blue gingham paper
- A5 sheet yellow card
- Large and small flower punches
- PVA glue

timing Set aside a quiet hour to make this special greetings card.

alternative Three-dimensional cards are very effective. Cut-outs that represent a hobby or interest would look good when used in this way.

1 Use the deckle-edge scissors to cut a 5 x 7.5cm (2 x 3in) rectangle from the sheet of white textured card. Edge with a line of blue 3D paint. Leave to dry.

2 Cut out a baby outfit and back it if necessary. Trace the coathanger template on page 232. Construct using the foam sheet and wire. Use double-sided tape to attach it to the sheet of blue deckle-edged card. Use 3D tape to attach the baby outfit giving the impression it is hanging up.

3 Score and fold the sheet of baby blue card to create the card base. Cut a 12.5 x 8cm (5 x 3¼in) rectangle of white card and a 12 x 7.5cm (4¾ x 3in) rectangle of gingham paper. Attach the white card using double-sided tape and the gingham paper using aerosol glue, in a central position on the base.

coordinating items *This design works well in pink as well as blue. You can make an array of items to match the card including gift-bags, tags and lined envelopes (see page 18).*

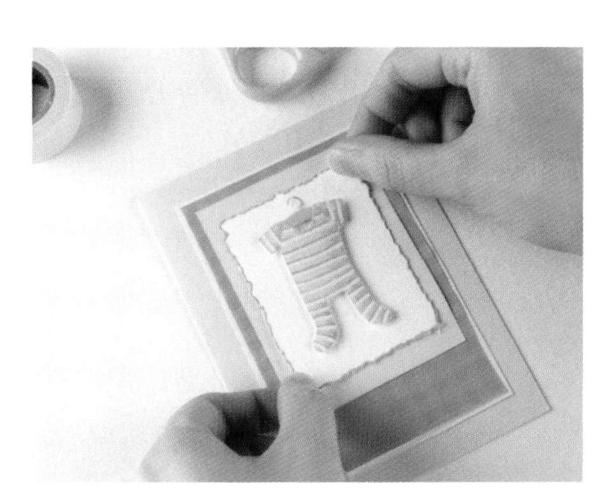

4 Cut out a 9 x 6.5cm (3½ x 2½in) rectangle of yellow card. Use double-sided tape to attach it in an upper central position on the gingham paper and finally stick the baby outfit motif on top of that.

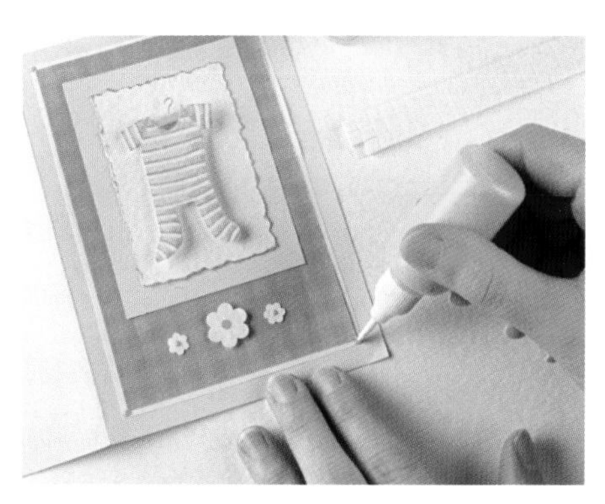

5 Punch out one large and two small flowers from the white card. Use 3D tape to stick the large flower underneath the motif. Glue the two small flowers either side of it. Paint yellow 3D centres in each flower and in the corners of the framed picture.

rocking horse

This framed rocking horse makes a lovely card. It would be wonderful to use for baby announcement cards or thank-you notes for new baby gifts.

you will need

- A5 sheet white textured card
- Metal ruler
- Stylus
- Sheet pink card
- Craft knife
- Cutting mat
- Double-sided tape
- Sheet white card
- Sheet silver card
- Peel-off sticker
- Embossing board and heart template
- Pink 3D paint

timing Peel-offs are very quick and easy to use so this is a good card to mass-produce.

alternative A photograph of a baby set on a blue or pink background would make a cute card.

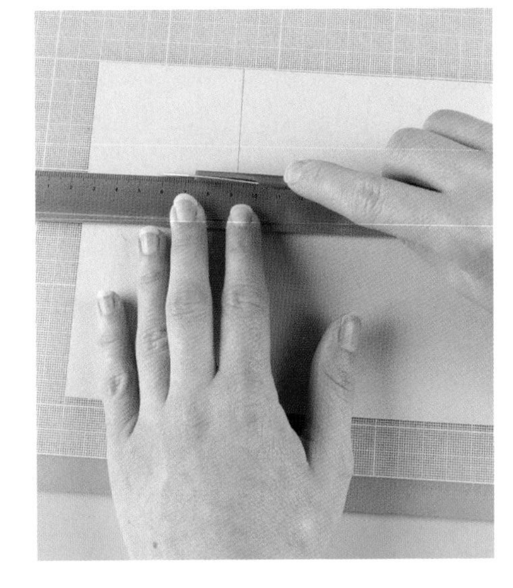

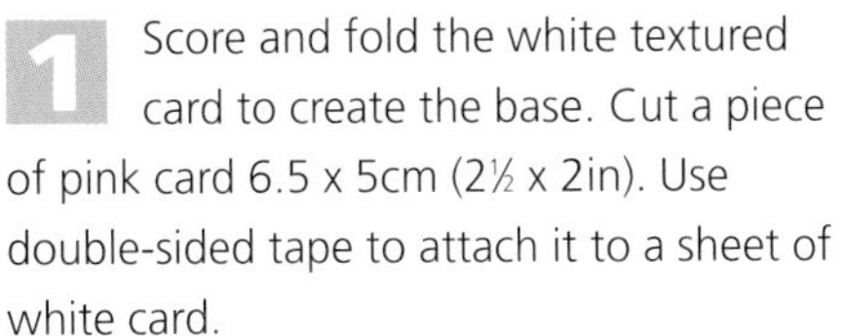

1 Score and fold the white textured card to create the base. Cut a piece of pink card 6.5 x 5cm (2½ x 2in). Use double-sided tape to attach it to a sheet of white card.

2 Cut away all but a narrow frame around the pink card. Use double-sided tape to attach it to silver card. Once again cut away all but a narrow border.

3 Stick the peel-off centrally on the frame. Use double-sided tape to attach the framed image in an upper central position on the card front.

4 Using the embossing board and template, emboss a small heart shape in a central position below the framed picture.

5 Use pink 3D paint to mark a dot in each corner, slightly outside the frame, to complete the card.

teddy bear

New-arrival cards are always a pleasure to make and this card is particularly special with the ribbon and rivet design. Ring the changes with a pink, lemon yellow or green background and use other peel-offs to decorate bags, tags and boxes.

you will need

- A4 sheet white textured card
- Craft knife
- Metal ruler
- Cutting mat
- Stylus
- Pencil
- Wooden board
- Rivet setting tools
- Hammer
- 6 silver rivets
- Small piece pale blue card
- Double-sided tape
- Scissors
- Small piece silver card
- Silver teddy bear peel-off
- Silver heart sequin
- PVA glue
- Thin pale blue ribbon

timing You need to spend a little time on this card as it is important to get the rivets positioned evenly and neatly.

alternative Turn this card into a wedding invitation – use a suitable peel-off to replace the teddy and insert printed invitation details.

1 Cut the sheet of white card in half. Score and fold one half to make the card base. Measure in 1cm (½in) from the folded edge of the card. Working down the card, mark light pencil dots at 1.5cm (½in), 4cm (1½in), 6.5cm (2½in), 8.5cm (3¼in), 11cm (4¼in) and 13.5cm (5¼in).

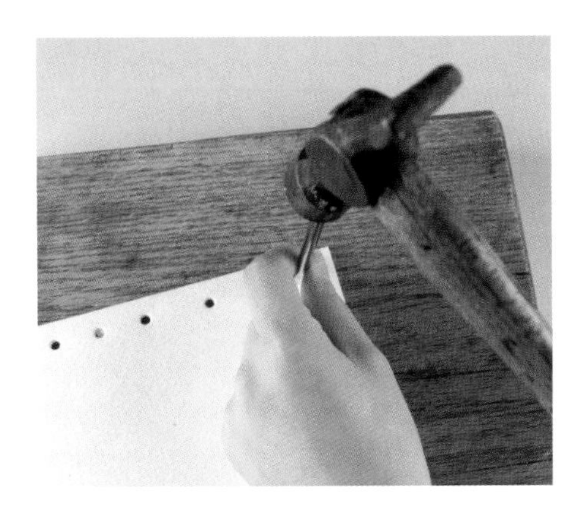

2 Place the card on a wooden board. Use the rivet hole maker and a hammer to make holes at the marked spots.

3 Press the rivets through the holes. Use a hammer and the rivet placement tool to secure the rivet.

4 Cut out a 4 x 3.5cm (1½ x 1¼in) rectangle from pale blue card. Use double-sided tape to attach this to a piece of textured white card. Cut away all but a narrow frame. Tape this on to silver card and cut away all but a narrow frame.

5 Attach the layers in an upper central position on the card front. Place the teddy bear peel-off sticker in a central position on the blue card. Glue a small silver heart 1cm (½in) beneath the framed picture.

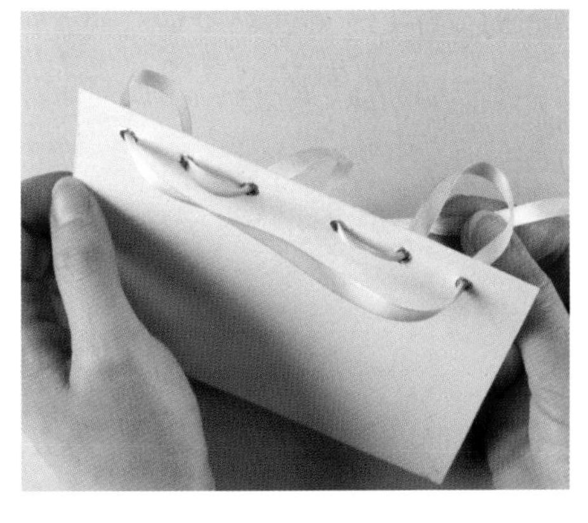

6 Thread the blue ribbon through the rivets and tie a bow.

witches abroad

I have used a selection of Hallowe'en-themed collage stickers on this card. If you cannot find suitable stickers or want to be even more creative, try creating your own collages using stickers and coloured paper.

you will need

- A5 sheet black card
- Craft knife
- Metal ruler
- Cutting mat
- Stylus
- Black glitter card
- Double-sided tape
- Scissors
- Lime green card
- Yellow card
- Hallowe'en collage stickers
- Gold 3D paint
- Star stickers

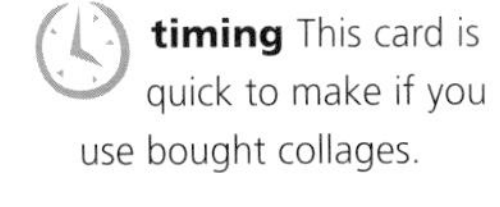

timing This card is quick to make if you use bought collages.

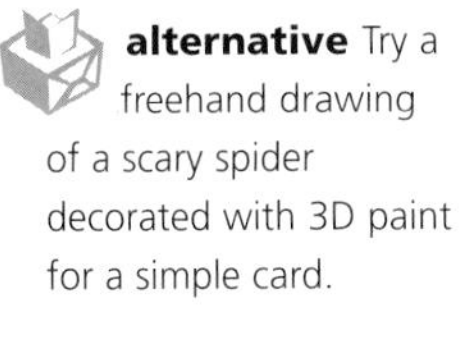

alternative Try a freehand drawing of a scary spider decorated with 3D paint for a simple card.

1 Cut a 15 x 11cm (6 x 4½in) rectangle from the black card. Score and fold to create the card base. Prepare the motifs. Cut a 2.5cm (1in) square from the black glitter card. Use double-sided tape to attach the square to lime green card. Cut away all but a narrow border. Then stick this to yellow card and again, cut away all but a narrow border. Repeat this process to make a second motif.

2 Use double-sided tape to stick the collage stickers in position on the motifs. Place the central sticker on the card first and then the two motifs.

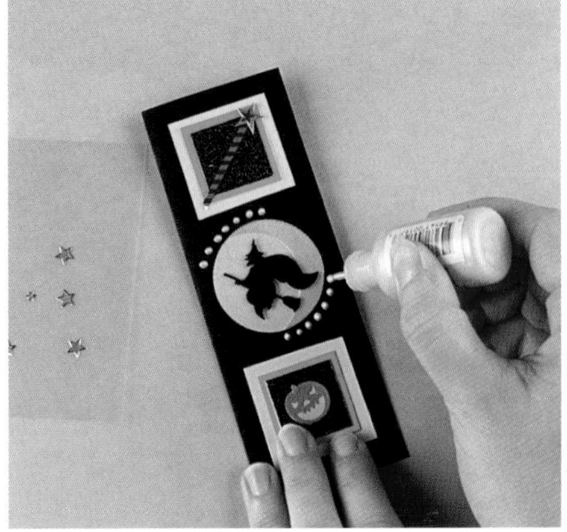

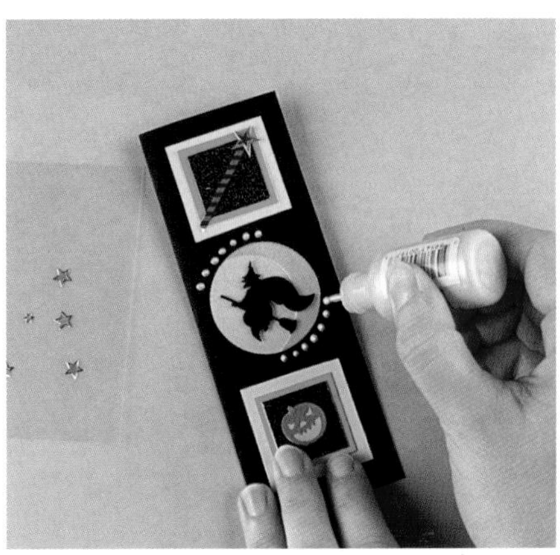

3 Use gold 3D paint to print dots around the central sticker – seven on the upper left and ten on the lower right.

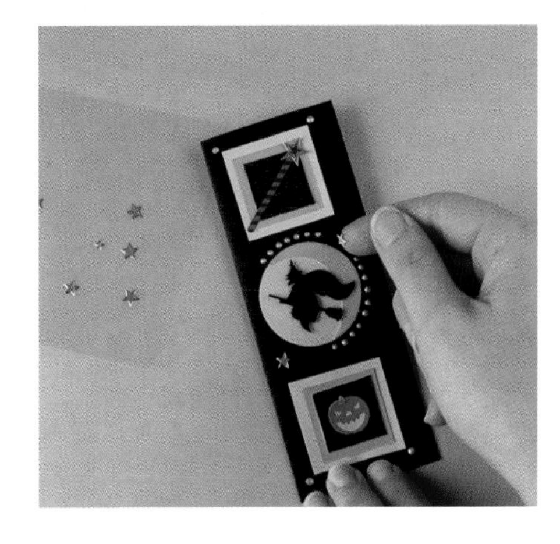

4 Print gold dots on the upper corners of the top motif and the lower corners of the bottom motif. Lay two stars decoratively on the upper right and lower left of the central sticker.

coordinating items

Decorate goodie bags with motifs and stars. Wrap gifts in corrugated card and make tags using single motifs.

happy hallowe'en

Celebrate Hallowe'en with this collage card. The card is made up of many elements – freehand drawing, rubber stamping and paper cut-outs. You can create many designs using a collage of different materials. Try using stickers as well.

you will need

- A4 sheet black card
- Craft knife
- Metal ruler
- Cutting mat
- Stylus
- Pencil
- Double-sided tape
- Scissors
- Sheet black glitter card
- Green, pink, white and blue gel pens
- Acetate
- Sheet white card
- PVA glue
- 2 tiny boggle eyes
- Sheet orange card
- Black fine liner pen
- Frog rubber stamp
- Green stamp pad

timing Take some time to practise your freehand drawing before you start making the card.

alternative Personalize a card with a photo of someone in fancy dress.

1 Cut the A4 sheet of black card in half. Score and fold one half to create the card base. Cut a rectangle of black card 7 x 10cm (2¾ x 4in). Use double-sided tape to attach it to a sheet of glitter card. Cut away all but a narrow border. Use double-sided tape to attach it centrally on the card base.

2 Draw a white gel pen spider web in the top right-hand corner of the card. Draw a spider in the centre of the web.

3 Trace the ghostly shape on page 232 and cut it out of white card. Use PVA glue to attach two boggle eyes. Tape the ghost in the top left-hand corner of the card.

4 Trace the pumpkin templates on page 232 and cut out in orange card. Draw lines on using a black fine liner pen to give them more shape.

5 Stamp a green frog on to the bottom right-hand corner of the card and use a blue gel pen to draw three ripples around it.

magic number

Number cut-outs make great card decorations. This card will work with any number and there are templates for numbers 0–9 on pages 234–5. If the number you want to use is in double figures, simply reduce the size of the numbers and overlap them slightly on the card.

you will need

- A5 sheet spring green card
- Metal ruler
- Stylus
- Yellow card
- Cutting mat
- Craft knife
- Pencil
- Double-sided tape
- Scissors
- Red card
- Blue corrugated card
- Yellow and blue 3D paint
- Tracing paper/ acetate
- Spotty wrapping paper
- White paper
- 3D tape
- Spring green paper

timing Take your time cutting out the number as the other elements of this card are quick and easy to put together.

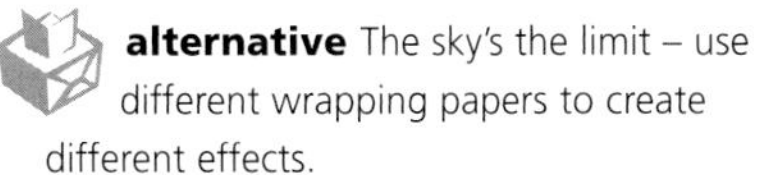

alternative The sky's the limit – use different wrapping papers to create different effects.

1 Score and fold the green card to create the card blank. Cut out a 10 x 8cm (4 x 3in) rectangle from the yellow card. Attach it to the card blank in an upper central position using double-sided tape.

2 Cut out a 9.5 x 7.5cm (3¾ x 3in) rectangle from the red card. Tape it on top of the yellow card. Cut out an 8.5 x 6.5cm (3½ x 2½in) rectangle of blue corrugated card. Attach this to the red card.

3 Use yellow and blue 3D paint to mark a dotty border on the red frame. Trace the number template on page 234 or 235. Cut the figure out of the wrapping paper. (If you are using translucent gift-wrap back it with a sheet of white copy paper before cutting out.)

4 Use 3D tape to attach the number to a sheet of green paper. Cut around the number to create a narrow border. Use double-sided tape to attach the number centrally on the card.

coordinating items
Number motifs brighten up plain white or brown bags wonderfully. I created the handle of the smaller bag using an oval cutter, template and board.

time to celebrate

projects

chick chick chicken

This card is decorated with an interesting button. For spring greetings mint green and yellow are a lovely colour combination. Look around for other motifs or buttons that would look good with these colours.

you will need

- A5 sheet pale green card
- Metal ruler
- Stylus
- Sheet white corrugated card
- Craft knife
- Cutting mat
- Chicken button
- 3D tape
- Sheet dotty paper
- Double-sided tape
- Scissors
- Sheet yellow translucent paper
- Sheet green translucent paper
- Daisy punch
- PVA glue
- Yellow 3D paint

timing Set aside an afternoon to make Easter cards for your friends.

alternative Look out for interesting buttons and coordinate them with suitable bases.

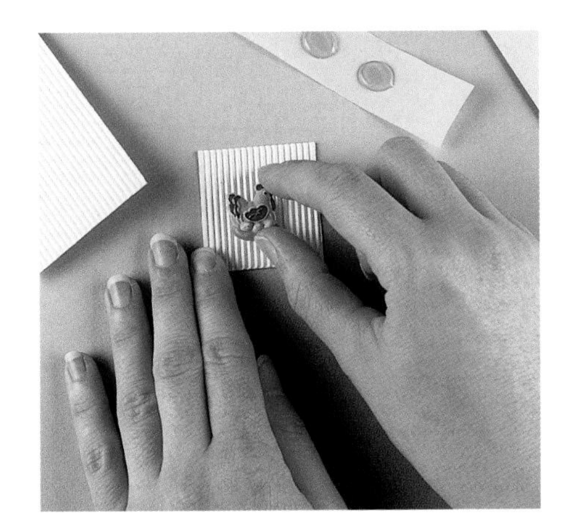

1 Score and fold the pale green card to create the card base. Cut a 4.5cm (1¾in) square of white corrugated card. Use 3D tape to attach the button in a central position on the square.

2 Cut a 6.5cm (2½in) square from dotty paper. Use double-sided tape to attach the motif in a central position on the dotty paper.

3 Use double-sided tape to attach the framed motif to a sheet of yellow translucent paper. Cut away all but a narrow frame. Tape this to a sheet of 8cm (3¼in) square of green translucent paper.

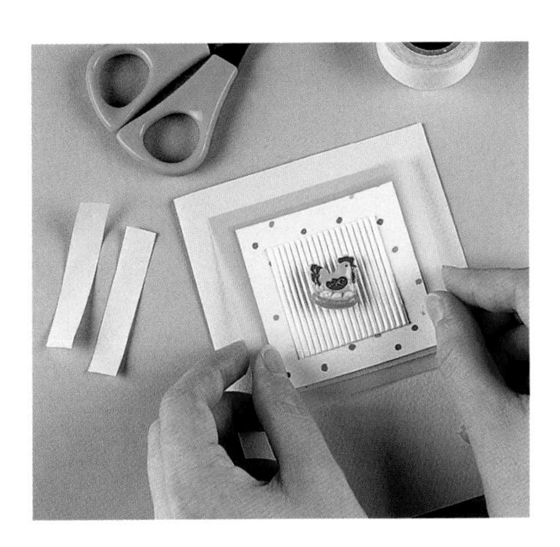

4 Attach the layered picture in an upper central position on the green card base.

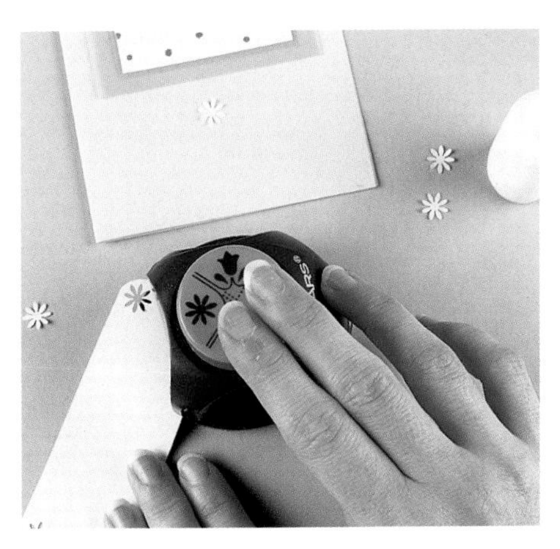

5 Punch out three white daisies and use PVA glue to attach them in a row beneath the picture.

6 Put dots of 3D paint in the corners of the framed picture and in the centre of each daisy.

easter bunnies

Use paper table napkins and wooden cut-outs to make this greetings card. If you cannot find wooden motifs use stickers or make your own paper cut-outs to achieve a similar effect.

you will need

- A4 sheet yellow card
- Metal ruler
- Pencil
- Craft knife
- Cutting mat
- Stylus
- A5 sheet green card
- Double-sided tape
- Scissors
- A5 sheet orange card
- Sheet yellow translucent paper
- A5 sheet white card
- 3 wooden rabbit cut-outs
- Easter paper napkin
- White paper
- Aerosol glue
- Green 3D paint

timing Preparing the elements of this card takes a little time.

alternative Make a card with a nautical theme – use sailboat motifs.

1 Cut a 19.5 x 16cm (7¾ x 6in) rectangle from yellow card. Score and fold it in half so that the card base is landscape. Cut a 19 x 7cm (7½ x 2¾in) rectangle of green card and use double-sided tape to attach it to the card base. Cut a 18.5 x 6.5cm (7¼ x 2½in) rectangle of orange card. Use double-sided tape to attach it centrally on the green card.

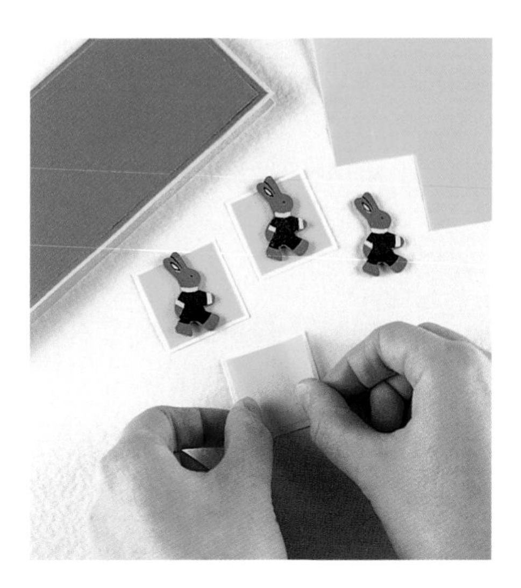

2 Measure and cut out three 3.5cm (1¼in) squares of yellow translucent paper and three 3.75cm (1½in) squares of white card. Use double-sided tape to attach the yellow squares to the white squares. Tape the rabbit motifs centrally on each yellow square.

3 Separate the decorated layer of the napkin from the other layers. Spray a sheet of white paper with aerosol glue and smooth the napkin on to it. Cut out four eggs.

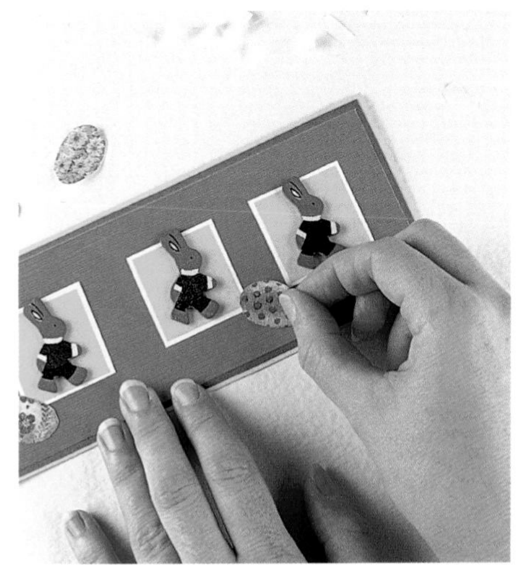

4 Use double-sided tape to attach the three motifs (position the central one first) and the eggs.

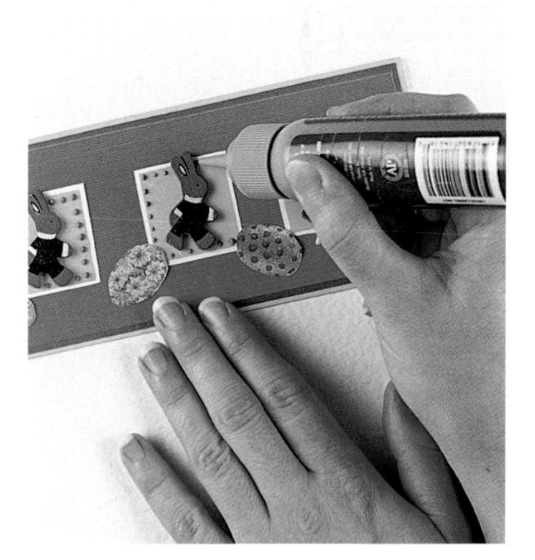

5 Paint a border of tiny dots around the yellow translucent paper squares.

nest egg

Three pretty Easter eggs in a delicate, gold wire nest adorn this card. I have used embossed stamped images to make the Easter eggs. If you don't have a stamp, cut out small ovals and decorate them with felt-tip pens or coloured foil. Use the decorated eggs to make alternative cards and gift-tags.

you will need

- A5 sheet blue card
- Craft knife
- Cutting mat
- Pencil
- Metal ruler
- Stylus
- A5 sheet textured white card
- Corner punch
- Blue and white polka dot paper
- Double-sided tape
- Scissors
- Gold card
- Decorative gold wire
- Super glue
- Embossing pad
- Small Easter egg rubber stamp
- Scrap of white card
- Scrap paper
- Gold embossing powder
- Tweezers or tongs
- Precision heat tool
- Felt-tip pens
- 3D tape

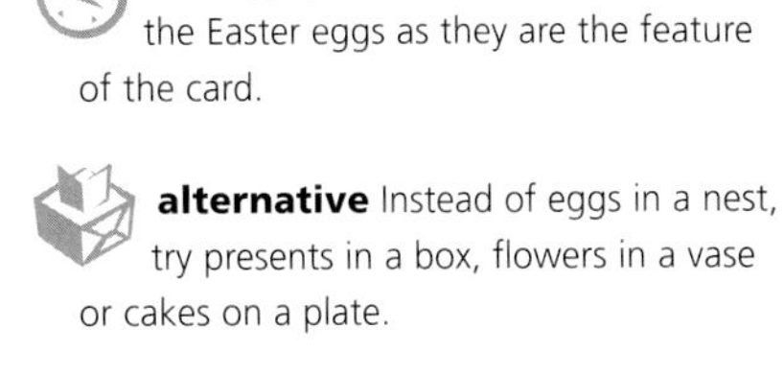

timing Spend a little time preparing the Easter eggs as they are the feature of the card.

alternative Instead of eggs in a nest, try presents in a box, flowers in a vase or cakes on a plate.

1 Cut a 16 x 13.5cm (6¼ x 5¼in) rectangle from the blue card. Score and fold to create the card base. Cut a 7 x 12.5cm (2¾ x 5in) rectangle from the white textured card. Use the corner punch to cut decorative corners.

2 Cut out a 7.5 x 2.5cm (3 x 1in) rectangle from the polka dot paper. Use double-sided tape to attach it to gold card. Cut away all but a narrow border. Use double-sided tape to attach the gold-framed polka dot paper in a central position on the white textured card and then tape the layers on to the card base.

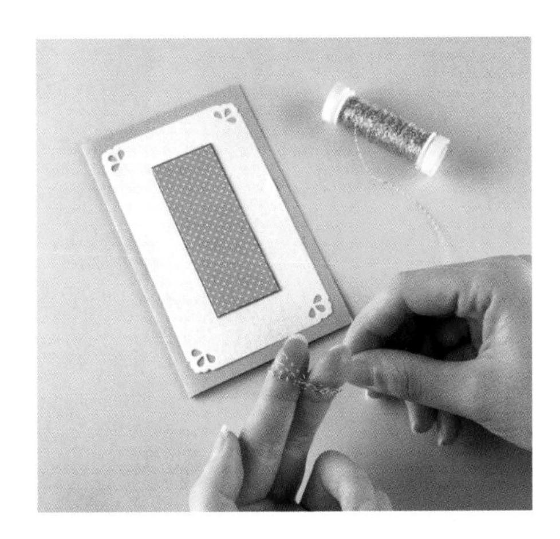

3 Make the nest by wrapping decorative gold wire around two fingers. Wrap the wire around about 10 times. Remove the wire from your fingers, then cut and wrap the ends around the wire oval. Shape into a flattened nest. Glue in place with super glue.

4 Use the embossing pad and stamp to print three eggs on to a scrap of white card. Fold a sheet of scrap paper in half and open it out. Put the stamped white card on to the scrap paper and sprinkle it with gold embossing powder. Shake the excess powder on to the scrap paper and return it to the container. Holding the card with tweezers or tongs, seal the designs with the precision heat tool (see page 14).

5 Use felt-tip pens to decorate the embossed eggs and cut them out. Place 3D tape on to the backs of the eggs and press in place in the nest.

easter eggs

Delicate spring flowers and pretty ribbon are the main features of this lovely Easter card. You might want to use a different colour scheme, maybe pink and green or powder blue and white with lemon yellow features.

you will need

- A5 sheet lilac card
- Stylus
- Metal ruler
- Oval cutter, template and board
- A5 sheet yellow and lilac spotted paper
- A4 sheet white paper
- Double-sided tape
- 7cm (2¾in) length of 1.75cm (¾in) wide pale blue organza ribbon
- 8.5cm (3¼in) of 1cm (⅓in) wide pink organza ribbon
- Aerosol glue
- Lilac blue blossom decorated paper
- Craft knife
- Cutting mat
- 3D tape
- Flower punch
- Scrap of lilac paper
- PVA glue
- Scrap of yellow paper
- Yellow and blue 3D paints

timing This card is very simple to make, but it does take a little time to assemble all the layers.

alternative Instead of an egg, wrap a Christmas present with ribbon and decorate with gold stars. Use festive wrapping paper for the layers.

1 Score and fold the lilac card to create the base. To make the egg, use the oval cutter, template and board to cut 7.5 x 5.5cm (3 x 2¼in) ovals from the spotted and the white paper. If you do not have an oval cutter use the template on page 229.

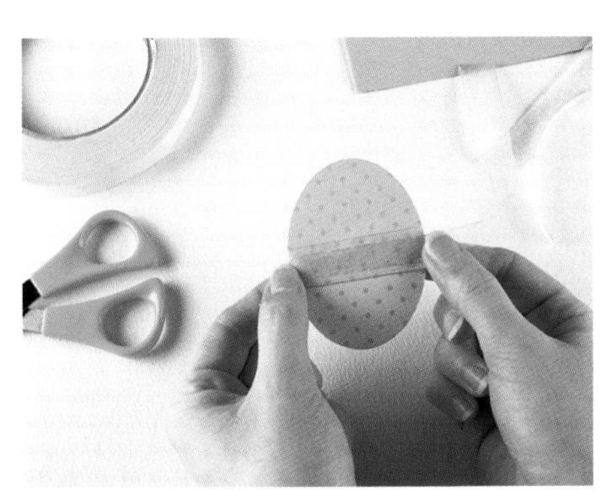

2 Attach a length of double-sided tape across the centre of the back of the spotted egg. Place the blue ribbon across the front of the egg, fold the edges around and attach them to the double-sided tape on the reverse. Attach the pink ribbon over the blue.

3 Spray aerosol glue on to one side of the white oval, attach this to the reverse of the spotted egg; this will help hold the ribbon in position and give the egg some substance. Set aside.

4 Cut a 7.5 x 9.5cm (3 x 3¾in) rectangle from the blossom paper. Use double-sided tape to attach it to spotted paper; cut away all but a narrow border. Layer this on to white paper and, once again, cut away all but a narrow border.

5 Use double-sided tape to attach this in an upper central position on the card base. Use 3D tape to attach the egg in a central position on the layers.

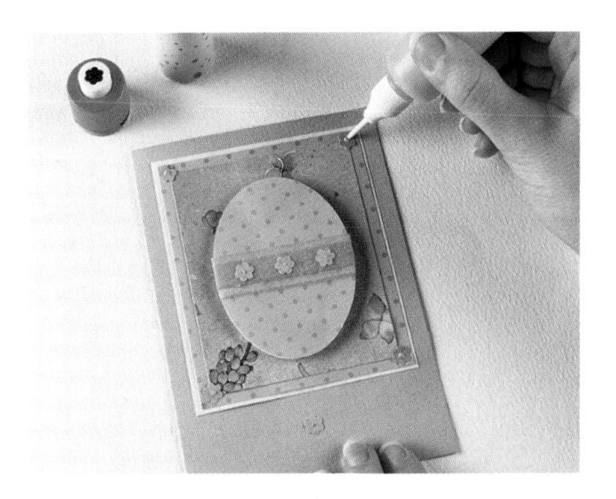

6 Punch out seven small flowers from lilac paper. Use PVA glue to attach three flowers across the centre of the pink ribbon and one in each corner of the frame. Punch out a yellow flower and glue beneath the layers. Squeeze a dot of yellow 3D paint on to each lilac flower and a blue 3D paint dot on to the yellow flower.

christmas trees

A stylish Christmas card made from simply decorated paper napkins.

you will need

- A5 sheet white card
- Craft knife
- Cutting mat
- Metal ruler
- Pencil
- Stylus
- Decorative paper napkin
- Aerosol glue
- A5 sheet white paper
- Scissors
- Double-sided tape
- Small piece red card
- Small piece green card
- Black fine point pen

timing This card is reasonably quick to make so it would be efficient to mass-produce.

alternative For a less seasonal look try this design using a different multi-image paper napkin, perhaps tiny flowers or balloons?

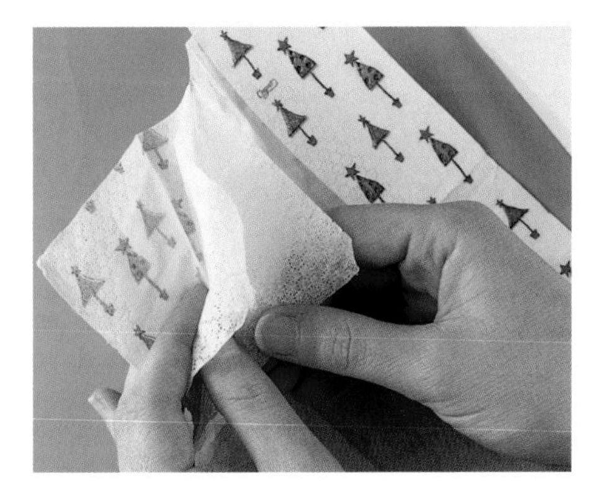

1 Cut a rectangle 20.5 x 11.5cm (8 x 4½in) from the white card. Score and fold to create the card blank. Take the napkin and separate out the patterned layer. Discard the plain layers.

2 Spray the reverse of the patterned layer with aerosol glue. Smooth it over the front of the card base and cut away the excess. Set aside. Stick the excess of the patterned layer on to a sheet of white paper. Smooth to attach firmly.

3 Cut out a single tree to be the focal point of your card. Use double-sided tape to attach the feature to a piece of red card. Cut away all but a narrow frame.

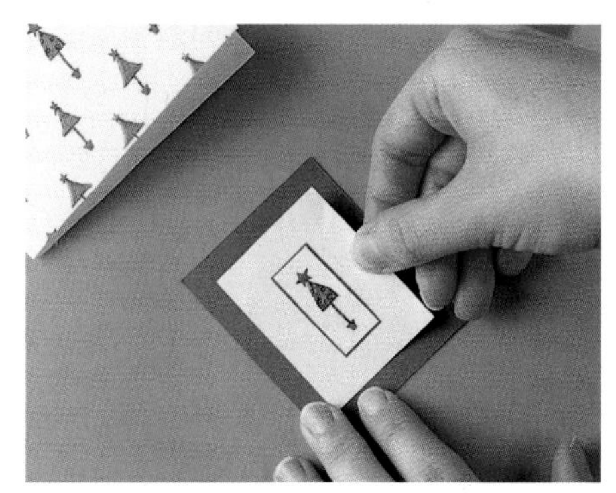

4 Use double-sided tape to attach the framed image to white card. Cut a 4.5 x 6cm (2¼ x 1¾in) rectangle. Cut a 6.3 x 7.3cm (2½ x 2¾in) rectangle of green card and attach the motif to it. Attach this to red card and cut a narrow frame.

coordinating items *Here is a set of seasonal stationery. I've used the central motif on different coloured blanks and layers. You can also use napkins as gift-wrap.*

5 Attach the layered motif to the card base. Draw a black line around the edge of the white card. Add small stars. You might want to attach a small feature to the back of the card to finish it off.

hark the herald angels

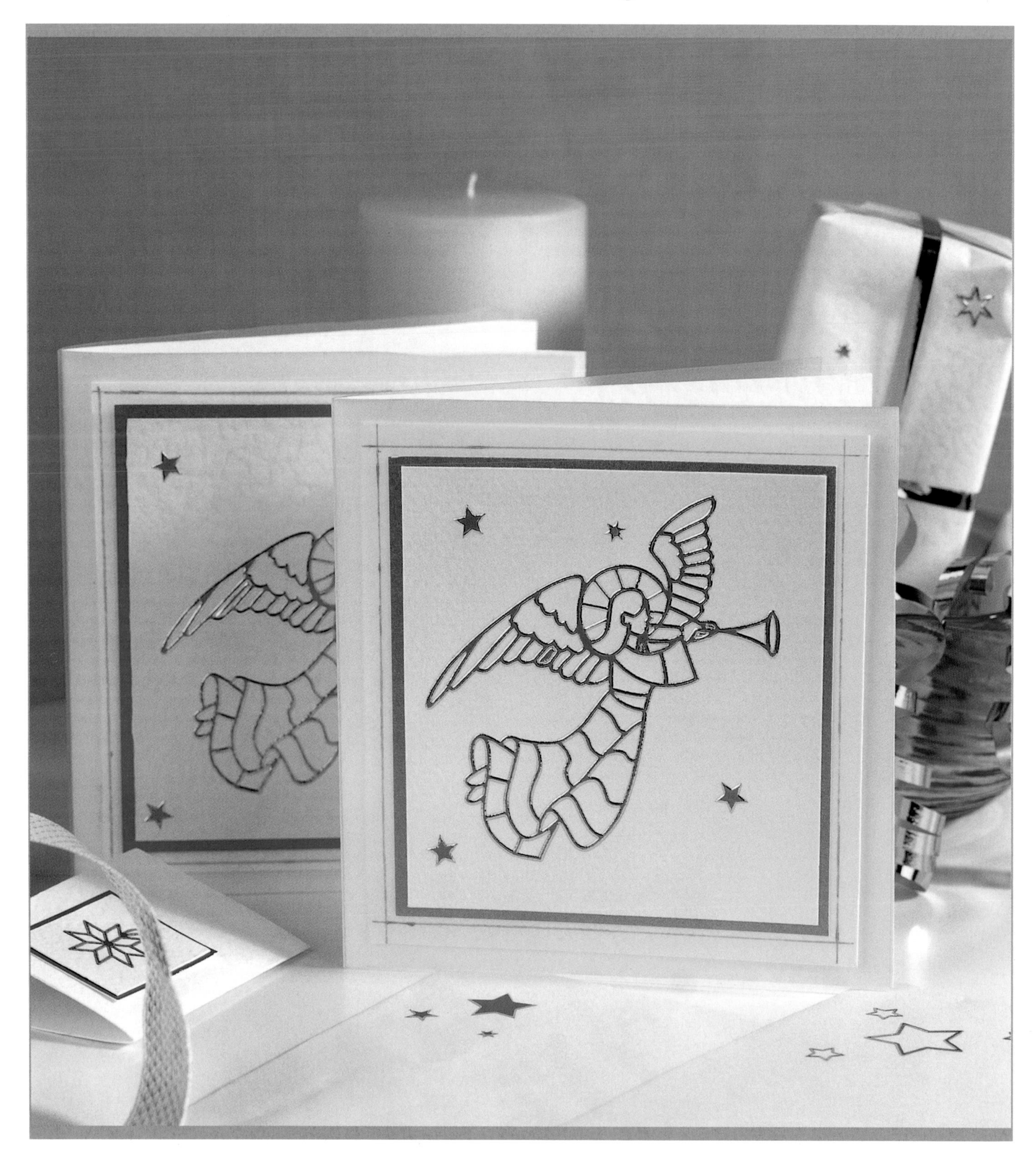

A sophisticated seasonal card using gold peel-off stickers, cream parchment and textured paper.

you will need

- A4 sheet cream textured paper
- Craft knife
- Metal ruler
- Pencil
- Cutting mat
- A4 sheet plasma
- Stylus
- Double-sided tape
- Scissors
- A5 sheet cream parchment paper
- A5 sheet gold card
- A5 sheet cream textured card
- Gold pen
- Angel peel-off sticker
- Gold star stickers

timing This card is quick and easy to mass-produce.

alternative White parchment, vellum and textured card would look good with silver angels and stars.

1 Cut out 24.5 x 13cm (9½ x 5in) rectangles of cream textured paper and plasma. Score and fold the paper and the plasma.

2 Place two strips of double-sided tape centrally on the inside front cover of the plasma. Match the fold of the cream paper to the fold of the plasma and smooth the cream paper on to the front cover of the plasma.

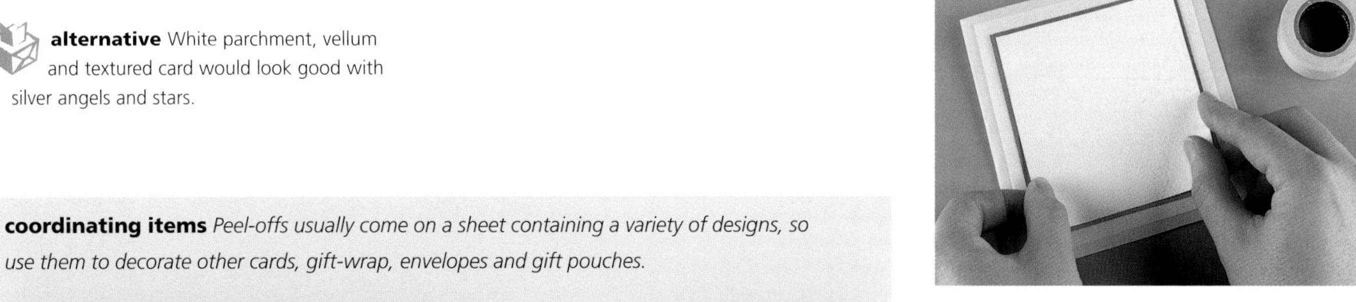

3 Cut out an 11 x 11.5cm (4¼ x 4½in) piece of cream parchment and use double-sided tape to attach it in a central position on the card front. Cut a piece of gold card, 9.5 x 10cm (3¾ x 4in), and tape it on the parchment. Finally, cut a piece of cream textured card, 9 x 9.5cm (3½ x 3¾in). Tape it on to the gold card.

4 Rule a thin, gold line around the edge of the parchment. Select your angel peel-off sticker and place it centrally on the card. Add a few gold stars to finish the design.

coordinating items *Peel-offs usually come on a sheet containing a variety of designs, so use them to decorate other cards, gift-wrap, envelopes and gift pouches.*

holly berries

Green textured handmade paper and a lovely holly sticker inspired this seasonal card.

you will need

- A4 sheet green handmade paper
- Metal ruler
- Cutting mat
- Craft knife
- Pencil
- Stylus
- Small piece gold paper
- Double-sided tape
- Scissors
- Small piece gold paper
- Small piece red card
- Gold card
- Green angel hair paper
- Suitable holly sticker

timing You could make enough of these cards in an afternoon to send to all of your friends and family.

alternative Use this design as a starting point, but vary the colours – creams, golds and earthy colours would look good with a star sticker.

1 Cut a 21 x 12cm (8¼ x 4¾in) square from the handmade paper. Score and fold it to create the card blank.

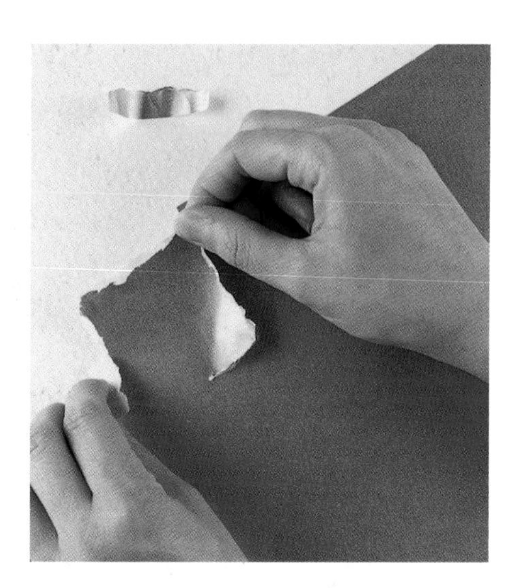

2 Tear out a 7.5cm (3in) square of gold paper. Tape it in a central position on the card so that it is a diamond shape.

3 Cut a 6cm (2½in) square of red card, attach it with double-sided tape centrally on the gold paper. Cut a 5.5cm (2¼in) square of gold card and tape it on top of the red card. Finally, cut a 5cm (2in) square of angel hair paper and place it on top of the gold card.

4 Place the holly sticker in a central position. To give your card a professional finish, place a sticker on the back of the card.

coordinating items *Use similar layered motifs to decorate gift pouches, boxes and tags. Make your own gift-wrap by stamping sprigs of holly on to tissue paper.*

winter wonderland

Stylized Christmas trees adorned with tiny silver jewels decorate this winter scene.

you will need

- A5 sheet silver card
- Craft knife
- Metal ruler
- Cutting mat
- Pencil
- Stylus
- Tracing paper or acetate
- A5 sheet green card
- Double-sided tape
- Scissors
- Tiny silver jewel stickers
- Red sequin stars
- PVA glue

timing Take time and care marking out the fold lines as precision is key when making a fold-out card.

alternative Use this idea to create your own designs; a row of sailing ships or pretty flowers would make effective cards.

1 Cut a 21 x 13cm (8¼ x 5in) rectangle out of the silver card. On the card front make light pencil marks at 3.5cm (1½in), 10.5cm (4¼in) and 17.5cm (6⅞in). Score lines at these points. These lines will form the hill folds.

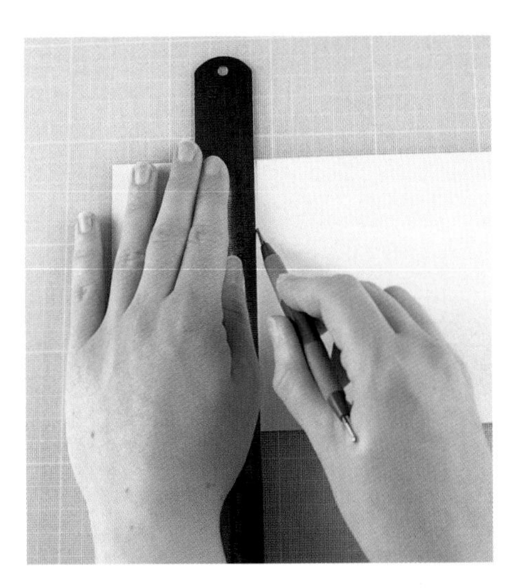

2 Turn the card over and mark points at 7cm (2¾in) and 14cm (5½in). Score lines at these points. These lines will form the valley folds. Fold along all of the lines you have scored to create the card base.

coordinating items *Use the decorated trees to embellish gift-bags and tags. Wrap gifts in plain, coloured gift-wrap and stick on decorated trees.*

3 Trace the tree templates on page 233. Use them to cut three large trees and four small trees out of green card. Referring to the photograph opposite, position the trees firmly in place using double-sided tape. Pay particular attention to how the trees overlap.

4 Decorate the trees with silver jewel stickers and star sequins. These jewels are tiny and extremely fiddly to use, so you may find sliding the jewel off the backing paper works better than lifting it.

star bright

Don't be afraid to use combinations of different materials on your cards. Foil, handmade paper, corrugated card, textured paper and stickers work well together on this sophisticated seasonal card.

you will need

- A5 sheet rich cream textured card
- Stylus
- Metal ruler
- Sheet gold foil
- Scissors
- Embossing board and star template
- Sheet natural handmade paper
- Sheet brown corrugated card
- Craft knife
- Cutting mat
- Double-sided tape
- Aerosol glue
- 3D tape
- Star peel-off stickers

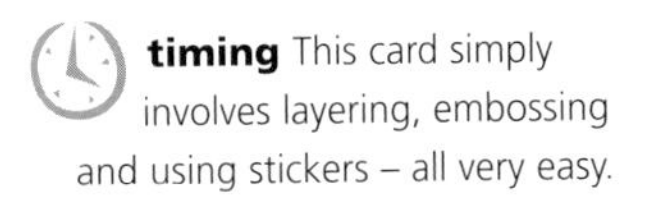

timing This card simply involves layering, embossing and using stickers – all very easy.

alternative For a housewarming card emboss a simple house shape and decorate with tiny flower stickers or stamps.

1 Score and fold in half the sheet of textured card to create the card base. Cut a piece of gold foil 2.5cm (1in) square. Place it under the star template on the embossing board and use the stylus to emboss the shape. Take your time over this and work over the star image thoroughly so that it will have a good shape.

2 Prepare the layers. Cut a 7cm (2¾in) square of gold foil, tear two squares of handmade paper – one 6cm (2½in) and the other 3.5cm (1½in) and cut a 4.5cm (1¾in) square of corrugated card. Put double-sided tape on the undersides of the foil and corrugated card and spray the handmade paper squares with aerosol glue.

coordinating items

Make gift-bags using the same handmade paper you have used for the card and decorate with the star motif. Print plain gift-wrap with a complementary stamped and embossed snowflake design. You can also make alternative cards in other shapes and sizes and decorate them with the same star motif.

3 Place the larger piece of gold foil in a high central position on the card base. Next glue on the largest handmade paper square, followed by the corrugated card and finally the smaller torn paper square. Use 3D tape to attach the embossed star square in a central position. Decorate the card with star peel-off stickers.

christmas robin

This robin redbreast will bring a little seasonal cheer to a Christmas mantelpiece.

you will need

- A5 sheet blue ribbed card
- Craft knife
- Metal ruler
- Cutting mat
- Pencil
- Stylus
- Tracing paper/ acetate
- Blue, white, red, brown and orange foam sheets
- Scissors
- Sheet red card
- Double-sided tape
- Tiny jewel stickers
- Gold star stickers

1 Measure and cut out a 21 x 10.5cm (8¼ x 4in) rectangle of blue ribbed card. Score and fold to create the base.

2 Trace the templates on page 233.

3 Use the templates to cut out the foam shapes for the robin and the background. When cutting the background cut out 8.5cm (3½in) squares from the blue and white foam sheets. Lay one on top of the other and place the background template on top. Cut through all three layers.

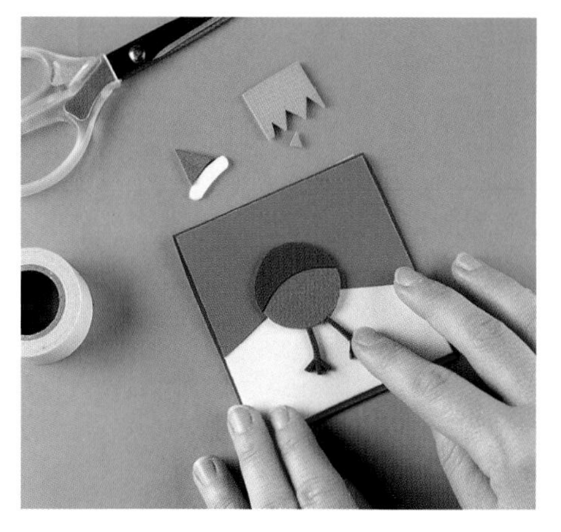

4 Cut a 9cm (3¾in) square of red card. Use double-sided tape to attach the sky and snow background to it. Next attach the body, legs and hat. Cut the beak from a scrap of orange foam and tape in place.

5 Stick on the tiny jewel eyes and place the gold star stickers on the blue sky background.

timing This card takes a little time to make so choose a few special friends to send it to.

alternative Create a country scene with green fields, blue sky and a white sheep. You could add some fluffy clouds too.

coordinating items
Use scraps of foam to create your own designs and use them to decorate cards, tags and boxes.

festive garland

This card is simple and sophisticated. The clean white card sets off the bright green holly garland and is highlighted by the brilliant red berries.

you will need

- A5 sheet white textured card
- Pencil
- Metal ruler
- Craft knife
- Cutting mat
- Stylus
- Holly leaf punch
- Green paper
- Pair of compasses
- PVA glue
- 3D red paint
- Red ribbon bow

timing Attaching the holly sprigs can be time consuming.

alternative Make this card in silver and hot pink to create an entirely different mood, or set the holly garland against a rich red background to put a little warmth on to a friend's mantelpiece. You might use a sticker or mini Christmas decoration instead of a bow as a feature.

1 Cut a 17 x 14cm (6¾ x 5½in) rectangle from the white textured card. Score and fold in half to create the card base. Punch about 40 holly sprigs from green paper.

2 Lightly draw a 5cm (2in) circle in an upper central position on the card. Squeeze dots of PVA glue around the circle. Lay the holly sprigs around the circle, working in one direction, but lean the sprigs to the right and left to create a thick garland.

3 Once the glue is dry, squeeze dots of red 3D paint in groups of two or three around the garland.

4 Attach the ribbon bow with PVA glue. For a professional finish you may want to glue a holly sprig on the back of the card and use it to decorate an envelope.

templates

The templates shown here are actual size unless otherwise stated. They may be easily enlarged or reduced on a photocopier if you wish to make a larger or smaller card.

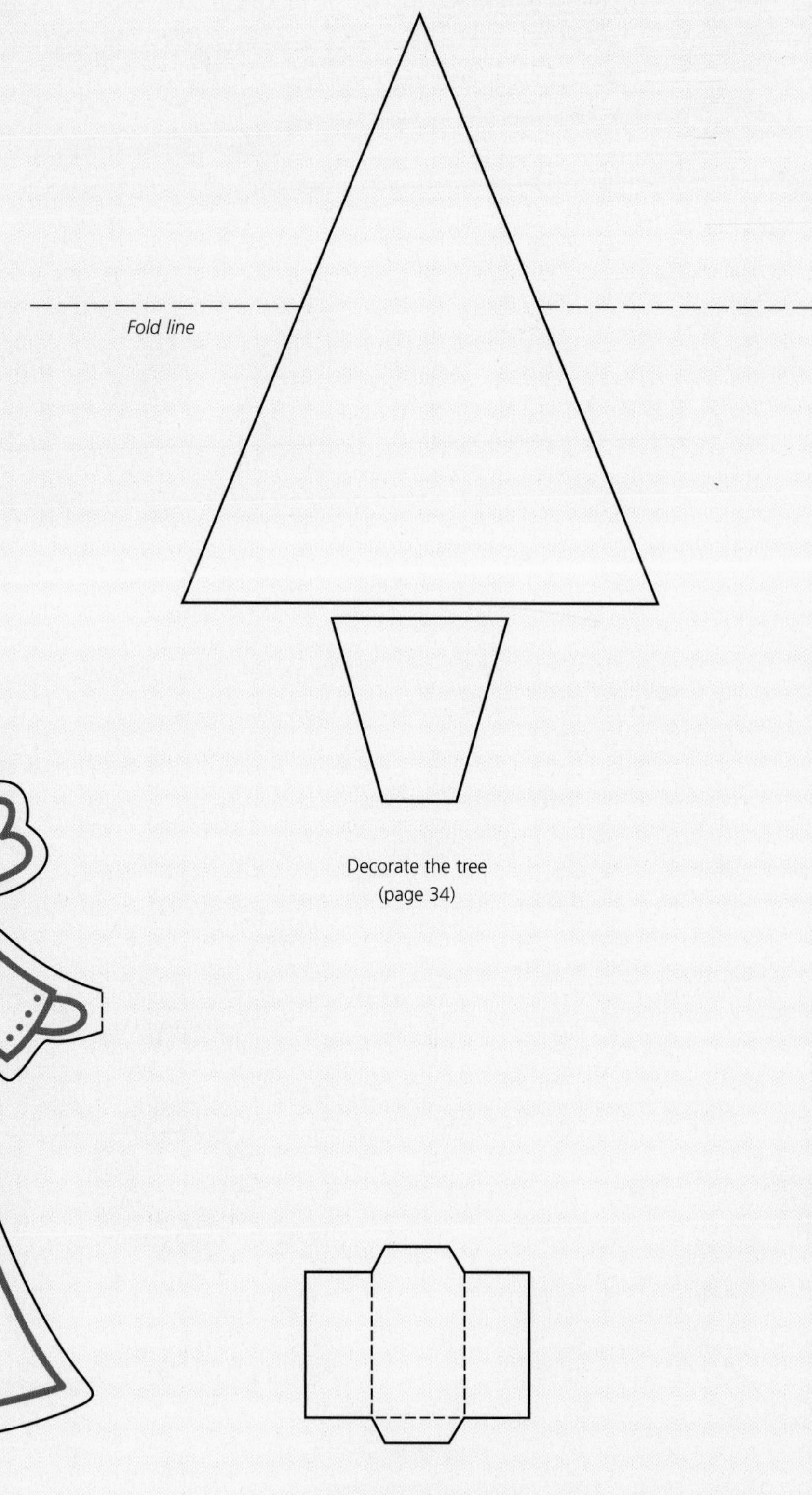

Decorate the tree
(page 34)

Host of angels
(page 32)

Gardener's memory album
(page 36)

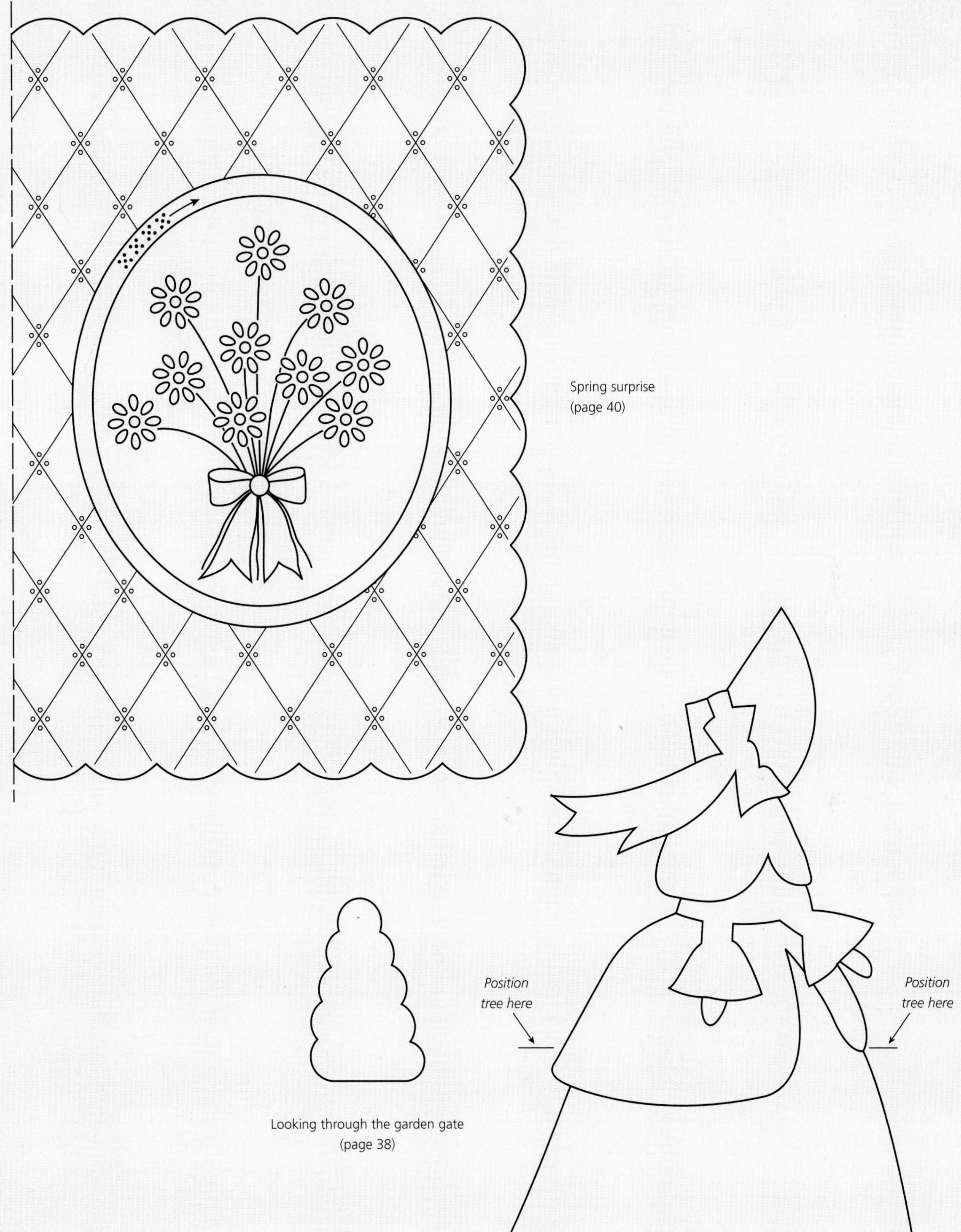

Spring surprise
(page 40)

Looking through the garden gate
(page 38)

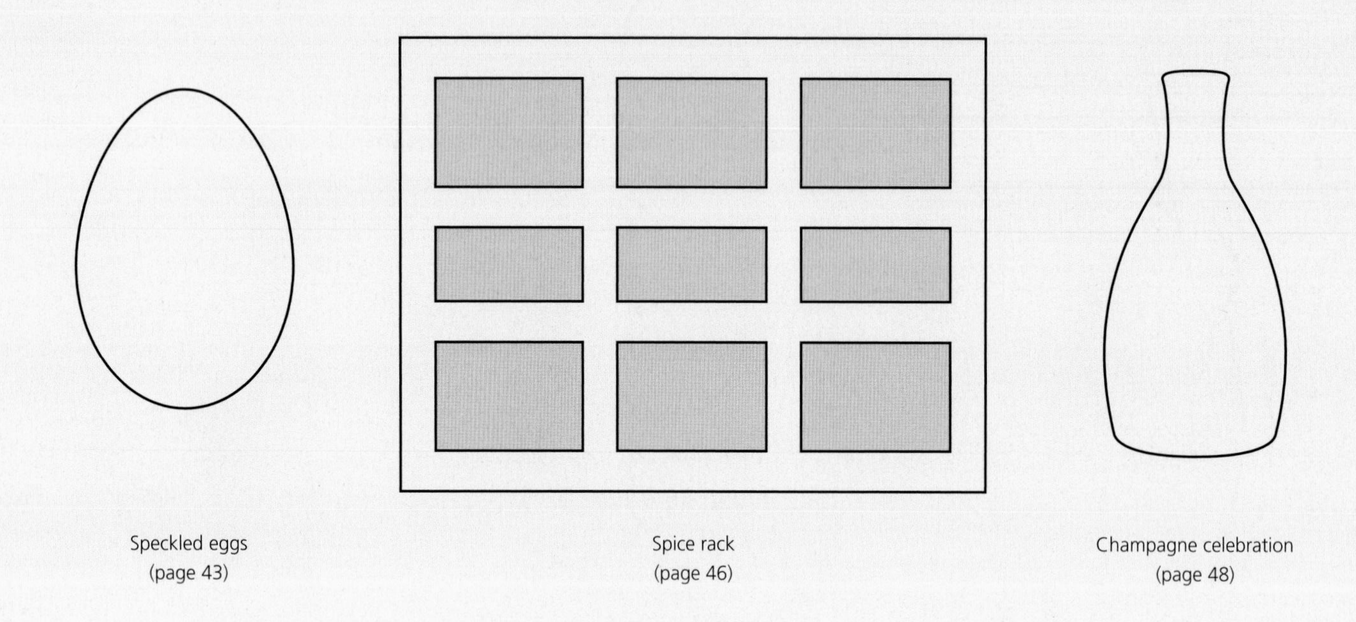

Speckled eggs
(page 43)

Spice rack
(page 46)

Champagne celebration
(page 48)

Pop-up parrots
(page 53)

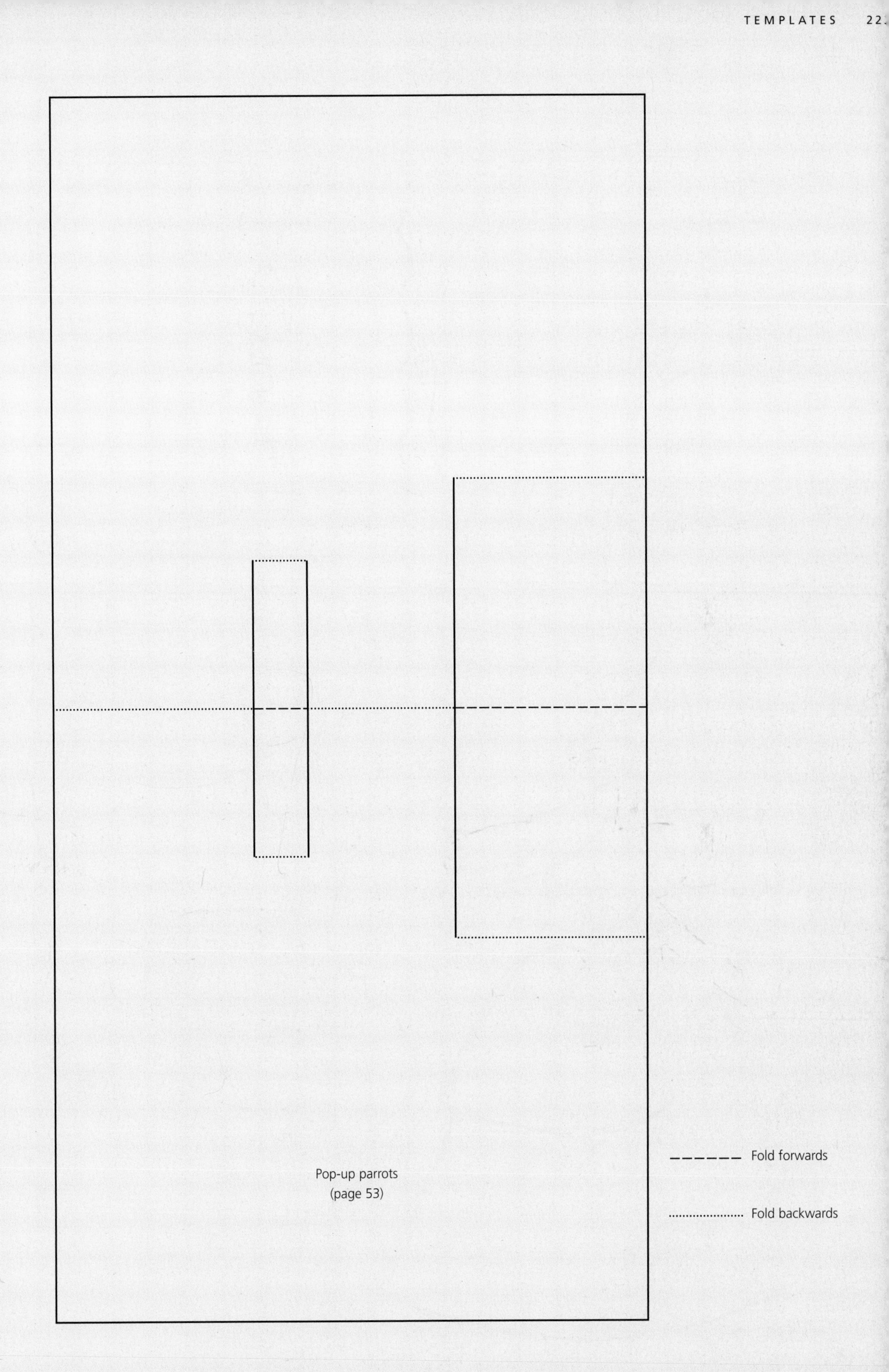
Pop-up parrots
(page 53)
Fold forwards
Fold backwards

Oriental flowers
(page 60)

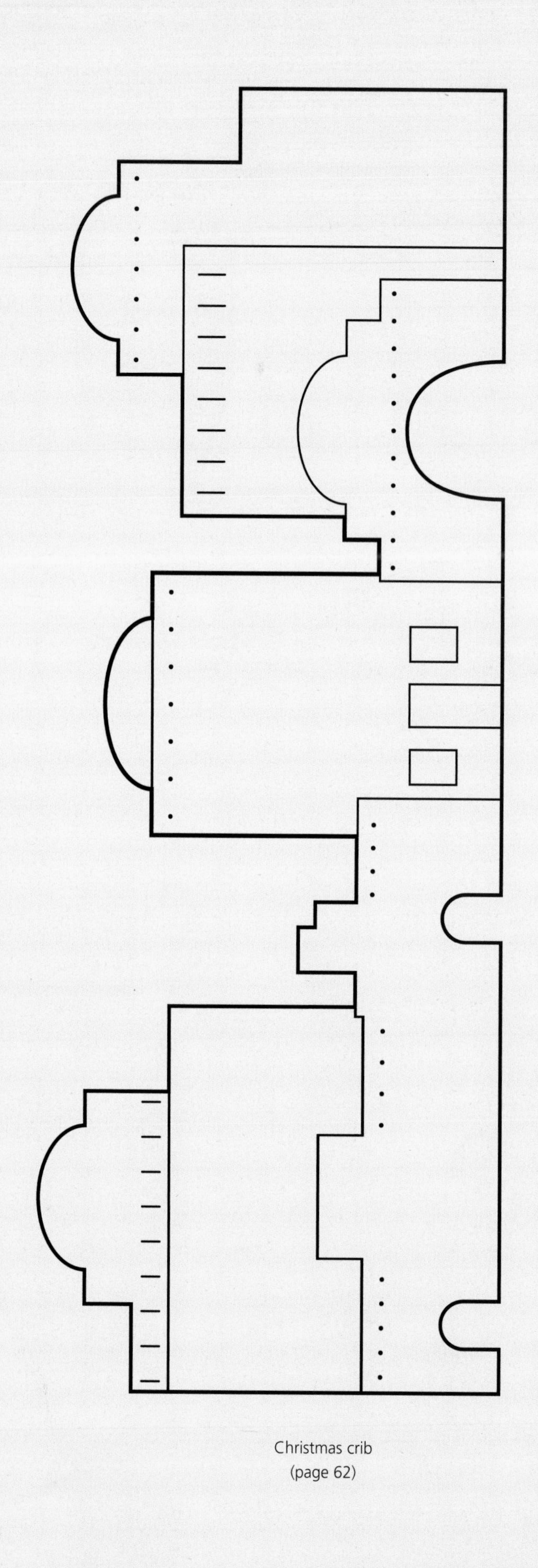

Christmas crib
(page 62)

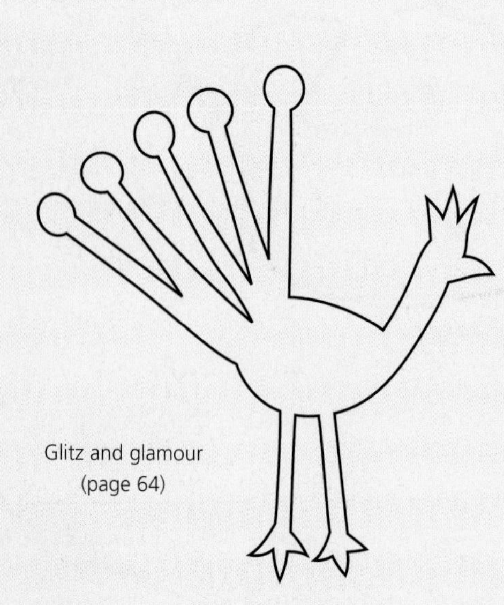

Glitz and glamour
(page 64)

Lines indicate edge of image

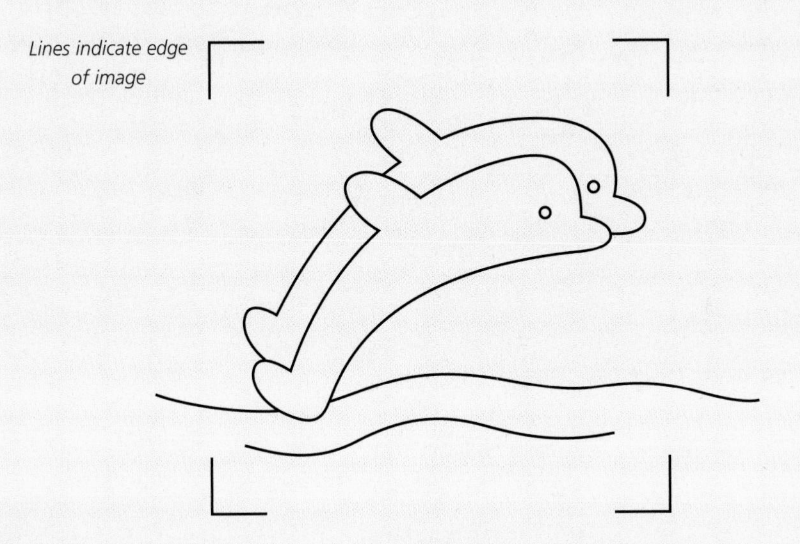

Dolphin display
(page 71)

Robin red breast
(page 66)

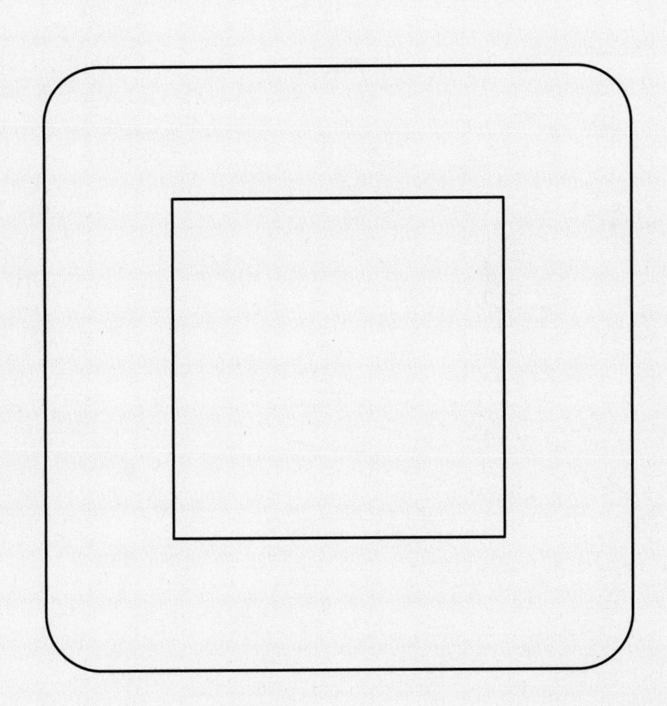

Christmas pudding
(page 78)

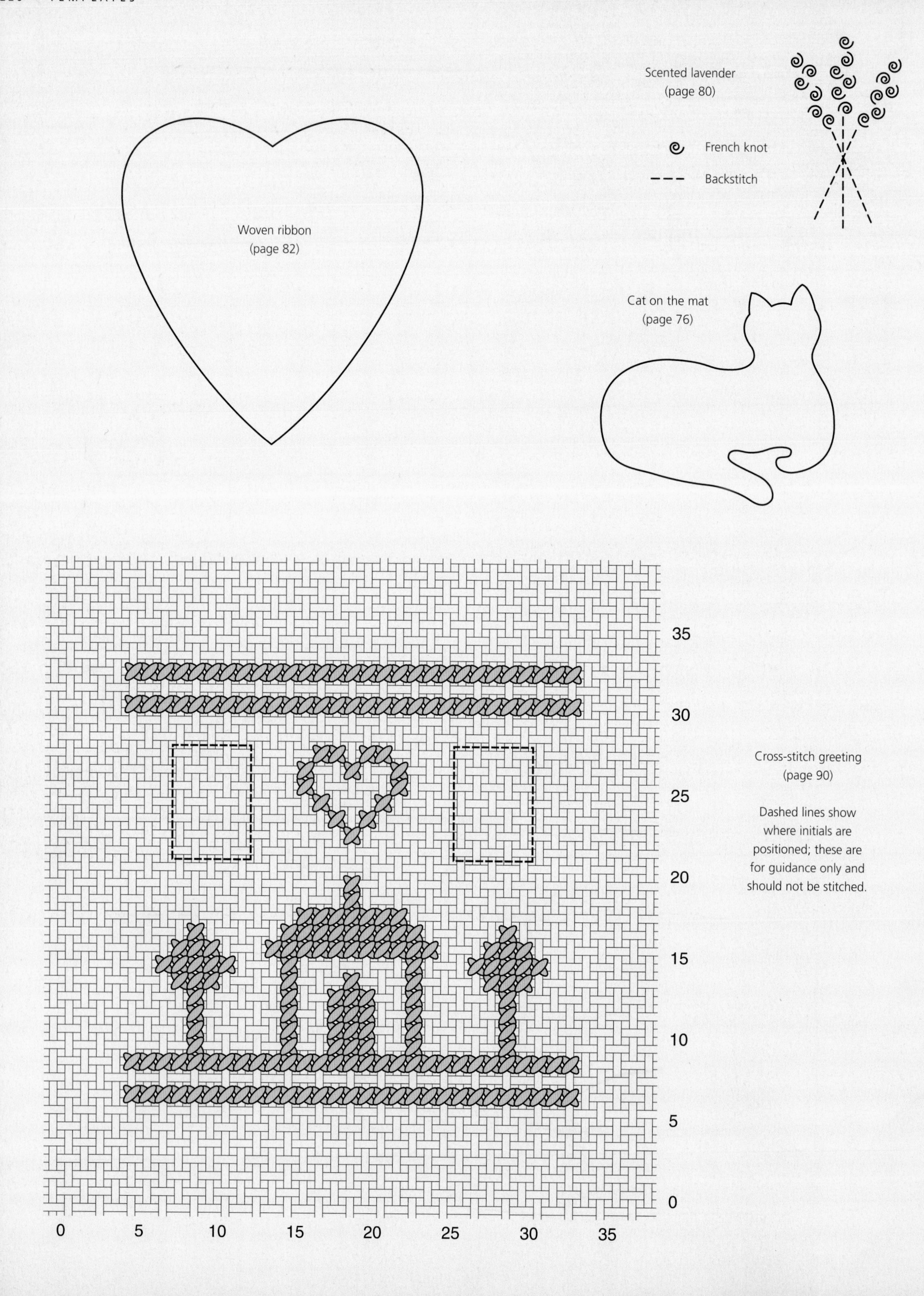
Scented lavender
(page 80)
French knot
Backstitch
Woven ribbon
(page 82)
Cat on the mat
(page 76)
35
30
25
20
15
10
5
0
0 5 10 15 20 25 30 35
Cross-stitch greeting
(page 90)
Dashed lines show where initials are positioned; these are for guidance only and should not be stitched.

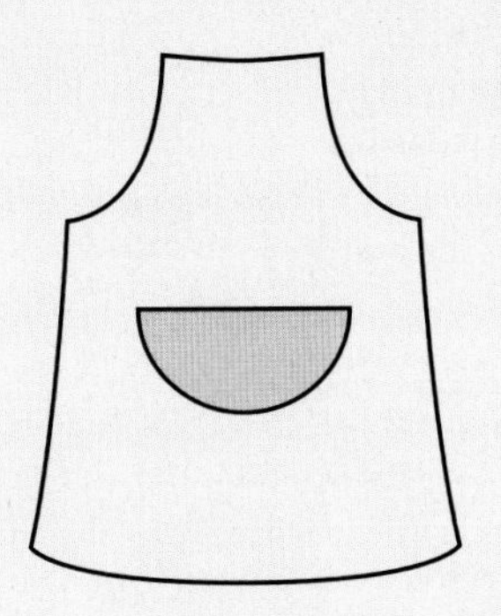

Card for cooks
(page 85)

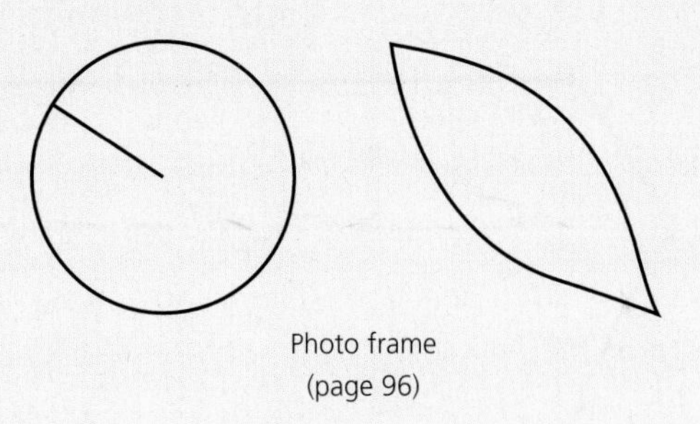

Photo frame
(page 96)

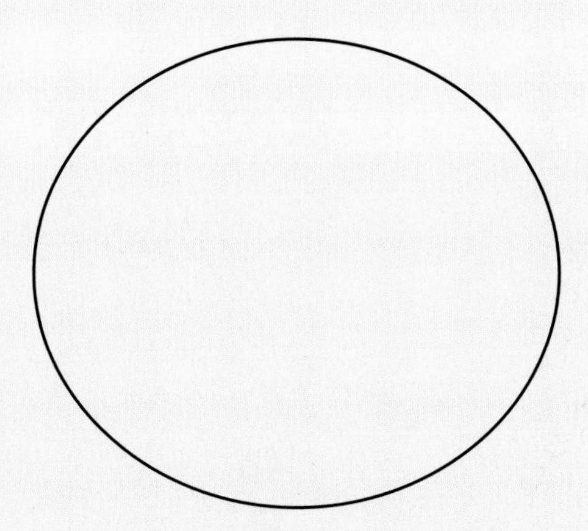

Welcome little stranger
(page 94)

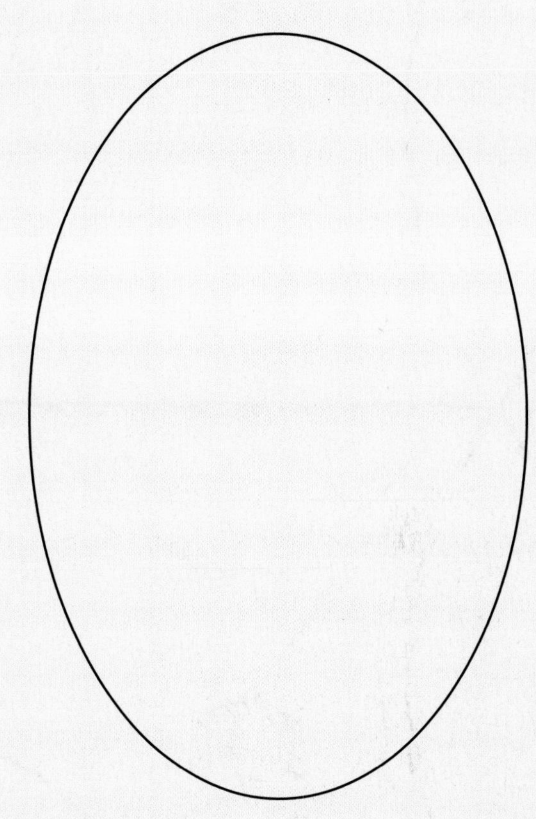

Tic-tac-toe
(page 110)

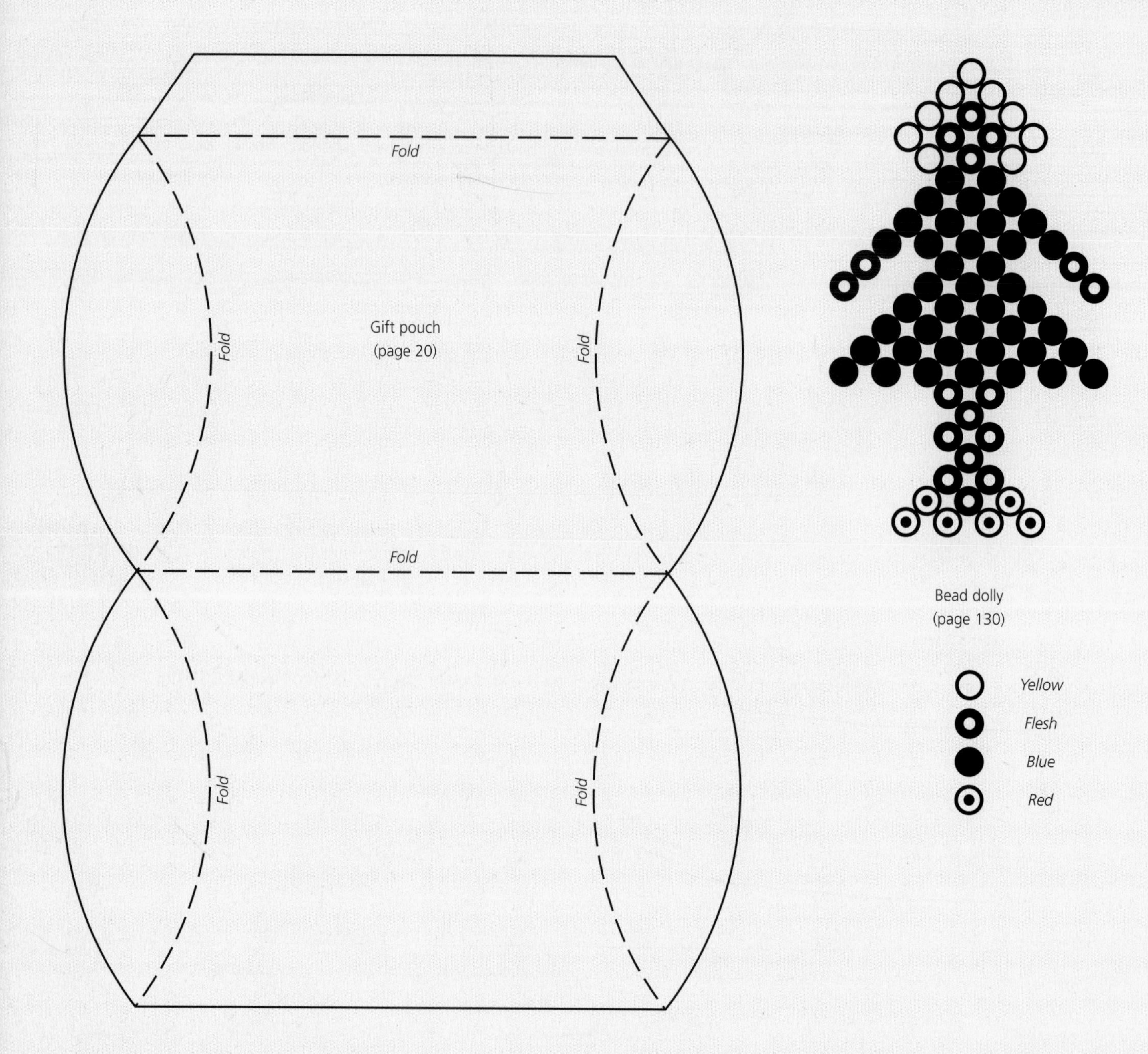

Gift pouch
(page 20)

Bead dolly
(page 130)

Olive branch
(page 132)

Blue oval

This oval is also used for Easter eggs
(page 204)
Photocopy, reducing to 74%

Olive green frame

Bookmark
(page 134)

Olive branch
(page 132)

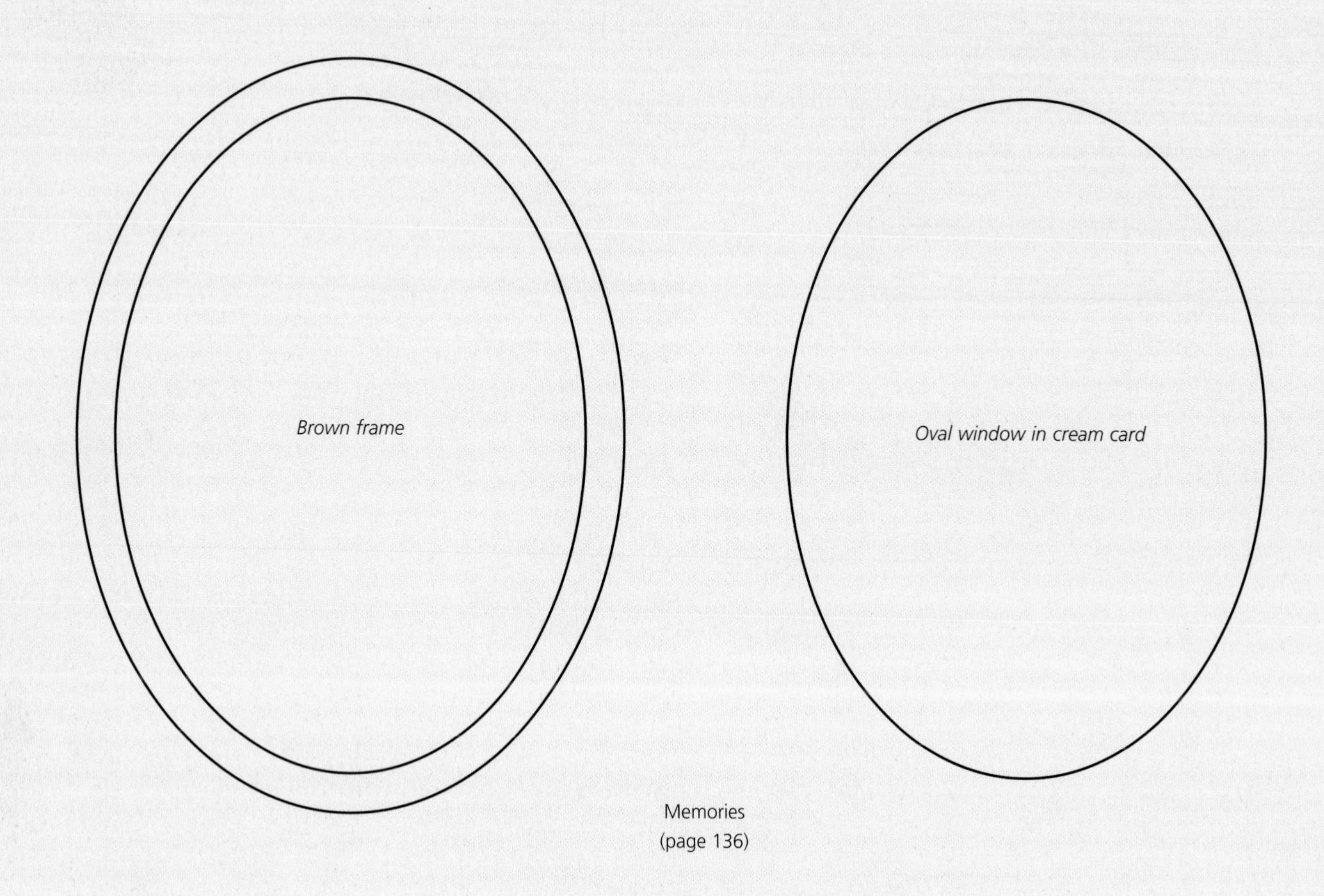

Memories
(page 136)

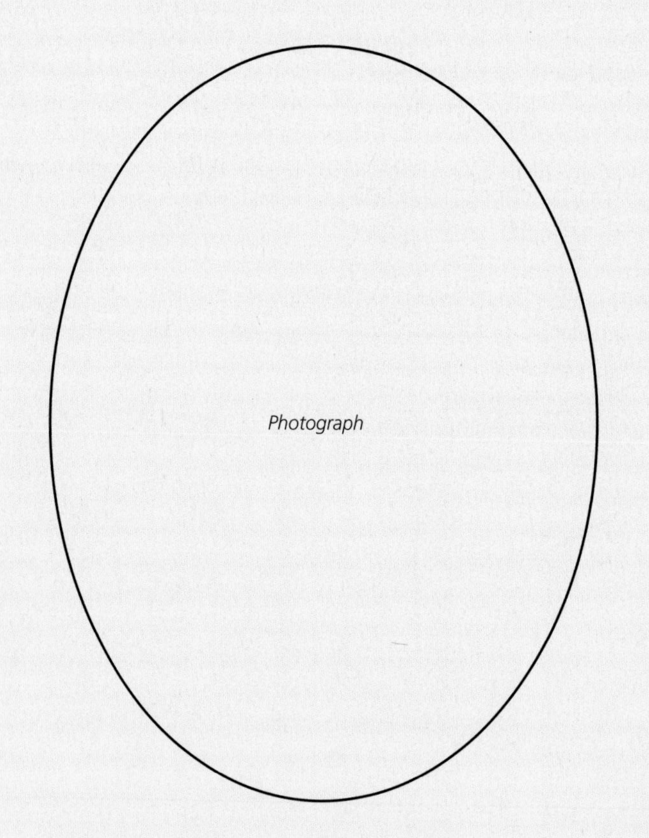

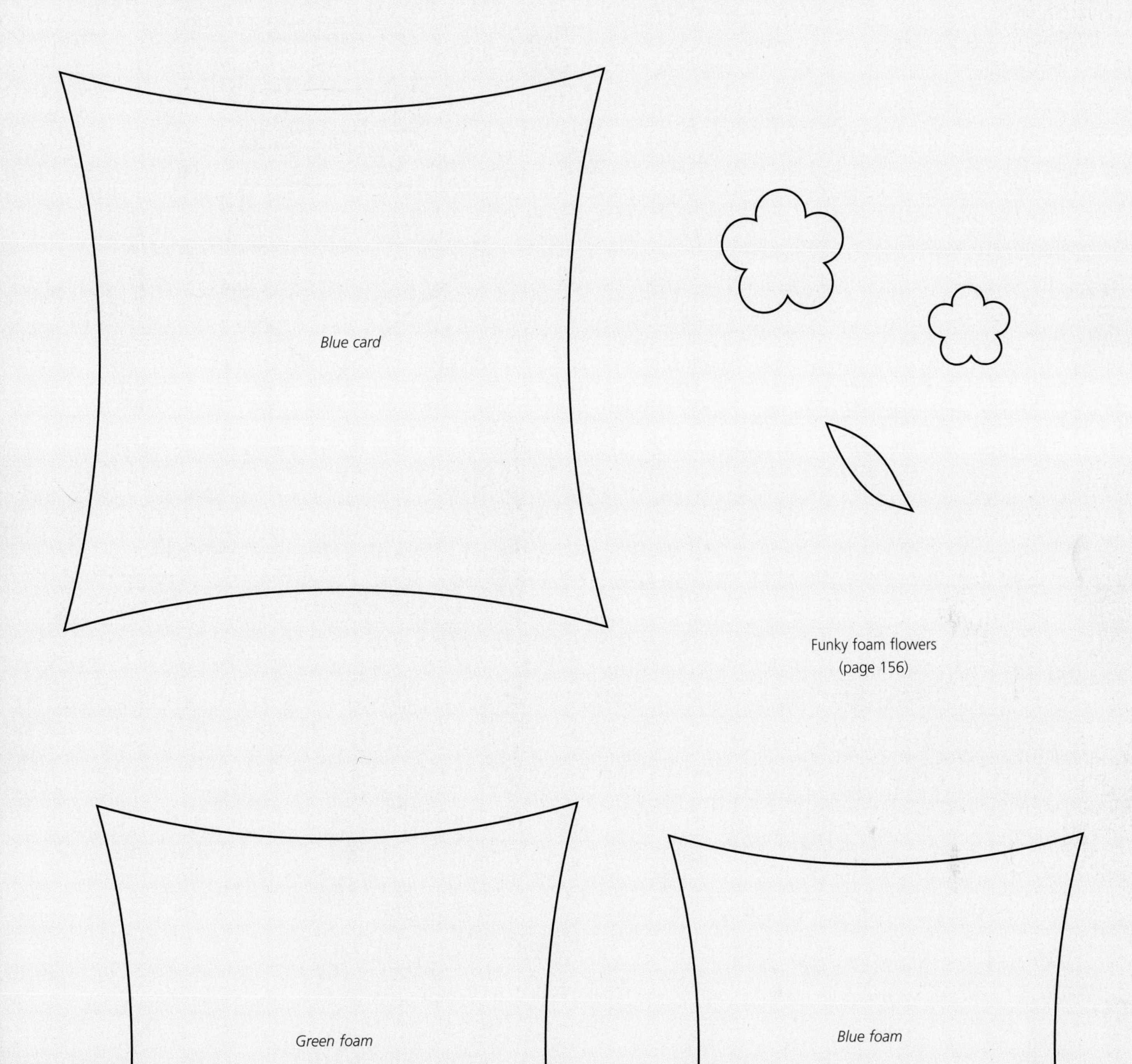

Funky foam flowers
(page 156)

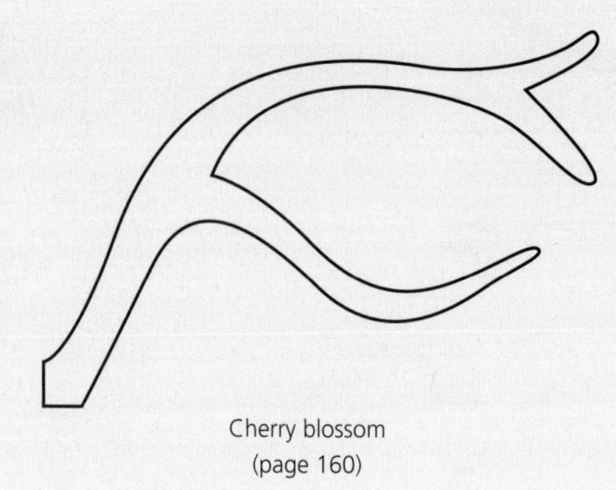

Cherry blossom
(page 160)

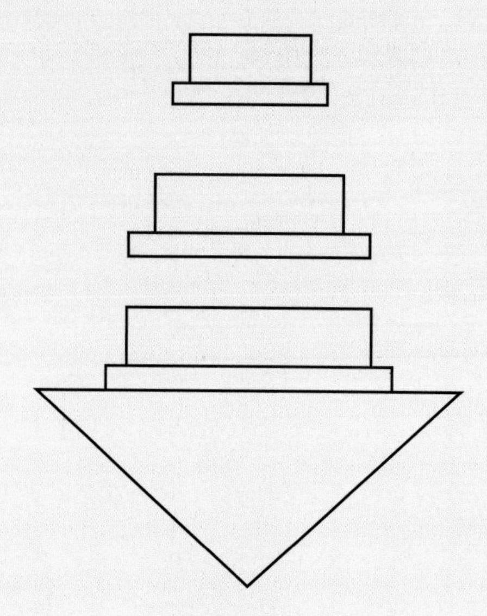

Wedding cake
(page 180)

Patchwork house
(page 170)

Tiny togs
(page 184)

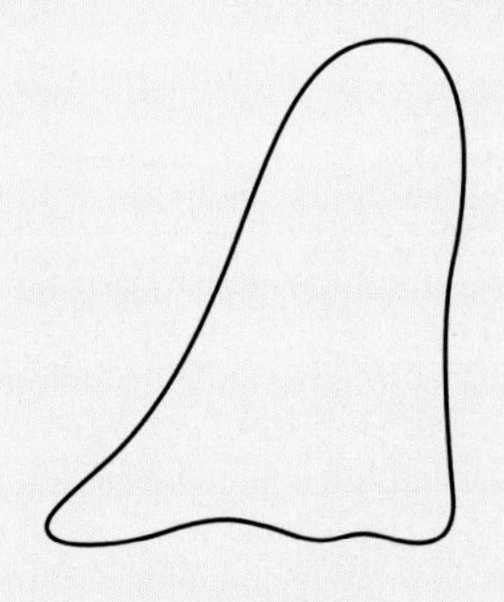

Sparkling hearts
(page 176)

Happy hallowe'en
(page 192)

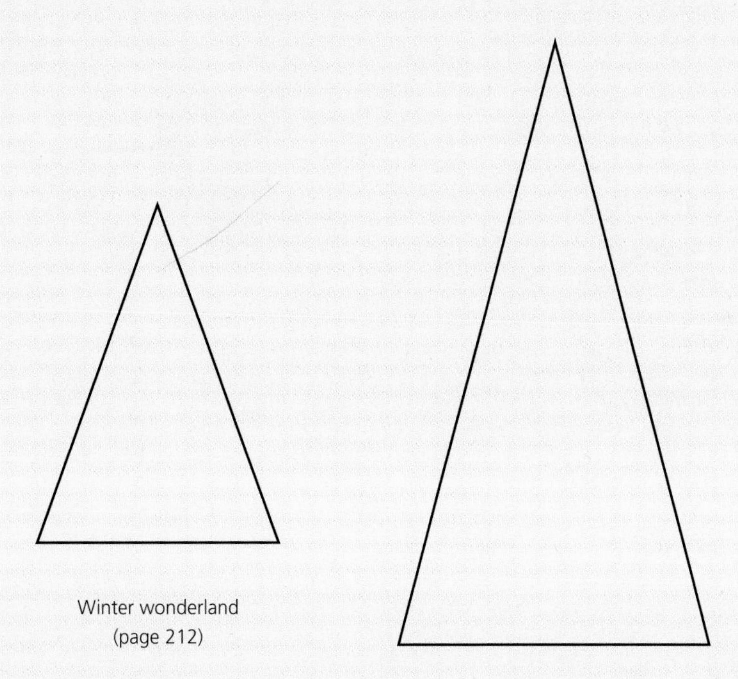

Winter wonderland
(page 212)

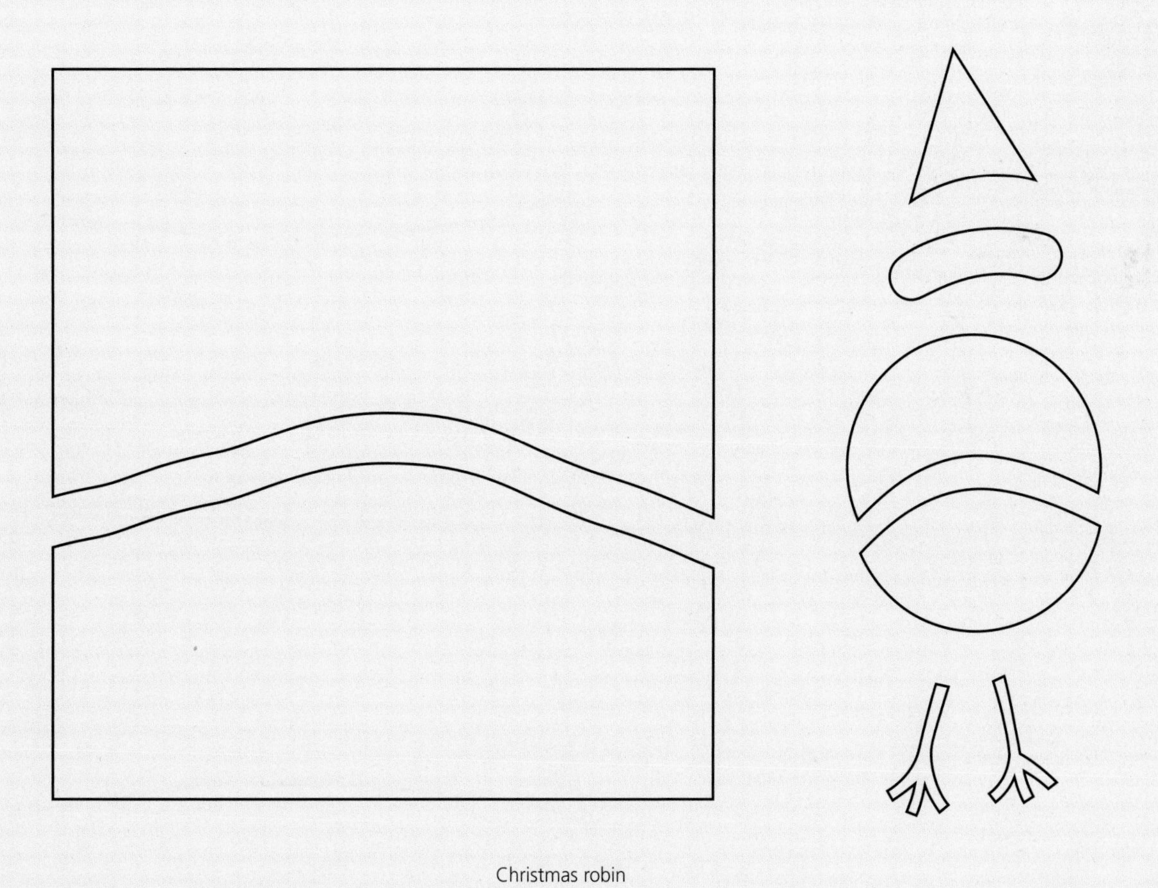

Christmas robin
(page 216)

Magic number
(page 194)

suppliers

United Kingdom

Colray Crafts
6B Main Street
Eastwood
NG16 3JH
Tel: 020 7794 3079
Email: sales@colray-crafts.com
www.colray-crafts.com
Specialist in cross-stitch, needlepoint and felt appliqué.

L. Cornelissen & Son
105 Great Russell Street
London
WC1B 3RY
Tel: 020 7636 1045
Email: info@cornelissen.co.uk
www.cornelissen.co.uk
General craft supplier. Also offers a mail-order service.

Cowling & Wilcox
26–28 Broadwick Street
London
W1F 8FG
Tel: 020 7734 9556
Email: art@cowlingandwilcox.com
www.cowlingandwilcox.com
General craft supplier.

Craft Creations
Ingersoll House
Delamare Road
Cheshunt
Hertfordshire
EN8 9HD
Tel: 01992 781 900
Email: enquiries@craftcreations.com
www.craftcreations.co.uk
General craft supplier. Mail-order service also available.

Cranberry Card Company
Unit 16
Dyffryn Business Park
Ystrad Mynach
Hengoed
CF82 7RJ
Tel: 01443 819 319
Email: info@cranberrycards.co.uk
www.cranberrycards.co.uk
Mail-order service offering a selection of card, paper and accessories.

The English Stamp Company
Worth Matravers
Dorset
BH19 3JP
Tel: 01929 439 117
Email: sales@englishstamp.com
www.englishstamp.com
Supplier of stamps, paints, inkpads and handmade paper. Mail order only.

Falkiner Fine Papers
76 Southampton Row
London
WC1B 4AR
Tel: 020 7831 1151
Carries a large range of handmade papers. Also offers a mail-order service.

Homecrafts Direct
PO Box 38
Leicester
LE1 9BU
Tel: 0116 269 7733
Email: info@homecrafts.co.uk
www.homecrafts.co.uk
Mail-order service. Offers a selection of hand-made papers and a range of craft products.

Lakeland Limited
Alexandra Buildings
Windermere
Cumbria
LA23 1BQ
Tel: 015394 88100
www.lakelandlimited.co.uk
Carries a range of craft products. Mail-order service and stores nationwide.

T. N. Lawrence & Son
208 Portland Road
Hove
BN3 5QT
Tel: 01273 260 260
Email: artbox@lawrence.co.uk
www.lawrence.co.uk
Supplier of a large range of papers, plus general artist's materials. Also offers a mail-order service.

Paperchase
Flagship store and main office
213–215 Tottenham Court Road
London
W1T 7PS
Tel: 020 7467 6200
Mail-order tel: 0161 839 1500
Mail-order email:
mailorder@paperchase.co.uk
www.paperchase.co.uk
Retailers of stationery, wrapping paper and art materials. Call for your nearest outlet.

Sew Simple
Unit 16
Taverham Nursery Centre
Fir Covert Road
Taverham
Norwich
NR8 6HT
Tel: 01603 262870
Email: sewsimpleuk@yahoo.co.uk
www.sew-simple.co.uk
Supplier of needlework and craft products.

The Stencil Store
41A Heronsgate Road
Chorleywood
Hertfordshire
WD3 5BL
Tel: 01923 285 577
Email: stencilstore@onetel.com
www.stencilstore.com
Supply wide range of stencil designs. Mail-order service also available.

Australia

Artwise Amazing Paper
186 Enmore Road
Enmore, NSW 2042
Tel: 02 9519 8237
Email: admin@amazingpaper.com.au
www.amazingpaper.com.au

Craft Warehouse Shop
50 Campbell Street
Bowen Hills, QLD 4006
Tel: 07 3257 1739

Edgeworth Craft Supplies
63 Edgeworth David Avenue
Waitara, NSW 2077
Tel: 02 9489 3909

Lincraft
Main Office
54–56 Rosebank Avenue
Clayton South, VIC 3169
Tel: 03 8558 9299
Email: customers@lincraft.com.au
www.lincraft.com.au
General craft supplier.
Phone for nearest store.

Paper Fantasy
256A Charters Towers Road
Hermit Park, QLD 4812
Tel: 07 4725 1272

Paper Wright
124 Lygon Street
Carlton, VIC 3053
Tel: 03 9633 8747

Spotlight
Tel: 1300 305 405
www.spotlight.com.au

New Zealand

Brush 'n' Palette
50 Lichfield Street
Christchurch 8001
Tel: 03 366 3088

Fine Art Papers
200 Madras Street
Christchurch
Tel: 03 379 4410

Gordon Harris
Flagship store and main office
4 Gillies Avenue
Newmarket
Auckland
Tel: 09 520 4466
Email: artsupplies@gordonharris.co.nz
www.gordonharris.co.nz

Northridge Plaza
Don McKinnon Drive
The Albany Centre
Albany
Auckland
Tel: 09 415 3406

31 Symonds Street
Auckland City
Tel: 09 377 9992

386 Anglesea Street
Hamilton
Tel: 07 834 3952

170 Victoria Street
Wellington
Tel: 04 385 2099

Littlejohns
170 Victoria Street
Wellington
Tel: 04 385 2099

Studio Art Supplies
81 Parnell Rise
Parnell
Auckland 1001
Tel: 09 377 0302

G. Webster & Co.
44 Manners Street
Wellington
Tel: 04 384 2134

South Africa

Art, Craft and Hobbies
72 Hibernia Street
George 6529
Tel: 044 874 1337

Art Shop
140A Victoria Avenue
Benoni West 1503
Tel: 011 421 1030

Articles Art Shop
290b Main Road
Paarl
Tel: 021 871 1493

Bowker Arts and Crafts
52 4th Avenue
Newton Park
Port Elizabeth
6045
Tel: 041 365 2487

Crafty Arts
Main Road
Walmer Park Shopping Centre
Port Elizabeth
Tel: 041 368 2528

Goodies Arts & Crafts
3 Veld Street
Glen Marais
Kempton Park
011 391 3419

Lolly's Arts and Crafts
2 Marconi Centre
460 Koeberg Road
Montagu Gardens
Tel: 021 552 8871

Party Themes Classic
25 Peter's Rd, Off Inanda Rd
Springfield Park
Durban
Tel: 031 577 0202 / 031 577 0206

index

Project names are in **bold**

First published in 2007 by
New Holland Publishers (UK) Ltd
London • Cape Town • Sydney • Auckland
www.newhollandpublishers.com

Garfield House, 86–88 Edgware Road
London W2 2EA
United Kingdom

80 McKenzie Street
Cape Town 8001
South Africa

14 Aquatic Drive
Frenchs Forest, NSW 2086
Australia

218 Lake Road
Northcote, Auckland
New Zealand

ISBN 978 1 84537 539 3

General editor: Anne Konopelski
Production: Hazel Kirkman
Photographer: Shona Wood
Design: Peter Crump and AG&G Books
Template illustrations: Stephen Dew
Editorial direction: Rosemary Wilkinson

1 3 5 7 9 10 8 6 4 2

Reproduction by Pica Digital Ltd, Singapore

Printed and bound by Times Offset, Malaysia